Dancing with Giants
China, India, and the Global Economy

Edited by

L. Alan Winters and Shahid Yusuf

A copublication of the World Bank and the Institute of Policy Studies (Singapore)

The International Bank for Reconstruction and
Development / The World Bank
1818 H Street NW
Washington DC 20433
Telephone: 202-473-1000
Internet: www.worldbank.org
E-mail: feedback@worldbank.org

The Institute of Policy Studies
29 Heng Mui Keng Terrace #06-06
Singapore 119620
Tel: +65 6215 1010
Fax: +65 6215 1014
Internet: www.ips.org.sg
E-mail: ips@ips.org.sg

ISBN-10: 0-8213-6749-8
ISBN-13: 978-0-8213-6749-0

eISBN-10: 0821367501
DOI: 10.1596/978-0-8213-6749-0

RCB Registration No.: 198704059K

Library of Congress Cataloging-in-Publication data has been applied for.

The Institute of Policy Studies (IPS) is a think-tank dedicated to fostering good governance in Singapore through strategic policy research and discussion. It focuses on Singapore's domestic developments and its external relations. It takes a multidisciplinary approach in its analysis, with an emphasis on long-term strategic thinking. IPS began operations in 1988. Key activities include research projects, conferences, and publications.

The institute's mission is threefold:
- Analysis: To analyze policy issues of critical concern to Singapore and contribute to policy development
- Bridge-building: To build bridges among diverse stakeholders, including government, business, academia, and civil society
- Communication: To communicate research findings to a wider community and generate a greater awareness of policy issues

Cover design: Rock Creek Creative, Bethesda, Maryland, United States.

Contents

Figures

Tables

Foreword

Hardly a day passes without a newspaper article, television show, or Internet blog story about the rise of China and India in the global economy. There are many reasons for this public interest. Never before have such large economies—with a combined population of 2.3 billion—grown so fast for so long: GDP growth in China averaged 9.1 percent over the last decade, and India averaged 6.1 percent. Some people are fearful: Will China and India dominate the world economy? Will they consume the earth's scarce resources? Will they bid down wages elsewhere? Others are curious: Can China and India sustain such impressive growth rates, especially in light of perceived fragilities (China's financial sector and India's public debt being notable examples)? Others seek lessons: Noting that neither China nor India is pursuing an "orthodox" model of development, they want to know how these economies did it, and whether there are lessons for other developing countries.

Because of this heightened interest among the general public, media coverage of China and India tends to emphasize the human dimension—stories comparing a factory worker in China with a software designer in India, or interviews with foreign investors comparing the two countries' prospects, or pictures contrasting the booming worlds of Shanghai and Mumbai with abject poverty in rural China and India.

Dancing with Giants considers the story from a different vantage point. It takes a dispassionate and critical look at the rise of China and India, and asks some difficult questions about this growth: Where is it occurring? Who is benefiting most? Is it sustainable? And what are the implications for the rest of the world? By bringing to bear the best available data and analytical tools, the book can provide answers that are much more nuanced than the typical news story. To take one example, the book demonstrates that, despite their similar size, the two Giants are not the same—China's role in the global economy is much greater than India's, with important implications for other countries.

Dancing with Giants considers whether the Giants' growth will be seriously constrained by weaknesses in governance, growing inequality, and environmental stresses, and it concludes that this need not occur. However, it does suggest that the Chinese and Indian authorities face important challenges in keeping their investment climates favorable, their inequalities at levels that do not undermine growth, and their air and water quality at acceptable levels. Discussion of how these issues affect the Giants has relevance as well to policy makers elsewhere. For example, despite their very different structures and traditions of governance, both countries have generated effective constraints on executive power, and that has played an important role in their growth.

Dancing with Giants also considers China's and India's interactions with the global trading and financial systems and their impact on the global commons, particularly with regard to climate. Examining the effects that they will have on the economic circumstances and fortunes of other countries, the various chapters find that

- The Giants' growth and trade offer most countries opportunities to gain economically. However, many countries will face strong adjustment pressure in manufacturing, particularly those with competing exports and especially if the Giants' technical progress is strongly export-enhancing. For a few countries, mainly in Asia, these pressures could outweigh the economic benefits of larger markets in, and cheaper imports from, the Giants; and the growth of those countries over the next 15 years will be slightly lower as a result.
- The Giants will contribute to the increase in world commodity and energy prices but they are not the principal cause of higher oil prices.
- The Giants' emissions of CO_2 will grow strongly, especially if economic growth is not accompanied by steps to enhance energy efficiency. At present, a one-time window of opportunity exists for achieving substantial efficiency improvements if ambitious current and future investment plans embody appropriate standards. Moreover, doing so will not be too costly or curtail growth significantly.
- From their relatively small positions at present, the Giants will emerge as significant players in the world financial system as they grow and liberalize. Rates of reserve asset accumulation likely will slow, and emerging pressures will encourage China to reduce its current account surplus.

Developed as a collaborative venture among the World Bank's research department and East and South Asia regions, and the Institute of Policy Studies in Singapore, this book is an important contribution to the global campaign for poverty reduction. With about a third of the world's poor people living in China and India, these countries' performance will be critical to alleviating global poverty. Moreover, the fact that China and India have been able to lift hundreds of millions of people out of poverty in the past few decades provides hope for the rest of the world. *Dancing with Giants* provides knowledge that will help turn that hope into reality.

François Bourguignon
Chief Economist and Senior Vice President, World Bank

Shantayanan Devarajan
Chief Economist, South Asia Region, World Bank

Homi Kharas
Chief Economist, East Asia and Pacific Region, World Bank

Contributors

Shubham Chaudhuri is Senior Economist, East Asia and Pacific Poverty Reduction and Economic Management Department, World Bank.

Betina Dimaranan is Research Economist, Center for Global Trade Analysis, Purdue University.

Elena Ianchovichina is Senior Economist, Economic Policy and Debt Department, PREM Network, World Bank.

Philip Keefer is Lead Economist, Development Research Group, World Bank.

Philip R. Lane is Professor of International Macroeconomics and Director of the Institute for International Integration Studies, Trinity College.

Will Martin is Lead Economist, Development Research Group, World Bank.

Kaoru Nabeshima is Economist, Development Research Group, World Bank.

Dwight Perkins is Harold Hitchings Burbank Research Professor of Political Economy, Department of Economics, Harvard University.

Martin Ravallion is Senior Research Manager, Development Research Group, World Bank.

Sergio L. Schmukler is Senior Economist, Development Research Group, World Bank.

Zmarak Shalizi is Senior Research Manager, Development Research Group, World Bank.

L. Alan Winters is Director, Development Research Group, World Bank.

Shahid Yusuf is Economic Adviser, Development Research Group, World Bank.

Acknowledgments

This book contains the output of a joint project between the East Asia, South Asia, and Development Economics Vice Presidencies of the World Bank, and the Institute of Policy Studies, Singapore (IPS). It was conceived as part of the background for the World Bank's September 2006 annual meetings in Singapore, titled "Asia in the World: The World in Asia." The project was directed by L. Alan Winters (director of the Development Research Group) in consultation with Arun Mahizhnan (deputy director of IPS), Shantayanan Devarajan (chief economist for South Asia), Homi Kharas (chief economist for East Asia and Pacific), and Shahid Yusuf (economic adviser, Development Research Group) of the World Bank.

Each of the chapters has drawn on input from many scholars, including papers commissioned from Chong-En Bai, Richard N. Cooper, Renaud Crassous, Betina Dimaranan, Joseph P. H. Fan, Masahisa Fujita, Vincent Gitz, Nobuaki Hamaguchi, Meriem Hamdi-Cherif, Jean-Charles Hourcade, Jiang Kejun, Louis Kuijs, Philip Lane, David D. Li, Sandrine Mathy, Taye Mengistae, Deepak Mishra, Devashish Mitra, Randall Morck, Victor Nee, Deunden Nikomborirak, Gregory W. Noble, Xu Nuo, Sonja Opper, Ila Patnaik, Dwight H. Perkins, Olivier Sassi, Ajay Shah, T. N. Srinivasan, Shane Streifel, Beyza Ural, Susan Whiting, Steven I. Wilkinson, Lixin Colin Xu, Bernard Y. Yeung, and Min Zhao. We are grateful to all these authors. Most of their papers are available on the *Dancing with Giants* Web site (http://econ.worldbank.org/dancingwithgiants).

We have benefited from discussions with the authors of the background papers, the chapter authors, and many other scholars around the world, but particular mention should be made of Suman Bery, Richard N. Cooper, Yasheng Huang, and T. N. Srinivasan, who were external reviewers for the whole manuscript; of Shantayanan Devarajan, Shahrokh Fardoust, Bert Hoffman, and Homi Kharas, who commented on the whole internally; and of Richard Baldwin, Priya Basu, Maureen Cropper, David Dollar, Subir Gokarn, Takatoshi

Ito, Henry Jacoby, Kapil Kapoor, Faruk Khan, Laura Kodres, Aart Kraay, Louis Kuijs, Franck Lecocq, Jong-Wha Lee, Jeff Lewis, Assar Lindbeck, Simon Long, Guonan Ma, Robert McCauley, Tom Rawski, Mark Sundberg, and Hans Timmer, who read parts of the manuscript. Audrey Kitson-Walters has provided excellent logistical support, and Trinidad Angeles and Andrea Wong provided equally excellent budgetary support.

Susan Graham, Patricia Katayama, Nancy Lammers, Santiago Pombo, and Nora Ridolfi have guided the publication, and Christine Cotting provided editorial services. We are grateful to all of them.

Chapters of the book have been discussed at the following venues and events: the World Bank China Office; "China and Emerging Asia: Reorganizing the Global Economy," World Bank headquarters; "Increased Integration of China and India in the Global Financial System," Indian Council for Research on International Economic Relations (ICRIER)–World Bank conference and "Dancing with Giants," ICRIER; the Center for Pacific Basin Studies' 2006 Pacific Basin conference (Federal Reserve Bank of San Francisco); "Production Networks and Changing Trade and Investment Patterns: The Economic Emergence of China and India and Implications for Asia and Singapore," the National University of Singapore SCAPE–IPS–World Bank workshop; "Rethinking Infrastructure for Development," the World Bank's Annual Bank Conference on Development Economics (Tokyo, May 2006); and "The Elephant and the Dragon" conference (Shanghai, July 2006). We are grateful to all participants for their useful feedback.

None of these people is responsible for the book's remaining shortcomings.

Background Papers

Bai, Chong-En. "The Domestic Financial System and Capital Flows: China."

Cooper, Richard N. "How Integrated Are Chinese and Indian Labor into the World Economy?"

Crassous, Renaud, Jean-Charles Hourcade, Olivier Sassi, Vincent Gitz, Sandrine Mathy, and Meriem Hamdi-Cherif. "IMACLIM-R: A Modeling Framework for Sustainable Development Issues."

Fan, Joseph P. H., Randall Morck, Lixin Colin Xu, and Bernard Yeung. "Does 'Good Government' Draw Foreign Capital? Explaining China's Exceptional FDI Inflow."

Fujita, Masahisa, and Nobuaki Hamaguchi. "The Coming Age of China-Plus-One: The Japanese Perspective on East Asian Production Networks."

Kuijs, Louis. "China in the Future: A Large Net Saver or Net Borrower?"

Lane, Philip. "The International Balance Sheets of China and India."

Li, David D. "Large Domestic Non-Intermediated Investments and Government Liabilities: Challenges Facing China's Financial Sector Reform."

Mengistae, Taye, Lixin Colin Xu, and Bernard Yeung. "China vs. India: A Microeconomic Look at Comparative Macroeconomic Performance."

Mishra, Deepak. "Financing India's Rapid Growth and Its Implications for the Global Economy."

Mitra, Devashish, and Beyza Ural. "Indian Manufacturing: A Slow Sector in a Rapidly Growing Economy."

Nee, Victor, and Sonja Opper. "China's Politicized Capitalism."

Nikomborirak, Deunden. "A Comparative Study of the Role of the Service Sector in the Economic Development of China and India."

Noble, Gregory W. "The Emergence of the Chinese and Indian Automobile Industries and Implications for Other Developing Countries."

Patnaik, Ila, and Ajay Shah. "The Interplay between Capital Flows and the Domestic Indian Financial System."

Streifel, Shane. "Impact of China and India on Global Commodity Markets: Focus on Metals and Minerals and Petroleum."

Srinivasan, T. N. "China, India, and the World Economy."

Whiting, Susan H. "Growth, Governance, and Institutions: The Internal Institutions of the Party-State in China."

Wilkinson, Steven I. "The Politics of Infrastructural Spending in India."

Zhao, Min. "External Liberalization and the Evolution of China's Exchange System: An Empirical Approach."

Acronyms and Abbreviations

AGE	applied general equilibrium
ALT	alternate scenario
BAU	business-as-usual scenario
BAU-H	business-as-usual scenario with high growth variant
BERI	Business Environment Risk Intelligence
CGE	computable general equilibrium
CO_2	carbon dioxide
CPC	Communist Party of China
EFTA	European Free Trade Association
EU25	25 countries of the European Union
FDI	foreign direct investment
FYP	five-year plan
GDP	gross domestic product
GE	General Electric
GIC	growth incidence curve
GTAP	Global Trade Analysis Project
GtC	giga tonnes of carbon
HIC	high-income country
HS	Harmonized System
ICRG	*International Country Risk Guide*
IEA	International Energy Agency
IIT	Indian Institute of Technology
IMF	International Monetary Fund
IT	information technology
LCD	liquid-crystal display
LIC	low-income country
mbd	million barrels per day
MFA	Multifiber Arrangement
MIC	middle-income country

MNC	multinational corporation
Mtoe	million tons of oil equivalent
NA	national accounts
NBS	National Bureau of Statistics
OPEC	Organization of the Petroleum Exporting Countries
PC	personal computer
PPP	purchasing power parity
R&D	research and development
SITC	Standard International Trade Classification
TFP	total factor productivity
TVE	township and village enterprise
USEIA	U.S. Energy Information Administration
WHO	World Health Organization
WTO	World Trade Organization

All dollars are U.S. dollars unless otherwise noted.

CHAPTER 1

Introduction
Dancing with Giants

L. Alan Winters and Shahid Yusuf

China and India share at least two characteristics: their populations are huge and their economies have been growing very fast for at least 10 years. Already they account for nearly 5 percent and 2 percent of world gross domestic product (GDP), respectively, at current exchange rates. Arguably, China's expansion since 1978 already has been the largest growth "surprise" ever experienced by the world economy; and if we extrapolated their recent growth rates for half a century, we would find that China and India—the Giants—were among the world's very largest economies. Their vast labor forces and expanding skills bases imply massive productive potential, especially if they continue (China) or start (India) to invest heavily in and welcome technology inflows. Low-income countries ask whether there will be any room for them at the bottom of the industrialization ladder, whereas high- and middle-income countries fear the erosion of their current advantages in more sophisticated fields. All recognize that a booming Asia presages strong demands, not only for primary products but also for niche manufactures and services and for industrial inputs and equipment. But, equally, all are eager to know which markets will expand and by how much. Moreover, the growth of these giant economies will affect not only goods markets but also flows of savings, investment, and even people around the world, and will place heavy demands on the global commons, such as the oceans and the atmosphere.

This book cannot answer all these questions, but it contains six essays on important aspects of the growth of the Giants that will, at least, aid thinking about them. Its principal aim is to highlight some of the major implications of the Giants' growth for the world economy and hence for other countries, drawing on new research and on the burgeoning literature concerning China and India: it is about dancing with the Giants without getting one's toes stepped on.[1] Three chapters focus on the Giants' interactions with other countries (via the evolution of their industrial capabilities, their international trade, and the international financial system), two chapters consider possible constraints and influences on their growth (inequality and governance), and one chapter combines the analysis of local constraints and global perspectives (on energy and emissions).

The question underlying the analysis is very simple. China and India account for about 37.5 percent of world population and 6.4 percent of the value of world output and income at current prices and exchange rates;[2] as their per capita production and consumption approach levels similar to those of today's developed economies—a standard to which, broadly speaking, both Giants aspire—major effects on global markets and global commons seem inevitable. We ask whether a continued rapid expansion of economic activity through 2020 is feasible, whether there are any hints about the form it will take, and how any such expansion will impinge on other countries. The last question is analyzed via the Giants' impact on global markets, systems, and commons rather than via their bilateral links with other countries. The effects on any individual country largely will be related to the nature of its engagements with these systems.[3]

Of course, the Giants will not grow in isolation—indeed, they probably never will contribute more than a minority share of world growth—so this raises a definitional question about what we mean by "the effects of the Giants' growth." In the two chapters in which we analyze the question formally, we postulate a plausible growth path to 2020 for everybody (which has implications for, say, world prices or carbon emissions), and then ask about the implications of "a bit more" growth for the Giants. One of these chapters uses a standard computable general equilibrium model to translate assumptions about future factor accumulation and technical progress into a picture of the world in 2020. It then increases the Giants' growth by about 2 percentage points per year after 2005 and calculates the resulting differences in the flows of goods and services between economies, the structure of production, and

---

1. One of the questions most commonly asked of World Bank country economists is, what does the rise of China and India mean for my country?
2. Unless stated otherwise, statistics in this chapter come from the World Bank's *World Development Indicators*.
3. We consider only tangible dimensions of impact, including services, but, of course, China and India also may influence norms, tastes, business models, and so forth.

economic welfare. The other chapter uses a different model, incorporating a detailed energy sector and endogenous technical progress, to explore energy/emissions scenarios up to 2050. It then similarly explores the consequences of adding about 2 percentage points per year to the Giants' growth.

In the long run and in aggregate, economies adjust fairly smoothly, so we expect the precise baseline chosen for these exercises to have rather little effect on the impact of the incremental growth. However, it is possible that there are critical economic and ecological thresholds, which mean that an extra 2 percentage points of annual growth from the Giants would have different effects, depending on whether they were introduced into a world already growing at, say, 2 percent or at 4 percent a year. For example, the supply of oil might act as a constraint, or faster growth might sufficiently increase incentives for innovation that this constraint becomes nonbinding. But, of course, no one knows whether and where such thresholds exist, so we proceed by assuming a plausible base and exploring a plausible increment, elaborating them with qualitative discussion where this seems appropriate.

The other chapters on the effects of the Giants' growth take a less quantitative approach. One describes current and foreseeable developments in industrial capability so as to identify sectors of likely future strength—and hence competitive advantage. It stresses the behavior of specific firms and sectors in promoting the very rapid changes in manufacturing and services capabilities in China and India, and hence supplements the more formal, model-based analysis of comparative advantage noted above. Another chapter quantifies the Giants' engagement in the international financial system and considers the factors—mainly their domestic policy reforms—that will influence it in the future. In the absence of predictions about such reforms, however, we eschew trying to make precise quantitative estimates of future financial stocks and flows.

The remaining two chapters are even farther from quantifying the future, but nonetheless address important factors underlying the Giants' growth. The first reviews the evidence on the Giants' poverty reduction, increasing inequality, and economic growth. It argues that increasing inequality could constrain growth—especially in China—and that governments should take steps to address it.[4] Precisely how they do so (for example, by trying to boost agricultural incomes or by encouraging migration out of rural areas) could affect

---

4. It is true that income inequality rose in the United Kingdom and the United States during their industrializations, without these trends being viewed as a constraint on growth. However, the scant evidence suggests that the increases were less than in China (for example, see Lindert [2000]). Furthermore, both technology and social norms were different then, and prevailing growth rates were lower, even for the most successful economies.

trade and hence the rest of the world. The last chapter similarly reviews past evidence—this time on governance and the investment climate—and concludes that, although problems of governance need not constrain growth in the Giants, certain fragilities exist. Both of these chapters are consistent with continuing rapid growth, but they identify circumstances in which it could be slowed.

From this discussion it will be clear that none of the chapters in this book makes unconditional predictions about the Giants or the world economy; rather, each chapter analyzes one aspect of growth and discusses, quantitatively or qualitatively, the type of factors that one should consider in projecting its continuation or its effects. Similarly, although the chapters all deal with the same events, they do not adopt a single analytical framework or data set. Analysis requires simplification, and the requisite simplifications vary from topic to topic. Likewise, different topics require different data and data sources, which often are somewhat at variance. Because we cannot produce a single statistical view of the Giants, we use data appropriate to each topic without seeking to impose an appearance of perfect mutual consistency. Except for the case of energy and emissions, our time horizon is the period between 2005 and 2020, long enough to identify longer-run trends and inform policy making over the next few years but, we hope, short enough not to be overwhelmed by the uncertainties of technology and politics.

We treat both China and India together as Giants because the essays are mainly concerned with the way in which the global economic environment facing *other countries* is evolving. From this perspective, the analytical apparatus required is similar for both China and India. We are not asserting, however, that the two Giants themselves are similar or that they have similar prospects. Indeed, as is noted below, even their scales are different over the 15 years that we consider. In some cases we will distinguish between the implications of Chinese and Indian growth for global outcomes or between the challenges they face in achieving growth, but for many other purposes we will refer to them collectively as the Giants.

The remainder of this introduction starts by observing that the Giants matter to the rest of the world because they are growing and because they are integrated or integrating with the global economy. It briefly discusses the forces shaping their growth and contrasts that growth with previous growth spurts in the world economy and with growth stimuli emanating from other countries; that is, it seeks to put the Giants in perspective. It next provides a brief overview of subsequent chapters, passing from industrial capability and international trade (that is, how the Giants' growth may be diffused through the world via goods and services markets); through their interactions with international financial markets, energy markets, and emissions; to the possible constraints to growth emanating from the environment, inequality, and the challenges of governance. Finally, we summarize the challenges that the growth of the Giants poses to governments of other countries, according to their different endowments and economic circumstances.

Much has been written about China's period of exceptional economic growth and India's recent takeoff, which space considerations deter us from discussing here. In a few cases, looking back is essential to looking forward, but except in such cases and where we need to measure growth rates from an historical point, we ignore these fascinating histories.[5] Thus, in this chapter we concentrate on where the Giants are now and where they are going.

Economic Growth

We are interested in the Giants because they are large and growing (and are expected to continue to do so), and because their growth impinges on other countries via their international transactions. This section considers the first of these reasons: How large and dynamic are the Giants, how does their growth compare with others' growth, and what determines the nature of their growth?

Putting the Giants in Perspective

We start by comparing the Giants with other large economies currently and in 2020. For comparing poverty or even economic welfare across countries, it is sensible to use purchasing power parity (PPP) exchange rates; but for assessing the effect of one economy on another, current actual exchange rates provide a better basis. Such international effects must operate via the international transfer of goods, services, or assets; given that the latter are tradable, their prices do not vary dramatically across countries, so PPP adjustment is not appropriate. The GDP data in table 1.1 suggest that China is perhaps one-

---

5. Among the many economic histories available, see Naughton (1995), Srinivasan (2003b), Panagariya (2004), Rodrik and Subramanian (2005), Frankel (2005), Friedman and Gilley (2005), Wu (2005), and Branstetter and Lardy (2006).

Table 1.1 Gross Domestic Product in Six Large Economies
percent

Economy	Share of world GDP (2004 $ and exchange rates)		Average annual real growth rates		Average contribution to world growth	
	2004	2020	1995–2004	2005–20	1995–2004	2005–20
China	4.7	7.9	9.1	6.6	12.8	15.8
India	1.7	2.4	6.1	5.5	3.2	4.1
United States	28.4	28.5	3.3	3.2	33.1	28.6
Japan	11.2	8.8	1.2	1.6	5.3	4.6
Germany	6.6	5.4	1.5	1.9[a]	3.0	3.3
Brazil	1.5	1.5	2.4	3.6	1.5	1.7
World	100.0	100.0	3.0	3.2	100.0	100.0

Source: World Bank 2005b, *World Development Indicators.*
Note: Average growth rates are calculated as the average of annual real growth rates (US$ constant 2000) for the period. Similarly, average contributions are calculated as the average of annual contributions. The calculation for the period 2005–20 is based on GDP in 2004 and the projected growth rates.
a. The World Bank projects an annual growth rate of 2.3 percent for the 25 countries of the European Union plus the European Free Trade Association, from which we derive the figure for Germany.

sixth as large as the United States in current dollars, and that India is one-sixteenth as large. In terms of impact, a given proportionate shock emanating from Germany or Japan would outweigh one from China, let alone one from India.

Turning to the growth of output and income, China and India have performed very strongly since 1995, especially compared with other large economies (see column 3 of table 1.1). China accounted for 13 percent of the world growth in output over 1995–2004; and India accounted for 3 percent, compared with the United States' 33 percent, whose slower growth rate is offset by its much higher starting share in 1995. Looking forward, the table projects GDP growth to 2020 based on the World Bank's central projections for the world economy as of early July 2006.[6] These projections are offered not as predictions but as plausible assumptions from which we can start to think about

6. It is very likely that these projections will be revised somewhat in *Global Economic Prospects 2007*. As argued above, however, the analysis of the effects of the Giants' growth is largely independent of the precise base to which it is applied. The projected decline in growth rates relative to recent experience reflects expert opinion as of early 2006, based on views about future accumulation, labor force growth, technical progress, and policy reform.

the relative magnitudes of the Giants' growth. The corresponding growth rates in factor inputs and productivity are given in table 3.4 (chapter 3).

The projections have China growing at an annual average of 6.6 percent over the period 2005–20 (an aggregate increase in output of 162 percent), and India growing at 5.5 percent a year (124 percent)—modest rates relative to the last decade but still formidable. The projections assume robust growth elsewhere (world average of 3.2 percent annually), so they imply a somewhat conservative view of the increase in the Giants' share of the world economy—from 4.7 percent to 7.9 percent for China, and from 1.7 percent to 2.4 percent for India. On these figures, the Giants account for larger shares of world growth in real terms over 2005–20 than over 1995–2004, but not dramatically so.[7] It is important to note, however, that these projections of real growth hold exchange rates constant at 2004 values. As the Giants become more affluent, the prices of their nontraded services and their equilibrium exchange rates will increase. Thus, by 2020 the Giants' shares at 2020 prices will exceed those in column 2 of table 1.1, probably substantially.[8] Nonetheless, over the time horizon we are dealing with, the Giants will not come to dominate the world economy. A given proportional change in North America or Western Europe, for example, still will be quantitatively larger.

It also is relevant to note that emerging economies' growth rates are typically more volatile than industrial countries' rates. As emerging economies become relatively larger in the world economy, this volatility will impinge more strongly on others, and unless it is negatively correlated with other growth shocks, overall volatility will increase slightly.

A different perspective on the Giants' growth comes from historical data. Looking at China's takeoff from 1979, one can compare its progress with previous large industrializations. (India's progress is too recent to be analyzed in this way.) Table 1.2 considers the United Kingdom and the United States over the 18th and 19th centuries, drawing on Maddison's (2003) statistics. Although, unfortunately, those statistics are in PPP terms and available only

---

7. If China's and India's growth rates were raised to 8.6 percent and 7.3 percent, respectively, as assumed in alternative simulations in chapter 3 and more in line with local predictions and plans, and if the world growth rate were reduced to 3.0 percent, China's and India's shares of GDP in 2020 would increase to 10.9 percent and 3.2 percent and their contributions to growth to 20.1 percent and 5.5 percent, respectively.

8. If we had applied these methods (that is, applied constant price growth rates to initial shares) to Japan over the period 1965–95, its share of world GDP would have appeared to rise from about 4.3 percent to 6.6 percent. In current prices, the increase was to 17.6 percent!

Table 1.2 Comparative Industrialization
GDP at PPP prices

Factor for comparison	China, WDI 1978–2004	China, Maddison 1978–2003	U.K. 1700–1820	U.K. 1820–70	U.S. 1820–70	U.S. 1870–1913
Industrializer's initial share (%)	2.9	4.9	2.9	5.2	1.8	8.8
Industrializer's annual growth (%)	13.3	7.5	1.0	2.1	4.2	3.9
World annual growth (%)	6.8	3.1	0.5	0.9	0.9	2.1
Growth differential	6.6	4.4	0.5	1.2	3.3	1.8
Number of years	26	25	120	50	50	43

Sources: World Bank 2005b, *World Development Indicators;* Maddison 2003.

for specific dates, they do suggest that neither country administered such a large shock to the global economy as has China. According to column 1, starting with 2.9 percent of world income, for 26 years China has grown an average of 6.6 percentage points per annum faster than the world economy. According to column 2, the country had an initial share of 4.9 percent and a growth differential of 4.4 percentage points. Historical growth rates were much lower, even for booming countries, and the nearest parallel to China was the United States over the period 1820–70, during which time the differential was 3.3 percentage points a year for 50 years (with a lower starting share).[9] In absolute terms, the Industrial Revolution was a revolution because, for the first time, it was possible that average per capita incomes might double in a couple of generations. In the United States' heyday, incomes more than doubled in a single generation; and at the Giants' current growth rates and life expectancies, incomes would rise a hundredfold in a generation!

Figure 1.1 offers the same analysis for more recent experiences, again using Maddison's data. (His data for China have been challenged as too conservative over growth—see Holz [2006].) Taking 1950 (the earliest point from which annual data are available) as the start of the growth spurts in the Federal Republic of Germany, Japan, and Taiwan (China); 1962 for the Republic

---

9. Because we cannot choose peak and trough years precisely, we undoubtedly overstate the difference between China and the others, but it is unlikely that our qualitative conclusion is wrong: $(1 + 0.065)^{26}$ exceeds $(1 + 0.033)^{50}$.

of Korea; and 1979 for China, we plot (figure 1.1a) the growth of output relative to world output (again at constant, PPP prices) taking the starting year as 1, and (figure 1.1b) the evolution of the target economy's share of world output.

Figure 1.1 China and Previous Growth Spurts Compared

a. Index of growth relative to world

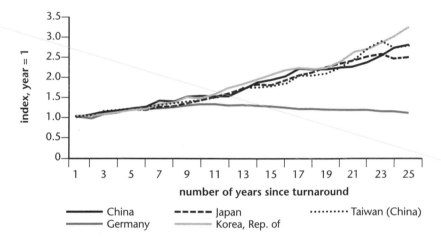

b. Evolution of share of world GDP

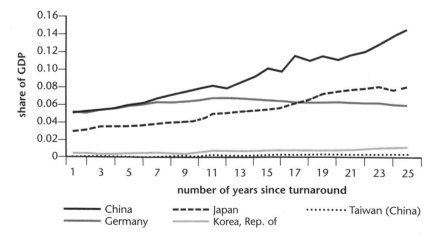

Source: Maddison 2003.

Japan, Korea, and Taiwan (China) all recorded domestic growth in excess of China's growth over their "first" 25 years, and Germany recorded rather less after the first 12 years, although in this case 1950 may be too late a starting point. After normalizing by world growth (that is, investigating the target economy's growth relative to the world's growth over its growth spurt [figure 1.1a]), all economies except Germany show fairly similar trends, at least for 20 years. In absolute terms, however, Korea and Taiwan (China) were tiny when their growth started, and even Japan, with an initial 3 percent share of world GDP, was smaller than China. Thus, in terms of an expanding share of world output, China's growth spurt has been much greater than any other spurt yet seen.

If we had data at actual prices rather than in PPP terms, China's initial share would have been much smaller and Japan's share would have been somewhat smaller, so the comparison would have been less extreme. Recall, however, that Maddison's (2003) data on China may be too conservative, and that Japan's growth spurt tailed off after 20 years. Although Japan's growth resumed in the 1980s, that country never achieved more than 9 percent of world GDP at PPP, whereas China already accounts for 14 percent.

These simple numbers suggest, indeed, that China's industrialization has been uniquely large, and this brings us only to the present. Projecting forward suggests an even larger shock to other economies. Moreover, it might be important that China and India are growing in a world that already may be pushing against the limits of resource availability. Although one might reasonably expect technical progress to continue to raise output per capita, one cannot deny that the global commons—frontier land, the oceans, the atmosphere—are under pressure.

If we do a similar exercise in terms of exports, the story is slightly different. Putting aside Korea's astronomical rate of export growth (50 times more than world exports over 43 years), China's export growth relative to the world's export growth was much the same as that of other countries for 25 years, edging into top place thereafter. In terms of shares of world exports, however, Germany had the greater increase (from 3.2 percent to 10.5 percent over 25 years, compared with China's increase from 0.8 percent to 7.3 percent and Japan's increase from 1.3 percent to 7.2 percent). China's share, of course, is expected to increase further in the future, whereas Germany's and Japan's shares fell away, and both of those were recovering rather than emerging economies. Hence, even in terms of exports, China is arguably the largest shock we have seen thus far, and its growth and that of India are projected to continue. In short, even though China is not the dominant force in the world economy, the shock it is administering to the world is unprecedented. Clearly, interest in the Giants is well justified.

Accounting for Growth

Now we turn briefly to the underpinnings of the growth rates assumed above for the Giants. The sources of growth include the growth of the workforce, the accumulation of physical and human capital tempered by any diminution of natural capital, the rate of technical change, and the allocation of resources across activities. The contribution of these sources to actual growth in China and India is affected by the incentive structure implicit in their domestic environments (for example, the functioning of factor and product markets, the breadth of access to these markets, economic and social infrastructure, and a range of policies) and by the nature and extent of their integration with world markets. We do not analyze the Giants' domestic environments or factor accumulation in any detail, taking as given projections of their likely magnitudes from other sources. We do need to ask briefly what those projections are, however, so that we may understand the nature of their growth.

In both Giants, population growth has been slowing and is expected to continue to do so. China's population grew by only 0.6 percent a year during 2000–05, to reach 1.32 billion[10]; it is expected to peak in 2032 and decline thereafter.[11] India's population grew by 1.4 percent in 2000–05, reaching 1.10 billion, and its growth is expected to slow to 0.7 percent a year between 2030 and 2040 (by which time it will have overtaken China). These trends reflect sharply lower fertility, with people age 15–64 accounting for 71 percent in China in 2005, falling to 69 percent in 2020 and to 62 percent in 2040. The corresponding percentages for India are 63 percent in 2005, and 67 percent in 2020. China's decline in the work cohort is likely to be at least partly offset by increasing employment participation rates, but India's younger profile is one reason to believe it will start to close the income gap by the second quarter of the century.

China has increased its urban population share from 21 percent in 1981 to 43 percent in 2005 (Cooper 2006), with absolute declines in the rural popula-

---

10. A billion is 1,000 millions.
11. For comparability we use United Nations population projections rather than local ones.

tion. Moreover, much rural employment is nonagricultural. Nonetheless, agriculture still accounts for approximately 45 percent of employment and industry accounts for 22 percent, so despite the importance of sectoral reallocation in China's past growth, we still see it as a potent force for the future. This is especially so given that agriculture accounts for a far lower share of GDP (13 percent) than of employment. Urbanization was much slower in India—from 23 percent to 28 percent over 1981–2001—with the number of rural residents increasing by more than 200 million. Agriculture provided 59 percent of employment in 2000 and industry provided only 16 percent. Again there is plenty of scope (and need) for future reallocation in India.

Given its size and its importance in poverty alleviation (see below) agriculture will remain an important sector in both Giants, even though the main drivers of growth will be elsewhere. In China, yields already are quite high and agricultural land is under pressure from urban and road expansion, so future growth will depend significantly on new crops and increased marketization. In India, the need for growth is greater but so is the scope. Indian yields are generally low, even by developing-country standards, and agriculture is hamstrung by poor infrastructure and excessive regulation (FAO 2006). Recent growth has been respectable in the sector, and achieving our projected growth rates (let alone those foreseen in official Indian plans) will require at least as much in the future.

Both China and India have made significant advances in basic education in the last two decades. In 2000, adult literacy was 84 percent in China and 57 percent in India, and youth (ages 15–24) literacy rates were 98 percent and 73 percent, respectively. Moreover, both countries are accumulating human capital rapidly, with secondary school enrollment rates of 50 percent and 39 percent, respectively, in 1998 (UNDP 2002, pp. 183–84). By 2005, India was producing 2.5 million new university-level graduates per year, 10 percent of whom were in engineering (Cooper 2006); China produced 3.4 million graduates, including 151,000 with postgraduate degrees (*Chinese Statistical Abstract* 2005, pp. 175–76). By 2004, approximately one-fifth of the relevant age cohort in China was entering tertiary education (Cooper 2006), although, as noted above, the cohort itself is already beginning to decline.

The prodigious growth in the number of graduates in China and India presages a significant increase in the Giants' shares of world skills and, hence, changes in their comparative advantages. The McKinsey Global Institute (2005) has suggested, however, that only about 10 percent of Chinese and Indian graduates currently would meet the standards expected by major U.S. companies; and, although undoubtedly this will change over time, at present one should not think of most of these graduates as very highly skilled workers.[12]

Turning to physical capital, the GDP-weighted average rates of gross capital accumulation were 42 percent and 24 percent for China and India, respectively, over 1990–2003. China's higher rate partly reflects its more capital-intensive structure and investment in infrastructure (including housing), and helps explain its faster growth (Srinivasan 2006). It was largely financed by China's prodigious domestic savings rate, and explains perhaps half of its growth rate. Total factor productivity (TFP), on the other hand, has increased at a respectable but not spectacular 2.5 percent annually in both China and India since 1995, although the recent revisions to the GDP data will increase the former's estimate. Much of the recorded TFP growth presumably reflects the reallocation of labor from agriculture and the state sector to market activities.

A natural question about any growth projection is, what are its margins of error? Overall, we believe that the estimates reported in table 1.1 are conservative and reasonably robust, but some commentators argue that there are serious vulnerabilities arising from the environment, income distribution, and governance, among other things. Hence, after analyzing the possible consequences of our central view, we return to consider these vulnerabilities. In the remainder of this introduction, we will contextualize and summarize the chapters in the rest of the book.

International Trade

China's and India's growth affect other countries through a variety of channels, but international trade is arguably the strongest and most direct. In chapter 2, the authors consider improvements in the Giants' industrial capabilities, and the authors of chapter 3 present a model of world trade into which we fit their growth.

Trade Expansion

China's trade expansion since 1978 has been legendary; and, since the early 1990s, India also has taken off. At 5.7 percent for exports and 4.8 percent for

---

12. In the long run, the apparent economies of agglomeration for very highly skilled workers suggest that China or India could become poles of attraction for science and engineering. Such a situation could transform countries' relative standings dramatically.

imports, China's share of world goods and services trade exceed its GDP share (see table 1.3). This is extraordinary for such a large economy, although in part it reflects China's integration into Asian production chains. Through this integration, perhaps as much as a third of the recorded value of exports (measured gross) comes from imported inputs rather than from local value added, which is what GDP measures.[13] With annual growth at 15.1 percent over 1995–2004, China provided almost 9 percent of the increase in world exports of goods and services (second only to the United States), and 8 percent of the increase in imports (also second to the United States).

Within these aggregates, China is a significant importer and exporter of manufactures, with market shares of 6.2 percent and 7.7 percent, respectively, in 2004. Manufactured imports comprise mainly parts and components for assembly activities and capital equipment, whereas exports substantially are finished goods. One notable feature of China's exporting has been technical upgrading. Devlin, Estevadeordal, and Rodríguez-Clare (2006) have shown how high-technology goods partly have displaced low-tech ones within the set of manufactured exports; Lall and Albaladejo (2004) forecast great competitive pressure from China at the lower end of the high-tech range (for example, autos, machinery, and electronics); and Freund and Ozden (2006) have found that China is displacing Central American exports mostly in sectors associated with relatively high-wage producing countries. Part of this upgrading reflects the import of more sophisticated components (see, for example, Branstetter and Lardy 2006), but part of it almost certainly arises from local improvements.

Even more striking is China's growth in imports of primary products. Soybean consumption has increased 15 percent a year recently, and soy and palm oil consumption by 20 percent and 25 percent, respectively (Streifel 2006). All largely are imported. China is a huge importer of fuels and minerals, accounting for nearly 40 percent of world market growth since 1995. Part of the increase in materials imports is balanced by corresponding declines in the countries from which China has displaced manufacturing, but most of the increase represents a net rise in demand: millions of Chinese consumers are starting to buy consumer durables and other goods as they grow richer, and low Chinese export prices are stimulating consumption elsewhere in the world.

---

13. Moreover, as Bergsten et al. (2006) have shown, much of the recent increase in the U.S. trade deficit with China is offset by declines in deficits with its neighboring supplying countries. This finding is consistent with the gradual transfer of assembly from the region into China.

Table 1.3 Trade in Goods and Services for Six Large Economies
percent

| Economy | Exports of goods and services | | | | Imports of goods and services | | | | |
	Share (2004)	Share of growth (1995–2004)	Projected growth rate (2005–20)	Share of growth 2005–20	Share (2003)	Share of growth (1995–2003)	Projected growth rate (2005–20)	Share of growth 2005–20
China	5.7	8.9	7.8	15.4	4.8	7.8	6.6	11.0
India	1.2	1.8	7.5	2.7	1.1	1.8	6.3	2.2
United States	11.2[a]	10.7	3.4	9.9	16.5	24.1	3.5	15.4
Japan	5.4[a]	-3.7	4.2	6.3	4.7	-0.8	3.5	4.4
Germany	9.1	7.7	1.8	3.8	8.2	3.6	2.0	3.9
Brazil	1.0	0.5	1.7	0.4	0.7	0.3	4.3	0.8

Source: World Development Indicators.
Note: Average contribution to growth for the period 2005–20 was calculated using projected average export growth rates.
a. 2003.

The data on the total consumption of various primary products presented in
table 1.4 reinforce the importance of China and India in world commodity markets. In metals and coal, China always is ranked first, with shares of 15 to 33
percent of world consumption, and the United States is ranked second or third;
in other energies, the United States is first and China is second or third. The
Giants also are important consumers of agricultural commodities, and here India figures prominently, leading the world in consumption of sugar and tea.

Increasing commodity demand from the Giants obviously supports prices,
other things being equal, but prices also depend on supply. Most analysts hold
that, in recent years, Chinese demand has increased most metals prices be-

Table 1.4 Shares in World Consumption of Primary Commodities
Percent by volume

Commodity	China	India	United States
Agriculture 2003			
Wheat	15.2	13.5	5.4
Rice	29.7	21.4	1.0
Maize	17.0	2.2	32.5
Soybeans	19.2	3.7	24.0
Soy oil	24.4	6.4	25.7
Palm oil	15.8	15.3	0.6
Sugar	6.6	15.2	12.5
Tea	14.4	17.5	3.8
Coffee	0.4	0.8	16.8
Cotton	31.2	12.8	6.9
Rubber	23.5	8.4	12.9
Metals 2005			
Aluminum	22.5	3.0	19.4
Copper	21.6	2.3	13.8
Lead	25.7	1.3	19.4
Nickel	15.2	0.9	9.5
Tin	33.3	2.2	12.1
Zinc	28.6	3.1	9.0
Iron ore	29.0	4.8	4.7
Steel production	31.5	3.5	8.5
Energy 2003			
Coal	32.9	7.1	20.6
Oil	7.4	3.4	25.3
Energy (total)	12.6	3.6	23.4
Electricity generation	11.4	3.8	24.3

Source: Streifel 2006.

cause supply growth has not kept up with demand.[14] The exception that (loosely speaking) proves the rule is aluminum, for which China is a net exporter and produces about 25 percent of the world total. Compared with price increases of 379 percent for copper from January 2002 to June 2006, aluminum prices have increased modestly—up only 80 percent (Streifel 2006).

India's trade in goods has not been remarkable to date, but it is starting to increase as barriers come down. The country accounted for about 2 percent in the growth of world exports and imports over the period 1995–2004. It will be significant for the evolution of prices, as the Giants' trade expands over the next few years, that the commodity compositions of India's and China's exports differ substantially. India's largest single export is gemstones (one-eighth of visible exports in 2004), but manufacturing is the largest export category and is now starting to grow strongly. The most dynamic export sector in India is information technology (IT)-enabled services for global companies, including call centers and software application, design, and maintenance. Such activities require qualified English-speaking labor, and India has an abundant, low-cost supply. The principal users of these services are U.S.-based global companies, but offshore software development contracts from Japan and Korea are expected to grow (Fujita and Hamaguchi 2006). Despite their dynamism, India's overall exports of commercial services ($40 billion in 2004) are less than those of China ($62 billion), although $17 billion of India's were in communications and software (arguably the high end of the sector), compared with China's $3.6 billion in software. However, both countries still have relatively small world shares (1.8 percent and 2.8 percent of world services exports, respectively).

Services account for only 41 percent of GDP in China (even after the recent revaluation), compared with approximately 52 percent in lower-middle-income countries, and this leaves plenty of room for growth if Chinese service providers start to master global service technology in the same way they have mastered manufacturing. In India, the service share of 51 percent is somewhat above the norm for low-income countries, and there is a dynamic export sector—business and IT services. The IT sector accounts for only 6 percent of service turnover, however, and employs perhaps 3 million people. Moreover, it tends to be focused at the low to middle end of the business (Commander et

---

14. Increases in some soft commodity prices also have been high (for example, rubber), but other factors appear to underlie this as well as China's growth (Streifel 2006).

al. 2004). Thus, services trade alone does not look likely to transform Indian economic performance.

Industrial Geography: The Evolution of Comparative Advantage

The key question going forward is how China's and India's international trade is likely to develop. Before getting to specific numbers, it is worthwhile to consider some qualitative trends in industrial and service capabilities: both India and China have demonstrated the ability to upgrade their performance in specific sectors, and this is the subject matter of chapter 2. As just noted, although services exports will be important for India, we do not see them presaging a completely new development model; and China's appetite for primary imports seems bound to continue growing. Hence, the future pattern of manufacturing production and exports is likely to be central to development in both countries.

The principal drivers in the Giants are large domestic middle-class markets (currently about $1 trillion per year in China and $250 billion annually in India), and large supplies of labor supplemented, at least in China, by improving industrial capability stimulated by domestic and foreign investment. The first driver creates a base for industries with large economies of scale, and the second will tend to keep wages down and help maintain labor-intensive industries. These features combine to favor certain mid-tech and high-tech sectors, such as autos, electronics, and domestic appliances—and, in the future, pharmaceuticals and engineering. Chapter 2 documents the rapid recent advances in technology and organization, and the strong future prospects of these sectors.

In China, the continuation of low-skilled, labor-intensive manufacturing seems feasible, but not in the traditional manufacturing centers along the eastern seaboard where production costs are rising. Some adjustment undoubtedly will prompt less-skilled sectors to relocate abroad, including to India, but it also is likely that some will move to inland centers where the large agricultural reserve of labor could be trained and mobilized for industrial work. The increases in outputs and incomes following this movement inland would be part of the payoff for recent huge investments in infrastructure.

Higher education also is booming in China, with a large share of its graduates in science and engineering and, of course, many skilled Chinese citizens who live abroad and could return. A concentration of the best Chinese brains could make China a major force in some sophisticated sectors, but the demand for skills in public service, general management, and education could constrain the emergence of such technological or innovative leadership for some time in many sectors. One consequence of this is that China will continue to import sophisticated goods, including capital goods, from abroad.

China currently sits at the center of production networks spanning Southeast and East Asia. The policy of offering duty-free access to imports of components for exports while protecting the local producers of both intermediate and final goods for the domestic market undoubtedly encouraged Chinese openness. This policy is beginning to unwind as protection levels fall and the domestic market grows, making it more attractive to bring components manufacture closer to assembly and to the market. Thus, the biggest uncertainty probably faces the suppliers of intermediates to Chinese industry, mainly in East and Southeast Asia.

India is smaller and poorer than China (with a gross national income per capita of approximately $3,000 PPP to China's $5,000 PPP) and, as argued above, India has not yet proved to be a major force in international manufacturing. So far, India has had export success in textiles and clothing, and, given its abundance of unskilled labor, it seems almost bound to continue to sustain a competitive edge in these industries. It is also a growing player in pharmaceuticals, building on its base of seasoned corporations, its ample supplies of graduates, and its potentially large home market. For the same reasons, India also is acquiring a reputation in some specialized engineering and services sectors. Other major industries show potential for expansion—steel, white goods, electronics—but probably mainly for the home market over our time horizon. Thus, although one may anticipate robust growth in Indian manufacturing over the next decade, there does not appear to be a strong likelihood of "disruptive" exporting occurring.

Despite this catalog of potential successes, China and India cannot have comparative advantage in everything. What, therefore, does all of this mean for other countries? To answer this question we need an approach that is grounded more firmly in the adding-up constraints of the Giants' and world economies.

General Equilibrium

In chapter 3, the authors consider the Giants' growth and capabilities and ask how they affect world trade. A number of approaches to answering this question are possible. Some scholars focus mainly on the bilateral trade links—for example, DfID (2005) and Jenkins and Edwards (2006). These links represent the most direct links between any two countries, but strong spillovers are likely between countries if they compete in the same third markets, even if there is no direct bilateral trade between them. Moreover, as Chinese demand grows, supply constraints will determine countries' exports to China more than their current shares of Chinese imports do.

Most studies consider global markets and compare the trade patterns of China and the studies' target countries. They argue that countries with export patterns similar to China's are likely to suffer losses as China grows, whereas those whose exports match China's imports are likely to receive a boost (see, for example, Lall and Weiss 2004; Goldstein et al. 2006; and Stevens and Kennan 2006). This also is informative for it recognizes that the principal mechanism connecting two countries' goods markets is the world market, and that, over the medium term, the exact locations where countries sell are secondary to the overall supply and demand balance. This approach, however, ignores China's main characteristic—its size. A flow accounting for, say, 1 percent of China's exports would outweigh Thailand's exports in that product even if it accounted for 5 percent of the latter's total exports. Also, because it is based solely on international trade data, this approach misses the resource constraints on China's future growth and their implications for relative prices, both of which will induce adjustments in initial patterns.

Our analysis of the trade consequences of the Giants' growth addresses these problems by using a computable general equilibrium (CGE) model. CGE models impose an internal consistency on their conclusions that requires, among other things, that trade imbalances do not grow unchecked and that demand equals supply for each good and factor of production. When considering such huge shocks as the more than doubling of the Giants' economies, this discipline is extremely important, although it comes at a cost, of course. The model has a simple constant returns-to-scale technology; productivity, labor force, and capital stock growth are all exogenous, and behavioral relationships are quite crude. Moreover, the modeling approach makes less use of detailed trade data than do the exercises discussed above, although a great deal of effort has gone into characterizing the trade links, the trade policy, the production structure, and the factor markets in 2001 (the model's base year) and into estimating the behavioral parameters in the various markets.

Chapter 3 starts by "rolling the world economy" forward from its base of 2001 to 2005, incorporating the enlargement of the European Union, the final liberalizations mandated by the Uruguay Round, India's recent liberalization, and Chinese accession to the World Trade Organization. It then postulates a continuation to 2020 of India's current tariff and trade reforms, and applies exogenously given estimates of the growth of productivity and factor supplies in all countries and regions. These estimates come from the World Bank "central projections" and thus imply the growth rates shown in table 1.1. In aggregate, they lead to yearly import growth rates of 6.6 percent and 6.3 percent for China and India, respectively, and to export growth rates of 7.8 percent and 7.5 percent, respectively (see table 1.3). These rates, in turn, imply that China will provide 15 percent and 11 percent of export and import growth, respectively, for 2005 to 2020, compared with the United States' 10 percent and 15 percent and with India's 2.7 percent and 2.2 percent. The excess of export over import growth rates does *not* indicate expanding trade surpluses for China and India because relative prices change. In fact, for technical reasons we assume that current account balances are frozen at 2001 levels as a percentage of GDP: +1.3 percent for China and +0.3 percent for India. As before, we reiterate that these growth rates are not predictions but are plausible magnitudes to identify orders of magnitude and provide a base for some thought experiments.

From this base, we next ask, what if India and China grew faster by 1.9 percentage points and 2.1 percentage points a year, respectively, as a result of faster productivity improvements (in all industries)?[15] This simulation gives a direct indication of the effects of the Giants' advance, and we analyze it both alone and with an added assumption that the productivity increase results in improvements in the range and quality of China's and India's export products. These improvements increase the productivity (or value) of Chinese and Indian goods for their users (or consumers), which in turn generates a real income gain for them. There are three broad effects on other countries: their exports face fiercer competition because the Giants' costs fall; their imports from the Giants become cheaper; and they benefit from aggregate demand increases, both in the Giants and from the (universal) increase in real income resulting from efficiency improvement. The balance of these forces varies from country to country, but because most countries import significant amounts from the Giants and all get a share of the increase in demand, most countries gain overall. In the simulation with growth alone, the exceptions are some Southeast Asian countries, the rest of South Asia, and Europe, which are projected to be net losers (see table 3.7, chapter 3). When we add

---

15. Average TFP growth increases from 1.9 percent annually in the base to 3.8 percent for India, and from 2.5 percent to 4.6 percent for China.

in the quality improvements, the Philippines' losses increase (because of their dependence on electronics in which they compete so directly with China), but every other country gains, although not by enough for Singapore and the rest of South Asia to become net gainers overall. For them, the effects of increased competition predominate.

Even for net gainers, however, not all is rosy in this particular garden. The Giants achieve major gains in their market shares in manufacturing, so most other countries experience declines in manufacturing output relative to base, especially in clothing and electronics, which are most sensitive to competition. Thus, even if the Giants' success is generally good news for other countries as a whole, there are adjustment pressures within those countries.

These results suggest that an important concern for other countries will be the extent to which the Giants, especially China, move up market into their "product space"—in terms of both products and quality within them—and this view is reinforced by simulations that restrict technical progress to the sectors identified in chapter 2 as gaining competitiveness. In these cases, world trade increases strongly because China and India receive a boost in their current exporting sectors; other countries adjust their output patterns to accommodate these shocks, often halving output in machinery and electronics and nearly doubling it in clothing, leather, and wood (again, relative to the base). As Freund and Ozden (2006) concluded for Central America, manufacturers' fears about Chinese and Indian competition often are well founded. However, only a general equilibrium analysis such as ours can show that the offsetting benefits from cheaper imports and stronger world growth are generally larger.

Modeling exercises are parables, not predictions. One should not take the precise numbers literally, and within each of our aggregates (say, electronics) there will be a wide range of effects across different products. The results do show, however, that the consequences of the Giants' rise could be large in particular sectors, but that suitable adjustments to the new circumstances could enable most countries to win.

International Financial Integration

China and India are actual or potential giants in international trade, but their positions in international finance are currently more mixed. As the authors of chapter 4 show (figure 4.3), China is the seventh-largest holder of foreign direct investment (FDI) liabilities (with 4.1 percent of the world total), and

China and India, respectively, are the first- and fifth-largest holders of reserve assets. Beyond these dimensions, however, they are minor players in the international financial system.

One major question about China's and India's financial flows is whether they might absorb FDI that otherwise would go to other countries. We have argued above that the Giants' growth will change patterns of comparative advantage and competitiveness, and hence change investment opportunities—and thus FDI. Some consequences may be negative for some partners (for example, a parts factory moving from Malaysia to China), but some could be positive (investing in commodity extraction or a processing plant to meet expanding Chinese or Indian demand). This type of effect is implicit in the trade discussion above.

But this is not the way in which the issue usually is articulated: the popular concern is that investment opportunities in other countries go unfilled for lack of resources. Clearly, if world savings were fixed, new opportunities in the Giants would displace less good ones elsewhere; but, in the face of high returns, savings may increase and the Giants may have access to capital that would otherwise not go to others. Moreover, one needs to consider whether it is plausible that the Giants' absorption of capital is large enough to squeeze other countries. The evidence on China so far suggests that such displacement has not occurred, and even though that country currently absorbs approximately 18 percent of world FDI inflows, as much as a third of that amount might be "round-tripping" (that is, it might be Chinese capital that is routed through Hong Kong [China] so as to reap the tax benefits of foreign investment), and perhaps another third comes from the diaspora and would not be invested elsewhere (Cooper 2006). As India becomes more attractive to FDI, we could expect significant inflows to bring its share of FDI liabilities (0.4 percent in 2004) toward its GDP share (1.7 percent), but the magnitudes are not huge over the next decade and, again, much seems likely to come from the diaspora.

China and India are also suppliers of FDI—small amounts at present, but potentially growing larger. The former has assets of approximately $45 billion and annual outflows of $5.5 billion (Broadman 2007), mostly in Asia (especially Hong Kong [China]) and Latin America. Africa also is starting to figure in the equation as China tries to consolidate its access to fuels and raw materials. FDI in developing countries sometimes is conjoined with official aid flows (Kaplinsky, McCormick, and Morris 2006). For India, the stock and flow are about $5 billion and $1 billion, respectively.

The notable feature of the Giants' current international portfolios is their asymmetry: assets are mainly in low-yielding reserve assets (67 percent and 82 percent of the totals, respectively, for China and India), whereas their liabilities are in higher-yielding areas of FDI and portfolio investment.[16] This differentiation reflects at least partly the restrictions on and limitations of their domestic financial systems, so that as financial liberalization proceeds, we would expect their portfolios to become similar and both to become larger investors in nonreserve assets abroad. On the basis of other countries' experiences and on the pressures to move to a more consumption-based model of growth, we also expect that China's present large current account surplus will fall (although there is no professional consensus on this). Hence, overall, the Giants' reserve accumulation seems most likely to fall in absolute terms. The effects of these changes on other countries will depend on their net financial transactions. Recipients of the new FDI will benefit, whereas those countries that depend on international borrowing will suffer because the declining demand for reserves is likely to raise interest rates somewhat.

Finally, we argue that two additional fears sometimes raised about the Giants' financial integration are exaggerated. First, although the Giants' financial integration introduces risks that would be absent if they remained autarchic (via, for example, their banking risks or contagion to suppliers if demand were suddenly to fall because protectionism cut their exports), these risks do not seem to be of different orders of magnitude from those in the normal operation of international capital markets. The second fear is that Chinese and eventually Indian FDI, lending, and official development assistance could undermine multilateral efforts to achieve higher common standards in aid (for example, against tying aid) or in investment (for example, business responsibility conditions). Even if the Giants do not adopt current developed-country norms, this does not seem likely at present, given the smallness of the flows; however, as the Giants increase their outflows, it may become an issue of debate.

Growth and the Environment

Environmental issues play two roles in this narrative. First, growing concern about local environmental quality—especially water and air quality—or even absolute limits on carrying capacity could constrain growth. Second, the Giants are large enough to affect the global commons. Their emissions generate

---

16. When risk is factored in, the imbalance in returns is reduced.

cross-border effects in terms of acid rain, for example, but most significant in the long run are greenhouse gas emissions. Furthermore, demand from the Giants may put increased pressure on world energy markets, although perhaps not to the extent popularly imagined. The author of chapter 5 addresses energy and emissions, but we begin here by briefly considering water.

Water is the most pressing environmental constraint in both of the Giants. In 2004, China's naturally available water flow was 2,206 m³/person and India's was 1,754 m³/person, compared with an average of 7,762 m³/person for developing countries and a world average of 8,549 m³/person (Shalizi 2006). Approximately 400 of 660 major Chinese cities currently face water shortages, a third of them severe ("China: Water Shortage" 2006); and water shortage in India has become a serious and recurring concern in many regions, including some major metropolitan areas. Briscoe (2005) has documented the poor state of water infrastructure and the unsustainable exploitation of groundwater sources, stimulated rather than contained by government actions, including the provision of free power.

In China, well over half the major lakes are severely polluted; only 38 percent of river water is drinkable; only 20 percent of the population has access to unpolluted drinking water; and almost a quarter of the people regularly drink water that is heavily polluted ("China: Water Shortage" 2006). Waste disposal is a serious source of water pollution, and the countryside suffers from the leaching of nitrates into groundwater. The problems are less pronounced in India (in part because urbanization and industrial development are lower), but, nevertheless, serious degradation in the quality of groundwater and river water has resulted from indiscriminate use of pesticides and chemical fertilizers and from salinity arising from overexploitation of groundwater. The deterioration is compounded by lack of proper effluent treatment for domestic waste water and industrial wastes (Government of India 2002; Briscoe 2005).

Continued rapid growth will exacerbate the water problems in each of the Giants, demanding resources, efficient utilization, and careful political management of the allocative process. This sector is arguably the most pressing of the environmental challenges.

Energy and emissions, on the other hand, present perhaps the largest policy challenge for the next century, and in chapter 5 the author considers the Giants' roles in this challenge over the period to 2050.[17] Despite considerable

---

17. The longer horizon used here than elsewhere in this book is necessary because policy options can be assessed sensibly only relative to long-run outcomes and because adjustment paths are so long.

progress in recent decades, China still appears to be energy inefficient. Its energy use per unit of GDP at market prices and actual exchange rates is 3.5 times that of the United States. India's is 2.7 times larger, and this factor has been increasing of late. Measured relative to GDP in PPP instead, China and India appear more efficient than the United States. However, given that most energy use is in tradable/marketed sectors and given the evidence of continuing inefficiency in industry (World Energy Council 1999), it still seems that the scope for and returns to economizing on the Giants' energy use are potentially large. China and India currently contribute 17 percent and 5 percent of global carbon emissions, respectively, and could account jointly for half of those emissions by 2050. If they alone pursued reasonable efficiency strategies, total world emissions could fall by approximately 20 percent, and their joint share could decrease to below 40 percent. Locally, air pollution is estimated to have caused more than 400,000 excess deaths in China in 2003 and more than 100,000 in India in 2000, and these figures will increase if action is not taken.

China and India both have huge investment programs under way or planned, and we argue that they currently have a one-time opportunity to raise energy efficiency for the sake of both local and global objectives by adopting higher standards now. Doing so undoubtedly will add to their costs, but because the efficiencies will be engineered from the beginning and from a low base, costs may not increase very significantly. Much depends on very specific details—for instance, whether locations that produce or burn dirty coal would have the water available to undertake pre-use washing. Moreover, apart from some transitional frictions, our results suggest that a less carbon-intensive energy policy would not curtail the Giants' growth seriously or place huge demands on global capital markets. The alternative of waiting until technology makes clean energy cheaper than at present may not be cost effective for the Giants (or for other major emitters of carbon) because delay has quasi-permanent effects on carbon dioxide accumulations.

Turning to global energy markets, the roles of China and India are less critical than often imagined. It is true that these countries have generated nearly half of the increase in oil use this century, but their shares of world oil consumption still were modest—7.4 percent and 3.4 percent, respectively, in 2003. Moreover, both through the recent past and in our forward-looking projections, the sensitivity of oil prices to the Giants' demand is fairly low. The spike in oil prices during the first half of 2006 owes more to constraints in, and concerns about, supply than to excessive demand increases.

Environmental stresses, both local and global, clearly require serious attention as the Giants grow—although not necessarily in the same way in China and India. However, our analysis suggests that, although addressing them will impose costs, it need not curtail growth rates seriously. Similarly, although high energy prices could reduce world growth slightly, the feedback from the Giants' growth onto energy prices and back to their growth will not be large enough to constrain them.

Inequalities

Another possible constraint on future growth could be rising income (and other related) inequalities and declining effectiveness in eradicating poverty. Both China and, to a lesser extent, India have coupled great success in reducing absolute poverty with increases in inequality. As the authors of chapter 6 argue, much of the latter is "good" inequality, reflecting a return to more direct incentives for effort, skills, investment, and entrepreneurship following periods in which the Giants' governments strove to suppress them. But at some point, increasing inequality is counterproductive. Inequality of opportunity wastes talent and ultimately reduces growth because it cuts the level of investment in education and business (World Bank 2005c). It also can lead to political stresses that hinder the pursuit of efficiency-enhancing reforms and even may cause unrest and dissent. Thus, the policy challenge for the future is to try to achieve a balance between good and bad inequalities, to avoid the worst exclusions while maintaining incentives to accumulate and to take risks. The questions of interest for the rest of the world are whether this is achieved, and how.

Growth rarely is balanced, either sectorally or geographically, and neither of the Giants is an exception. In China, primary sector growth (mostly agriculture) appears to be the most pro-poor, but it has lagged behind other sectors over the last two decades. Similarly but not identically, rural areas have lagged behind urban areas. Policy to improve the rural economy via improvements in health, education, and infrastructure services seems likely to help those who are worst off, both by encouraging rural activity (agricultural or otherwise) and by facilitating migration to the cities. To the extent that the former route would increase agricultural output, it would reduce net food imports, although China's already high yields and declining areas of cultivation will limit the extent of that reduction unless the shift is made strongly to nontraditional cash crops. Migration, on the other hand, could stimulate increases in output in tradable secondary and tertiary sectors. Which route will dominate has implications for trade and the rest of the world. We certainly expect more migration, but the precise balance is impossible to forecast at present.

In India, land inequality is higher than in China, and so primary growth is less poverty alleviating than is growth in the tertiary sector. Nonetheless, the weight of rural poverty is so great that rural policies are necessary in the same areas as noted for China. The requirement is not for generic redistribution policies, however; rather, it is for targeted interventions that address identified restrictions on opportunities.

One concern is that targeting rural areas or the primary sector would reduce urban growth without boosting rural growth because the latter is already close to its maximum. The evidence in both China and India suggests that in the aggregate there has been no trade-off between growth in these pro-poor sectors or regions and overall growth; and, at the level of individual policies, we believe that careful analysis and design also can avoid the trade-off. Both of the Giants are seeking to address their growing inequalities, but success is far from easy. Constant evaluation is necessary to ensure that policies are effective and appropriate. One useful component will be to ensure that governance—capacity, accountability, and responsiveness—improves at local levels.

Growing inequality within the Giants attracts a good deal of attention both locally and globally—perhaps more than it deserves relative to other factors that determine growth and welfare. The challenges are real, and the ways in which they are resolved may influence trade patterns and hence other countries, but we do not expect addressing them to disrupt medium-term growth significantly.

Investment Climate and Governance

Current development theory gives governance a central role in accumulation and resource allocation, and hence in growth. Governance processes differ dramatically between China and India, but in neither country have either processes or outcomes corresponded to conventional views of optimality. Therefore, in chapter 7 the author asks whether governance problems could derail growth and whether the Giants refute the hypothesis that governance matters for growth. In both cases the answer is a qualified "no."

Three factors help explain the Giants' growth takeoffs in the face of only average governance indicators. First, in the 1980s and 1990s, policy prohibitions on certain economic activities were relaxed and the Giants' size as potential markets and labor forces was sufficient to encourage activity. Second, although only average globally, governance indicators as measured by security of property rights are significantly better in China and India than in other poor countries; consequently, when capital inflows were no longer discouraged or prohibited, investors looking for low-wage locations found China and India relatively attractive. Third, improvements in governance in the late 1970s (albeit only from poor to average levels) could have fostered growth from the late 1970s (China) or mid-1980s (India). Although no direct measures of governance are available for the 1970s, political events and policy decisions in both countries suggest the emergence of institutional and political constraints on opportunistic behavior.

The constraints on opportunism were achieved in quite different political settings in the two Giants. China navigated the challenges without open political contests through a series of internal Communist Party conventions and policy decisions. Particularly in the 1980s, policy decisions allowed cadres to reap rewards from investment (for example, by encouraging township and village enterprises [TVEs], giving localities the lion's share of tax revenues, and granting them authority over land allocation decisions that were key to implementing the Household Responsibility System). At the same time, though, internal party institutions were developed that, consciously or unconsciously, aligned individual cadre incentives with those of the broader party. Significant investments in institutionalized cadre promotion and evaluation reassured cadres that the returns to the investments they oversaw (such as those in TVEs) would not be expropriated and that they would be rewarded for growth-promoting land management decisions. In the 1990s, increasing institutional checks and balances (also largely within the party and largely at the center) increased the security of foreign investors, and FDI replaced TVEs as a major driver of manufacturing growth.

Growth in India fell in the 1970s, not only with the abrupt and broad introduction of intrusive microeconomic regulations (ranging from licensing to the nationalization of banks) but also with the increasing centralization of power within the ruling party and within the formal institutions of government. Growth resumed when the erosion of major governance institutions that provided political checks and balances was reversed with the lifting of the Emergency of the 1970s, with elections that removed the Congress Party from office for the first time since independence, and with the restoration of such key institutional checks as the legislative review authority of the judiciary. These events also put a halt to, and very partially reversed, the introduction of counterproductive industrial policies.

Turning to the future, the governance challenges continue to differ. In India, the reform process moves at a stately pace, with vigorous debate but ultimately sufficient consensus and legitimacy to make reforms fairly robust. As political competition comes to rely less on (still important) clientelist promises and sectarian appeals, the political incentives to reform will increase.[18] Even then, however, increasing concerns about equity and distribution will condition policy and will demand resources for rural infrastructure, education, and so on. The challenge of improving the investment climate—whether infrastructural or regulatory—will remain significant. The core governance problems in the investment climate—the threat of expropriatory activity and the arbitrary treatment of firms—will continue to dwindle, both in absolute terms and relative to the regulatory hurdles confronting entrepreneurial activity.

The future governance challenge in China is to maintain the intraparty institutions that link individual cadre interests to those of countrywide equitable growth. This appears to have become more difficult in the 1990s than it was in the 1980s, and it may become yet more difficult in the future. The Communist Party of China has formalized its practices and enhanced political checks and balances at the top of the party, it has allowed local elections, and it has increased the oversight activities of different intraparty legislative institutions. All of these changes have increased the security of larger investors (for example, foreign direct investors) who can appeal to the central government. However, local cadres still have enormous authority in their jurisdictions. This only matters because, as the party and citizens more broadly have begun to care more about issues of equity, social service provision, and such public goods as environmental quality, cadre incentives seem to be more strongly related to economic growth than ever before.

The 1990s' fiscal reforms that largely reversed the generous 1980s' fiscal policies of allowing China's local governments to retain large tax shares have increased local governments' incentives to maximize the revenue potential of local assets. Promotion criteria for cadres, though increasingly reflective of the central government's desire to see better social service provision and better husbandry of the environment, still place a priority on economic growth. And the fast growth of the economy has driven up the value of the outside

---

18. Democracy has an intrinsic as well as an instrumental value, but that is not an issue we take up here.

options of cadres faster than the value of internal party rewards. All of these circumstances give cadres strong incentives to pursue economic growth at the expense of other social goals. For example, local officials have stronger incentives to reallocate assets under their control (such as farmland) to more highly valued uses at the expense of current beneficiaries. The rapid increase in inequality is a potential source of stress and, especially when associated with corruption or arbitrary official behavior, could reduce high levels of popular support for the government. This, in turn, makes it more expensive for the party leadership to maintain cadre loyalty with promises of future rewards.

While incomes expand rapidly, these stresses look manageable; but if growth were to falter or if there were an exogenous decline in government popularity, the political equilibrium could be disturbed. To be sure, China has weathered several economic shocks well, but Huang (2003) has argued that political crises have harmed the private sector in the past, and private investment is more important to growth now than previously. The objective prognosis is that China could continue to grow strongly, and on that basis continue to experience adequate and improving governance. Although we do not believe that governance failures will undermine growth, the weaknesses outlined in chapter 7 undoubtedly increase China's vulnerability to negative shocks and so may induce some caution on the part of private investors.

Dance Steps: Responses to the Rise of China and India

The rise of China and India as major trading nations in manufacturing and services will affect world markets, systems, and commons substantially, and hence change the environment in which other countries make their economic decisions. The question that remains is, how should other countries respond to these new opportunities and challenges—how should they dance with the Giants? Part of the answer is generic. Any country will be better placed to take advantage of new markets and to weather competitive pressure if it creates a healthy investment climate and invests soundly in infrastructure and human resources. And, given the impossibility of predicting precisely in which subsectors threats and opportunities will arise, there will be a premium on flexibility—creating circumstances in which entrepreneurs are able to experiment, expand on success, and withdraw cleanly from failure.

Within this broad rubric, however, the answer varies with the income and the resources of the country concerned because these are what determine its interaction with the world economy.[19] For the lowest-income countries without natural resource wealth and with a limited endowment of human capital, the challenge is to develop manufacturing capacity in low-wage, labor-intensive industry that can compete with these industries in China today; this would position them to cut into China's trade shares a decade from now as wages in China climb above the level needed to keep these industries competitive. China's rising wages should be seen as an opportunity in these sectors for countries such as India, Indonesia, Vietnam, and possibly a number of the poorest countries in Africa (such as Ethiopia), just as the rise in wages in Korea, Taiwan (China), and Hong Kong (China) two decades ago was an opportunity for China. To compete, however, these low-income countries will have to enhance governance, improve their infrastructure, and remove the many bureaucratic obstacles that hamper efficiency and prevent achievement of the timing and quality standards required by purchasers in high-income countries.

Countries (whether low- or middle-income) with large natural resource exports are in a different position. Their real exchange rates will be driven upward by natural resource exports, which, in turn, will hinder their industrial sectors from competing with the manufactured exports of other low-income countries. One sees elements of this already in certain African countries. Incomes have risen with exports of raw materials and their prices, but at the expense of higher commodity price volatility; stagnant exports of low-tech, labor-intensive goods; and declines in the prices of those low-tech goods (Reisen, Goldstein, and Pinaud 2006).

Clearly, increases in income are desirable and efforts should be made to share their benefits widely within society. Steps also should be taken to insulate the public sector and aggregate demand from the worst volatility of commodity prices. To the extent that manufacturing jobs are sought, import-substituting industrialization is not the route to sustainable exports of manufactures. Rather, policies to encourage business in general are required—policies such as reducing transport and trading costs, easing access to finance, strengthening energy and IT infrastructure, and raising the quality of human resources. These countries generally will not be able to develop large manu-

---

19. Country- and region-specific analyses of impacts and policy options may be found in other World Bank studies of the effects of the growth of China and India: Broadman (2007) on Africa and World Bank (forthcoming) on Latin America.

facturing sectors, but some activity certainly will be feasible on the basis of local markets and niche exports.

The biggest challenges posed by China and, to a lesser degree, India are probably to the middle-income countries in Asia and Latin America. These are the countries into whose product space China in particular looks likely to expand; they are the members of production networks that may be threatened by China's move into component manufacturing; and they are the recipients of FDI designed to create export platforms for the multinational corporations. Wages in these countries are typically much higher than in China and India (and are likely to remain so for at least the coming decade), although their education levels often are not much higher than where levels in China will be a decade from now.

For East Asian countries, exports already are being squeezed by competing Chinese exports in the global market, mostly in low- and medium-tech and resource-based products at present but prospectively also in higher-tech products. China currently emphasizes the final stage of production while importing raw materials and parts from its neighbors. Hence, although East Asian countries may face tougher competition in the final destinations, they may be able to gain by refocusing their efforts on supplying firms based in China. The current data suggest that those countries are maintaining their positions in skill-intensive components and that the trend for skill intensity is on the rise. Thus, preparedness would require a focus on human capital, facilities for high-tech production, and a welcoming attitude toward FDI, even from China.

Similar comparisons between China and Latin America suggest that, so far, the direct "threat" from China is muted. This situation may not persist, however, unless Latin Americans invest heavily in the skills and technological capability of firms. They might draw lessons from Korea or Taiwan (China), which are less likely to be hurt by Chinese and Indian competition because they are far enough ahead in technology and human resources—and are making sustained efforts to stay ahead. These lessons would emphasize technological capability, diversifying the product mix, and upgrading the quality of products and expertise in design. Successful emulation of these two models might suggest, among other things, more reliance on domestic businesses (especially large and dynamic ones) and homegrown technology rather than almost total reliance on FDI, at least in the export of manufactures.

The challenge for high-income countries (other than a handful of oil exporters) will be to adjust to the rise of China and India without excessive, politically motivated interventions in the economy. Over the next decade and a half, Japan, North America, and Western Europe, for the most part, have little to fear from Chinese and Indian competition in the high-technology and high-skill sectors in manufacturing and services, especially where those sectors rely on highly educated and experienced workforces, accumulated tacit knowledge, and innovation supported by heavy investment in research and development (Lardy 2004). Indeed, they have much to gain from specialization in these areas.

The high-income countries have not been competitive in the manufacture of garments, shoes, and consumer electronics for a long time, and so they have been strong gainers from the price reductions that the Giants have engendered and will continue to engender. But one would not know this from the political discussions in the United States and parts of Europe that import large quantities of goods from China.[20] The U.S. current account deficit, roughly one-quarter of which is with China, largely is due to the lack of domestic savings and not to China's barriers to imports (which, in fact, have come down dramatically in recent years) or to an undervalued Chinese exchange rate (which is a real but fairly recent problem).

We anticipate a decline in the growth rate of China's exports—a decline that will not be made up fully by India. This will ease some of the political economy problems just alluded to. It also is likely to be accompanied by a switch to lower reserve accumulation, which could raise global interest rates somewhat. This will adversely affect some of the world's richest countries, which are among the biggest borrowers, and some of the poorest; and both groups would do well to start adjusting their fiscal and external positions in anticipation.

Finally, China and India contribute to, but are not the primary causes of, increasing energy prices and carbon emissions. All countries should continue to pursue their own energy-efficiency strategies both for domestic reasons (such as balance of payments and local pollution) and for global ones.

---

20. Trade with India, in contrast, is not yet large enough to play a major role in these debates.

CHAPTER 2

China and India Reshape Global Industrial Geography

Shahid Yusuf, Kaoru Nabeshima, and Dwight H. Perkins

China's meteoric climb as an exporter of manufactures since the mid-1990s, and India's ability to claim a sizable fraction of the global market for tradable information technology (IT)-enabled services over the past six years have contributed to the changing pattern and the volume of global trade (table 2.1).[1] By 2004, China's share of the world's manufacturing exports was 8.3 percent; that of India was 0.9 percent. The two countries' shares of global imports were 6.3 percent and 0.8 percent, respectively. In commercial services, which include IT services, China's share of exports and imports was 2.9 percent and 3.4 percent, respectively; that of India was 1.9 percent and 2.0 percent, respectively (tables 2.1 and 2.2).

China's manufacturing sector accounts for more than 41 percent of gross domestic product (GDP), and in 2005 manufactured goods constituted 93 percent of exports or almost a quarter of the gross value of industrial output. Machinery and transport equipment accounted for 45.2 percent of total exports. These statistics reflect the large gains in manufacturing capability facilitated by heavy investment in plants and equipment embodying the latest technologies and the codification of knowledge on production processes.

The authors are greatly indebted to Jimena Luna and Wei Ha for their assistance with research and production; and to Richard Cooper, Masahisa Fujita, Nobuaki Hamaguchi, Greg Noble, and T. N. Srinivasan for insightful background papers.
1. India's IT-enabled services are principally business processing services and activities associated with the writing, testing, and debugging of software.

Table 2.1 China's and India's Shares of World Exports

World exports	1980 China	1980 India	1990 China	1990 India	2004 China	2004 India
I. Manufacturing	0.8	0.5	1.9	0.5	8.3	0.9
1. Iron and steel	0.3	0.1	1.2	0.2	5.2	1.6
2. Chemicals	0.8	0.3	1.3	0.4	2.7	0.7
2.1 Pharmaceuticals	—	—	1.6[a]	1.2[a]	1.3	1.0[b]
3. Office machines and telecommunications equipment	0.1	—	1.0	0.8	15.2	0.6
4. Auto parts	0.0	0.0	0.1	0.1	0.7	0.1
5. Textiles	4.6	2.4	6.9	2.1	17.2	4.0
6. Clothing	4.0	1.7	8.9	2.3	24.0	2.9
II. Commercial services	—	—	—	—	2.9	1.9
1. Transports	—	—	—	—	—	—
2. Travel	—	—	—	—	4.1	—
3. Other	—	—	—	—	2.4	3.1

Source: Srinivasan 2006.
Note: — = not available.
a. Pertains to 2000.
b. Pertains to 2003.

Table 2.2 China's and India's Shares of World Imports

World imports	1980 China	1980 India	1990 China	1990 India	2004 China	2004 India
I. Manufacturing	1.1	0.5	1.7	0.5	6.3	0.8
1. Iron and steel	2.7	1.0	2.5	1.0	8.2	1.0
2. Chemicals	2.0	—	2.2	—	6.5	—
2.1 Pharmaceuticals	—	—	0.9[a]	—	0.8[a]	—
3 Office machines and telecommunications equipment	0.6	0.2	1.3	0.3	11.2	0.5
4. Auto parts	0.6	0.0	0.6	0.1	1.7	0.3
5. Textiles	1.9	—	4.9	0.2	7.4	0.6[b]
6. Clothing	0.1	0.0	0.0	0.0	0.6	0.0
II. Commercial services	—	—	2.5[a]	2.1[a]	3.4	2.0
1. Transports	—	—	—	—	4.2	2.2
2. Travel	—	—	—	—	3.3	2.4
3. Other	—	—	—	—	3.5	2.1

Source: Srinivasan 2006.
Note: — = not available.
a. Pertains to 2000.
b. Pertains to 2003.

Relative to China, India's formal manufacturing sector accounts for a far smaller share of GDP—less than 16 percent. Investment in new industrial capacity and industrial growth since 1990 has been slower, and exports of manufactures are a fraction of China's exports in absolute terms and are a smaller fraction of total exports. India undoubtedly has achieved competitiveness in a few manufacturing subsectors, and some of those are technologically quite advanced, but, on balance, manufacturing capability has lagged. As described later in this chapter, India's breakthrough is in the export of certain business process services and software, the tradability of which has been enhanced greatly by advances in telecommunications and the advent of the Internet.[2]

These developments point to ongoing and impending shifts in worldwide industrial geography. In this chapter we explore the likelihood of a continuing concentration of major industrial activities in China and India and the implications for other economies if such concentration materializes.

The balance of this chapter is divided as follows: The next section describes the size of the domestic markets in China and India, especially for the relevant manufacturing products. The third section focuses on the overall strategy and patterns of development in the two Giants, and then we briefly examine the development of a few of the leading industrial subsectors in both countries. In our concluding observations, we report on longer-term implications for China, India, and their trading partners.

Large Domestic Markets

The evolving international competitiveness of Chinese industry—and eventually of Indian industry—will depend on a number of factors, including the expansion of domestic markets, infrastructure improvements, strengthening of the innovation system, and the dynamism of major firms. Businesses and the press regularly talk about the enormous size of both the Chinese and the Indian markets, given their huge populations. Large markets create a competitive advantage for any product that has substantial economies of scale, such as white goods or automobile assembly. Scale economies can be achieved without a large domestic market by relying from the start on exports, of course, but access to the domestic market and lower entry barriers can be significant advantages. So just how large are the Chinese and Indian markets?

---

2. Exports not only of software and services but also of goods have benefited (Clarke and Wallsten 2006).

Table 2.3 Households Owning High-income Consumer Durables in China, 2004

Consumer durable	Number per 100 urban households	Number per 100 rural households
Washing machine	95.9	37.3
Refrigerator	90.2	17.8
Color television	133.4	75.1
Camera	47.0	3.7
Mobile phone	111.4	34.7
Automobile	2.2	—

Source: National Bureau of Statistics of China, *China Statistical Yearbook 2005.*
Note: — = not available.

For many industrial producers the size of their market is much smaller than the total GDP, however that is measured.[3] Much of the purchasing power a family has is spent on food rather than on industrial products. Low-income families in both rural and urban areas do purchase manufactured products, such as garments and footwear, but they do not purchase automobiles and the more expensive consumer durables. It is precisely in the area of white and brown goods where economies of scale are important. Thus, the market for these latter household labor-saving and entertainment products is made up mainly of people in upper income groups who have high income elasticities of demand for such products and who live in urban areas in China and India or abroad. Data on the ownership of consumer durables and automobiles in China are presented in table 2.3 and for India in table 2.4.

How big is the income of these higher income groups or the "middle class" in China and India? One way to approach this question is to measure the cumulative income of the highest-income decile of the population and the share of that income spent on nonfood products. That calculation results in a market purchasing capacity of $550 billion for China and less than $150 billion for India.[4] To this figure could be added the share of investment that goes to

---

3. For an industrial firm selling its products in the market, the purchasing power parity measure of GDP is irrelevant. A foreign firm in particular will want to know what its sales are worth in a convertible international currency, such as U.S. dollars. If a domestic firm is engaged in international trade as either a seller or buyer, it will want to know prices converted into its domestic currency using the official exchange rate. Thus, the relevant GDP concept in U.S. dollars is the one obtained by using the official exchange rate.

4. A billion is 1,000 millions.

Table 2.4 Households Owning Selected Assets in India, 2001
percent

Asset	Total households	Urban households	Rural households
Electronics			
Radio, transistor	35.1	44.5	31.5
Television	31.6	64.3	18.9
Telephone	9.1	23.0	3.8
Transportation vehicles			
Bicycle	43.7	46.0	42.8
Scooter, motorcycle, moped	11.7	24.7	6.7
Car, jeep, van	2.5	5.6	1.3
None of the specified assets	34.5	19.0	40.5

Source: Office of the Registrar General 2003.

purchase machinery and equipment and such key inputs as steel and cement. This would result in a market for industrial products of another $400 billion for China and $100–150 billion for India.

Thus, industrial producers in China face a potential market of nearly $1 trillion. Indian industrial producers face a potential market that is a quarter to a third of China's size.

Two Rapidly Industrializing Economies

What are the implications of recent trends for the future international competitiveness of Chinese and Indian industry and services and the likely resulting industrial geography?

China Ascending

To begin with, China will remain primarily an exporter of manufactures over the next 10 to 15 years. Regarding imports, China is a major buyer of primary products, of sophisticated equipment, and of parts and components. China's demand for new materials and energy (discussed in chapters 1 and 5) has increased its imports from the least developed countries (see figures 2.1 and 2.2). In 2002, China absorbed $3.5 billion in exports from those countries and was their third-ranked market (Yang 2006). The main question with respect to

primary goods imports is the pace at which China will become a major importer of food and related agricultural products. China's grain output peaked
in 1996 and 1998, and although it has fallen in absolute terms since that time,
it was a net exporter of 19.9 million tons of grain in 2003 and only a small net
importer of 5 million tons in 2004. Overall, however, China remained a net
exporter of $9.7 billion of food and live animals as of the end of 2004.

China imports machinery, plant equipment, and components that have
fueled its massive expansion of industrial capacity and served as conduits for
technology transfer. The first two imports—that is, complex capital goods
bought almost exclusively from the advanced countries—are likely to continue to flow into China over the foreseeable future because, given the importance of learning, tacit knowledge, and cumulative research, the country's
comparative advantage in these items will materialize only gradually. With regard to electronic components, currently the principal export of several East
and Southeast Asian economies, the situation is less clear. Exports of such

Figure 2.1 Product Structure of Exports

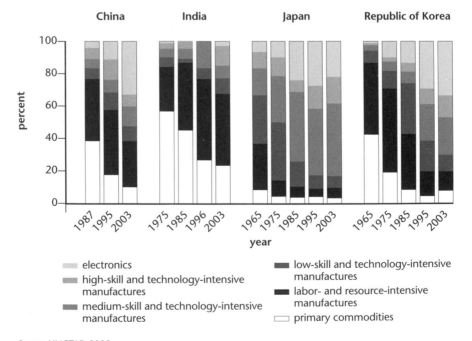

Source: UNCTAD 2005.

Figure 2.2 Product Structure of Imports

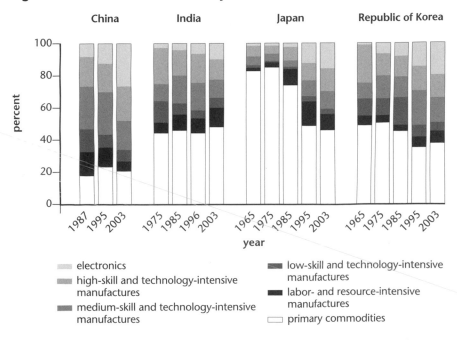

Source: UNCTAD 2005.

components have risen steeply since 1995. China is one of the principal trading partners of the newly industrializing countries and its openness to trade is contributing to the interdependence of the East Asian region (Branstetter and Lardy 2006; Petri 2006; Yang 2006). More recently, however, elements of the supply chain are migrating to China as manufacturers of intermediates move closer to markets and final assemblers. This process, especially with regard to the auto industry, could fuel foreign direct investment (FDI) in China during the next decade.

On the export side, China is likely to remain competitive in labor-intensive products in 2010 or 2015, even as wages rise. In 2004, real wages were 2.11 times their level in 1989; and the rate of wage increase accelerated in 2004 and 2005, especially in the coastal regions—although productivity is rising as well.[5] This trend is likely to be contained because China still has a

5. The figures cited refer to the change in the real average wage of all workers and staff so it includes both wage increases within various job categories and changes in the share of par

large surplus of 350 million agricultural workers, many of whose incomes are a small fraction of the wages earned by urban workers.[6] To take full advantage of these underutilized workers and the lower cost of land, however, China will have to move the labor-intensive factories closer to its interior, as is being attempted now in the southwestern provinces through investment in the transport infrastructure (Chan and Gu 2006). Assuming this effort succeeds (and the process could take time), China's dominant world position in the export of textiles, garments, shoes, and toys is not likely to change much in the coming years.

China is the second-largest market for, and the largest exporter of, electronics/information and communication technology products (Ma, Ngyuen, and Xu 2006). The potential growth of these markets has attracted most of the leading multinational corporations (MNCs) producing electronics, autos, and consumer durables, as well as those in Taiwan (China) and the Republic of Korea. China's three largest exporters in 2003 were subsidiaries of Taiwanese electronics firms, such as Foxconn (Hon Hai) and Quanta. Several auto assemblers and manufacturers of auto parts have shifted their regional headquarters to China and are planning to move some of their research and design facilities as well—for example, Toyota and Volkswagen.

A recent study of China's trade by Roland-Holst and Weiss (2005) showed that the country is out-competing its neighbors in the Association of Southeast Asian Nations. The latter are losing shares in export markets although their exports continue to grow in absolute terms. Rodrik (2006b) similarly found that the growing sophistication of China poses a considerable challenge for other Southeast Asian countries.

With more than 5 million people graduating each year from senior secondary schools, the Chinese labor force is going to have a large number of people capable of taking on jobs well above the low-skilled, labor-intensive assembly operations associated with light manufactures.

China's gross enrollment rate for higher education rose from 19 percent of the relevant age cohort in 2004 to 21 percent in 2005 (Min 2006; data from

---

ticular job categories in the wage bill. They are based on the Chinese official wage indexes for enterprises in the urban areas (see National Bureau of Statistics of China, *China Statistical Yearbook 2005*, p. 151).

6. The marginal return to labor in 2001 was 365 renminbi (RMB) in agriculture, whereas it was 11,884 RMB in urban industry, 4,672 RMB in rural nonfarm industry, and 2,009 RMB in urban services. These data point to large distortions in the labor market, especially between agriculture and urban industry (Tan 2004).

UNESCO Institute for Statistics, 2006). Currently, China is graduating 600,000 people in science and engineering mainly at the undergraduate level. Over the next decade, the total of such graduates could be more than 5 million ("Up to the Job?" 2006). The very top Chinese students in sciences and engineering (like those from India) are competitive with the best in the world and are beginning to make a mark through scientific publications and patenting (Chen and Kenney forthcoming). The increasing stock of scientists and engineers is enabling China to enter a limited number of higher technology areas (such as nanotechnology [see Zhou and Leydesdorff 2006]) at an earlier stage of development than would be the case in a smaller country. Significant numbers of graduating students can staff world-class research laboratories abroad and should enable China to enter other high-technology fields if these experienced researchers come back to China after years of studying abroad. The lure is rising research and development (R&D), which reached 1.4 percent of GDP in 2005 (compared with 1 percent in 2000), together with numerous incentives for returnees with service and technology skills (Yusuf and Nabeshima 2006a, 2006b; Yusuf, Wang, and Nabeshima 2005).

There remains a question about the quality of the graduates from many Chinese tertiary institutions. Based on surveys by McKinsey, that quality does not seem to be particularly high. Only 10 percent are considered sufficiently well trained to be hired by MNCs in China ("China's Hi-Tech Success" 2005). These graduates (along with graduates in less technical fields) have to staff managerial and technical jobs in more than 200,000 industrial enterprises, a wide variety of service sector businesses, government agencies, and universities.

What Is India's Model for Catching Up?

As noted above, relative to China, the Indian business environment has been less conducive to the growth of manufacturing and exports, and this is immediately apparent from the stark contrast in absolute numbers from the two countries as well as from the shares of manufacturing production and the volume of exports of manufactures (see figure 2.1). Hence, for a country of its size, India's impact on the rest of the world has been modest—at least as measured by population. Among its exports of manufactures, only textiles has achieved a scale sufficient to impinge on the prospects of other Asian countries, producers elsewhere, and the market for raw cotton. IT-enabled services is the only other area in which Indian exports have established a substantial and growing presence. Because of the still relatively small size of its economy and its modest level of industrialization, India's imports of raw materials, machinery, intermediate products, and consumer goods are fewer than those of Brazil, Mexico, and Korea (which were approximately comparable in size using constant dollars in 2004).

It is certainly true that India's global footprint has expanded since the beginning of the century. Looking forward, its economy and trading relations will become more visible on the global stage, but even a doubling of GDP in 10 years will result in an economy that is less than two-thirds the size of the Chinese economy today, in nominal dollars. India's future impact on the rest of the world needs to be taken seriously, however, because it has the labor resources, a growing base of human capital, the domestic market potential, and the nascent industrial strength to become an industrial powerhouse that is comparable to China today. Whether this actually materializes and India begins significantly influencing the fortunes of other countries and natural resource use, global externalities will depend on the country's competitiveness and on the dimensions of a number of industrial subsectors. This outcome appears unlikely.

Were India to proceed along the growth path chalked by the dynamic and fast-growing East Asian economies, then manufacturing would lead the way. Given its factor supplies, India would need to expand its labor-intensive consumer industries rapidly while building the basic materials industries (such as petrochemicals and metallurgy) and the downstream engineering and transport industries. Moreover, although the domestic market is and would remain a major outlet for all these industries, rapid growth would likely rest on FDI in manufacturing industries and on success in export markets (as is the case in China).[7] If India is to conform to the East Asian model, the share of manufacturing in GDP (currently less than 16 percent) would need to double possibly within 15 years. That would call for sector growth rates in the double-digit range, which also would help generate urgently needed jobs ("Risks Mount" 2006), and for export of a significant portion of the output produced.

A second and untried model would project growth on the basis of high and accelerating expansion of the services sector fueled by domestic and international demand. It certainly is plausible that key services subsectors could lead growth. Overall, services is by far the largest part of the Indian economy (50 percent); some parts have been expanding at a rapid clip and

---

7. The low level of FDI in Indian industry, relative to Chinese industry, has influenced the development of the manufacturing sector and growth of exports (Huang and Khanna 2005; Mukherji 2005; Swamy 2005).

there is much scope for increased investment and gains in productivity (Gordon and Gupta 2005).

These two models have different implications for global industrial geography and for India's impact on the rest of the world. Which model is more likely rests again on the future industrial capability of key subsectors, their competitiveness, and demand for their products—domestic and foreign.

It is easier to tackle the second model. Around 1990, India's services sector had a share in total GDP similar to that of other countries at an equivalent income level. Since then, it has risen at an above-average pace, and the share in 2005 was a bit above the norm for lower-income countries. Business services and software have spearheaded this growth, and Indian firms in those areas now rank among the largest in the world. IT services account for 6 percent of the services sector GDP as a whole, and in fiscal 2004/05 had revenues of $30 billion ("Now for the Hard Part" 2006). Exports reached $12 billion in fiscal 2003/04. Both turnover and exports have risen swiftly since 2000, averaging 30 percent and 31 percent a year, respectively. Employment too has climbed and is now a respectable 3 million, concentrated in five or six urban centers. In other words, the performance in the past five years is remarkable in the context of the Indian economy, but the IT sector is still fairly small, and the capability of the services sector as a whole does not extend much beyond software application development and maintenance and low-value-added processing services (financial, legal, medical, accounting, and others). Instead of computer architecture and operating systems design, the sector is dominated by call center services, professional services, document entry and transcription, and software maintenance activities. That this has been achieved in a short span of time points to the latent capability that could evolve rapidly if spurred by the activities of India's homegrown firms such as TCS and Infosys and by MNCs that are expanding their presence in India. Intel's largest chip design center is in Bangalore, and both IBM and Cisco Systems have opened major chip design facilities there. Advanced Micro Devices and Texas Instruments are planning to follow (Arora and Gambardella 2004; "Big Players in Chip Design" 2006; D'Costa 2006). It is also worth noting that India accounts for only 3 percent of world exports of business services.

Software and IT-enabled Services

The roots of the Indian software/business-processing services sector reach back to some decisions made many decades ago and to other developments in the more recent past. In early 1950, the first Indian Institute of Technology (IIT), modeled on the Massachusetts Institute of Technology, was established at Kharagpur in West Bengal. Six other IITs were set up in selected cities across the country after the Indian Institute of Technology Act passed in 1956. The seven IITs, with a total enrollment in 2004 approaching 30,000 (17,000 undergraduate and 13,000 graduate students), have provided India with the nucleus of a world-class technological elite. These schools and other training institutions (such as the six Indian Institutes of Management and several Indian Institutes of Information Technologies in conjunction with the universities) have provisioned India's labor markets with engineering, management, and IT-relevant skills.

India's capacity to train accredited engineers rose from 60,000 in fiscal 1987/88 to 340,000 in 2003. For IT professionals, it rose from 25,800 to 250,000 over the same period (Arora and Gambardella 2004). In addition, the many graduates from the IITs who work abroad or previously have studied and worked abroad have contributed to the growth of the IT services industry in three substantive ways. First, the quality of their training and skills has created a positive reputation in North America, the United Kingdom, and beyond. Second, many former graduates, having acquired further education and experience abroad, have returned to India and are setting up their own businesses or working for local or multinational firms operating in India. In fact, 71 of 75 MNCs operating in Bangalore's software park were headed by Indians who had lived overseas, and many of the smaller companies are owned by Indian entrepreneurs presently living in the United States. Third, the Indian diaspora of professional and business people has shown great initiative in creating opportunities for Indian firms and in funneling contracts to them. As a source of capital and of expertise and guidance on technologies, the Indian diaspora is second only to the efforts of Chinese citizens overseas. Much like their Chinese counterparts, expatriate Indians have become increasingly adept in playing the roles of intermediaries, venture capitalists, and angel investors with secure footholds in strategic clusters, such as Silicon Valley (California) and the Boston (Massachusetts) area (Saxenian 2006).

Indian firms were motivated to look overseas for business because the domestic market for their services was very limited in the 1980s and 1990s. The links forged with major U.S. companies that established subsidiaries in India led to a buildup of contract work for American firms. The work, usually done on-site by Indian professionals, focused on software enhancement and maintenance, the writing of code, engineering design, and other related projects that harnessed specific plentiful and very-low-priced skills.[8] The shortage of computer hardware in India, caused by steep duties and other import restrictions, also made on-site work at the facilities of American companies necessary.

The falling cost of telecommunications and the vistas opened by the Internet made it feasible to outsource a host of services: back-office services, all types of information processing, engineering, some kinds of retail, and medical services. Companies based in the United States have taken a lead in outsourcing services.[9] Not many countries had India's mix and volume of skills and English language capabilities. Moreover, Indian IT professionals and companies had the added advantage of long exposure and involvement with U.S. companies that took the lead in adopting IT, in reengineering corporate structures, and in outsourcing services.[10] It was during this period that more Indian firms began to enter the field, and IT services clusters (for instance, in the software parks) began to take shape in Bangalore and other cities with a concentration of engineering talent (Arora and Athreye 2001). The growth of the industry, however, was spearheaded by a number of medium-size firms established much earlier. The first, Tata Consulting Services, was created in 1968; Wipro in 1980; Infosys in 1981; and Satyam in 1987. The leading firms now account for the lion's share of turnover and exports (Khanna and Palepu 2004). Only one-fourth of the top 20 exporters are foreign multinationals. Thus, the past association dating back to the 1980s and reinforced by the presence of thousands of Indian professionals in the United States, gave Indian firms a flying start in the global marketplace, and it accounts for the heavy dependence on exports and on the U.S. market. The government helped by containing the rates for telecommunication services and modifying India's stringent labor laws to give IT firms greater flexibility in hiring and laying off workers.

As the IT sector has expanded, one of the most serious constraints that has emerged is the shortage of needed technical and managerial skills, which goes

---

8. The Y2K threat and the euro conversion greatly expanded the demand for technicians to write code and debug software.

9. Only 3 percent of India's retail business is conducted by large chain stores and in shopping centers (although such chains as Big Bazaar and Pantaloons and malls such as Phoenix-Mills are multiplying). By comparison, 20 percent of China's retail business is conducted in such venues. ("Here Comes" 2005).

10. During the period 1999–2001, roughly half of the petitions for H1B visas (work authorization for skilled workers in the United States) were granted to Indians (Cooper 2006).

in tandem with high and disruptive labor turnover. Thus, India needs to invest heavily in skills and in technology, and firms will need to cultivate links with universities and research institutes if they are to sustain high growth rates.[11] The quality of technical graduates in India also leaves much to be desired. Possibly 20 percent are world-class and, according to a recent survey, three-fifths are "lamentable" ("Now for the Hard Part" 2006; "Up to the Job?" 2006). Other middle-income countries also are looking to services to provide economic momentum and jobs— Brazil, the East European economies, Mexico, and the Russian Federation. China is producing more engineers and IT technicians than India; and ambitiously is expanding its IT-enabled services and software sectors, assisted by FDI from Indian IT firms ("Watch Out, India" 2006). India also can expect to encounter strong competition from Ireland, Israel, several European countries, and the United States as it pushes into the high-value end of IT, as it now is attempting—for instance, with digital signal processing software. Hence, projecting the likely future geographical distribution of business and IT services is no easy matter. It is beginning to seem, however, that other South and Southeast Asian economies and those from Eastern Europe and Latin America will have to struggle to find lucrative niches in an IT services market dominated by MNCs and Indian firms.

Other Services

India's banking, finance, telecommunications, and hotel and restaurant services have grown at or near double-digit rates (Gordon and Gupta 2005). There is plenty of scope for developing India's finance, telecom, commercial and retail, medical, moviemaking, and logistics services on the strength of buoyant domestic and overseas demand. Each of these industries also stands to benefit from advances in IT that will raise productivity and generate demand for the firms supplying the services. It is an open question, however, whether India is likely to emerge within the next decade as a significant exporter of any of these services. India's economy is only a sixth as monetized as China's economy. India holds 1 percent of the global financial assets, but less than one-half are in the form of bank deposits (Farrell and Key 2005). India's banking and finance sector, although improving and apparently more dynam-

---

11. Only a small fraction of those employed by the IT industry have more than five years' experience ("Now for the Hard Part" 2006; "Up to the Job?" 2006).

ic than China's, remains inefficient by international standards, and Indian institutions have not made any headway overseas.

Telecommunications also is a domestic industry, even though India has created a production base for hardware technologically attuned to the needs of lower-income countries. But unlike Chinese firms such as Huawei and ZTE, Indian companies have yet to venture abroad, to offer the kind of full-service packages (including financing) that Chinese firms now offer, and to invest significant sums equal to 8–10 percent of sales in R&D to stay abreast with the frontrunners in this rapidly advancing field ("Global Transformation" 2006).[12]

Moviemaking is a thriving national industry, and India is the biggest producer of films in the world. This industry also caters to the large overseas Indian diaspora and has acquired a niche market in some of the Middle Eastern countries as well. But it has yet to broaden its appeal to consistently reach a global audience and compete with Hollywood or with producers in Greater China (China, Hong Kong [China], and Taiwan [China]) and Korea, despite the international acclaim enjoyed by a few movies (most notably *Bend It Like Beckham*).

Very recently, Indian firms have begun supplying IT services for the international movie industry and producers of video games (for example, for cell phones)—a business that could grow in line with the demand for special effects and video content. With the exception of the business services processing and software industries, it is far from obvious that India is positioned to make a mark in the global market with its services industry, at least during the next 10 years.

Prospects of Key Manufacturing Industry

It is very likely that the impact of China and India on the geography of the world's tradable services industry will be modest and not especially disruptive. The same cannot be said for manufacturing if India picks up speed. And so we come back to the conventional manufacturing sector-led model of development that underlies the development of China and other East Asian economies.

Whether Indian manufacturing can become the principal leading sector and whether India can join China as a leading industrial economy will depend largely on the medium-term performance of a number of manufacturing

---

12. Indian software firms' average investment in R&D as a percent of sales in 2000 was 3.5 percent (Radhakrishnan 2006).

Table 2.5 Industry Exports as a Percentage of Total Exports, China and India

Industry export	1995	2000	2004
China			
Pharmaceutical products	1.1	0.7	0.6
Iron and steel	3.5	1.8	2.3
Electrical equipment	5.9	9.7	10.0
White goods	0.7	1.1	1.3
Road vehicles	1.8	2.6	2.8
Textiles	26.0	21.4	16.2
India			
Pharmaceutical products	2.3	2.8	2.9
Iron and steel	3.0	2.9	6.0
Electrical equipment	1.3	1.8	1.9
White goods	0.0	0.0	0.1
Road vehicles	2.8	2.0	2.8
Textiles	27.0	27.2	17.4

Source: United Nations Commodity Trade Statistics database, accessed via the World Bank's World Integrated Trade Solution (WITS) software.
Note: Textiles is defined as the combination of 26, 65, and 84 of Standard International Trade Classification (SITC), Rev. 3. White goods is defined as the combination of 7751, 7752, 7753, and 7758 of SITC, Rev. 3. Pharmaceutical products, iron and steel, electrical equipment, and road vehicles are defined, respectively, as 54, 67, 77, and 78 of SITC, Rev. 3.

subsectors in both countries, and on the parallel development of infrastructure in India particularly.[13]

The pertinent subsectors are textiles and clothing, white goods, pharmaceuticals, autos and auto parts, steel, and electronics. Together, these subsectors account for close to a third of the merchandise exports of both India and China (see table 2.5), as well as for 48 percent of the sales of industrial products in China and 41 percent of industrial employment (see table 2.6).

---

13. Power shortages are a major concern for Indian firms. A survey of Indian manufacturing firms in 2003 revealed that 61 percent still rely on their own generators for electricity. In China the share is 27 percent. The same survey also found that firms in India faced an average of 17 significant power outages a month, far more frequent than in Malaysia (1 a month) or China (fewer than 5 a month). The loss from power outages in India was 9 percent of total output, compared with 2 percent in China (World Bank 2004a), and electricity costs twice as much as in China. Deficiencies in infrastructure provisions are costing India 3–4 percentage points in lost growth ("An Urgent Political and Moral Imperative" 2006).

Textiles and Clothing

Textiles and clothing account for 7 percent of world exports. China is the leading producer, followed by India. China's advantage derives from its integration with the global production network through foreign investment and direct contacts with the retailers in Organisation for Economic Co-operation and Development countries. Wal-Mart, for example, purchased $18 billion worth of goods from China in 2004. In contrast, Indian firms have far less direct contact with the retailers (Whalley 2006).

In 1950, India was a leading exporter of cotton textiles, but thereafter it lost ground and the industry's fortunes only began to reverse course when reforms were introduced in the early 1980s (Roy 2004). Now, India's textiles and clothing sector is the second-largest employer, with 35 million workers responsible for 20 percent of industrial production (Ananthakrishnan and Jain-Chandra 2005). However, India's textile industry still trails well behind that of China. In 2005, exports of textiles and garments amounted to $9.5 billion and $7.5 billion, respectively, versus China's respective $77 billion and $40 billion. The average firm in India's formal sector often has been constrained from fully exploiting scale economies and new technologies; little foreign capital has flowed into the sector; and because Indian firms are less well integrated into global production networks than are Chinese firms, they have benefited less from technology transfer. Hence, the productivity level of India's textiles and clothing sector is only 35 percent that of the United States, whereas China's is 55 percent (Ananthakrishnan and Jain-Chandra 2005). The overall productivity of India's apparel industry is 16 percent that of producers in the United States (Padhi, Pauwels, and Taylor 2004).

As with several other Indian industries, the partial dismantling of domestic regulations and of the Multifiber Arrangement (MFA) have created openings that firms are rushing to exploit. Indian exports—some of which compete against exports from China—are rising and the two countries are moving to dominate the world market to an even greater extent than in the past. Both increased their market shares in the European Union, Japan, and the United States in 2005. China's gains were larger because Chinese producers had invested in anticipation of the lifting of quotas and were better prepared and more competitive ("Air-conditioners Wilt" 2005; "India: China Eats" 2005; Yang 2006). As the backloaded MFA phaseout started in 1995, China was able to take advantage of the phased removal of quotas on various apparel categories, even though it was not yet a member of the World Trade Organization (WTO). India did not (Srinivasan 2003a, 2006).

Table 2.6 Indicators of All State-owned and Non-state-owned Enterprises in China, by Industrial Sector, 2004

Sector	Enterprises		Industrial products		Employees	
	Number	Percent of total	Sales revenue (billion yuan)	Percent of total	Number (millions)	Percent of total
Manufacture of textiles	17,144	7.8	934.7	5.0	5.19	8.5
Manufacture of textile wearing apparel, footwear, and caps	10,901	5.0	388.0	2.1	3.20	5.3
Manufacture of raw chemical materials and chemical products	15,172	6.9	1,198.3	6.4	3.16	5.2
Manufacture of medicines	4,397	2.0	321.3	1.7	1.19	1.9
Smelting and pressing of ferrous metals	4,947	2.3	1,590.7	8.5	2.61	4.3
Manufacture of transport equipment	9,389	4.3	1,327.2	7.1	3.28	5.4
Manufacture of electrical machinery and equipment	11,760	5.4	1,005.6	5.6	2.99	5.0
Manufacture of communication equipment, computers, and other electronic equipment	6,638	3.0	2,146.3	11.4	3.33	5.5
Subtotal of these selected sectors	80,348	36.7	8,912.1	47.8	24.95	41.1
National total	219,463	36.6	18,781.5	47.5	60.99	40.9

Source: National Bureau of Statistics of China, China Statistical Yearbook 2005.
Note: Firms included in the tables are those with sales of 5 million yuan or more.

Even if there is a full liberalization, India may not soon be able to take advantage of the opportunities made available because Indian firms remain hampered by suboptimal scales of production, labor market rigidities, and other impediments to trade, particularly with respect to logistics (Schiff et al. 2006).[14] The minimum delivery time from India to the United States is 24 days, compared with 18 days from Thailand, 15 days from China, 12 days from Hong Kong (China), and 3 days from Mexico. In addition, customs delays on imports eat up 10 days in India, compared with 7 days in Korea and Thailand (Ananthakrishnan and Jain-Chandra 2005).

Looking ahead, India—and China—very likely will remain among the most competitive producers of garments and textiles because of their elastic labor supplies, assuming that labor laws and shortages do not push up wages more rapidly than what has occurred over the previous decade. There is considerable latitude for raising productivity, quality, and design in the industry. Niche products surely will continue to offer opportunities for suppliers in other countries.[15] But even against the high-value textiles and fashion garments produced by Italy, pressure from China and India will mount because of the levels of investment, the design and engineering skills being mobilized locally and from overseas sources (as the design industry is becoming globalized and design services can be outsourced), the increasing sophistication of domestic consumers, and the immense domestic markets. This is strikingly supported by China's capacity to diversify its product offerings in textiles and enter new markets. Since 1990, at the 10-digit level the number of textile product varieties has risen from 6,602 to 12,698 (World Bank Office 2006).

White and Brown Goods

The market for white goods worldwide amounted to more than $100 billion in 2002. One-third of demand for large appliances was from the Asia Pacific region, of which half came from China, the fastest growing market (Nichols and Cam 2005). Seeing the opportunities, foreign firms are entering the Chinese market; and in durables, such as washing machines, their market share has in-

---

14. Even large firms, such as Gokaldas, are unwilling to expand employment because it is difficult to lay off workers ("Now for the Hard Part" 2006).

15. For instance, knitwear from Bangladesh and carpets from Pakistan have held up well so far in the U.S. and European Union markets after the abolition of the MFA (Whalley 2006).

creased from 15 percent in 2000 to 25 percent in 2003 (Nichols and Cam 2005). General Electric and other such firms are planning to shift a third of their production capacity to Asia, with China the primary destination.

Similarly, the Indian market is expanding and domestic producers, such as Godrej and Videocom, and MNCs have created two large clusters to produce white goods in Noida (near Delhi) and Pune (near Mumbai), with help from government-provided incentives. The household ownership rate for refrigerators in India was just 15 percent in 2004 and it was low for other durables ("Japanese White Goods" 2006). Haier is attempting to enter the Indian market where Korean producers (such as market leader LG and Samsung) currently have a strong presence. In 2004, LG announced plans to make India its second-largest global production base after China (Nichols and Cam 2005). The company already accounts for more than a quarter of the market for air conditioners and color televisions, and more than a third of the market for washing machines, refrigerators, and microwaves ("Now for the Hard Part" 2006). Sanyo will start marketing white goods in India, using existing partnerships with local distributors for their TVs ("Sanyo Seeks India Boost" 2006). Sharp and Toshiba are planning to do the same ("Sharp India Chalking Out" 2006; "Toshiba Forays" 2006).

In the past, local production was the rule worldwide because of freight costs. Given that freight charges are typically quoted with reference to cubic capacity, it is relatively expensive to ship finished white goods over a long distance, especially larger goods (Nichols and Cam 2005), so the size and growth opportunities of the domestic market determined how the white goods industry developed. However, low wages and production costs coupled with the adoption of modern technology has enabled China to export refrigerators and wine coolers to the United States (Nichols and Cam 2005). Parallel to the increase in trade of finished goods, intraindustry trade has increased, reflecting the development of global production networks for white goods.[16]

Although demand is strong, especially from China and India, the unit price of white goods has been in decline, and firms are adopting a number of strategies to cut labor costs, to outsource, to strip production down to an assembly operation, and to bring in modern management techniques (especially total quality management) to reduce the number of defects (Nichols and Cam 2005). Others are trying to move up the technology ladder by offering

---

16. For instance, Maytag dishwashers assembled in the United States use motors made in China (by GE) and wire harnesses from Mexico (Nichols and Cam 2005).

more functions in each unit, better designs, integration with the whole kitchen as a system, and even Internet-enabled refrigerators (Nichols and Cam 2005).

China

In 1981, the urban penetration rate of refrigerators and washing machines per 100 families in China was only 0.2 and 6.0, respectively. The "big three" home appliances at that time were the bicycle, the wristwatch, and the sewing machine (Zhao, Nichols, and Cam 2005). In 20 years, the penetration rate of white goods in China increased dramatically to reach 87 refrigerators and 92 washing machines per 100 urban families in 2002. In some cities, such as Beijing, the penetration rate that year was 107.4 refrigerators and 102.8 washing machines per 100 families (Zhao, Nichols, and Cam 2005). Although the urban market is fast becoming saturated, white goods ownership among rural households is still low, with 13.6 refrigerators and 29.9 washing machines per 100 rural families (Zhao, Nichols, and Cam 2005).

In the early 1980s, most firms were small-scale state-owned or collectively owned enterprises. To meet the rising demand, these firms imported factories from Italy and Germany. By the mid-1990s, more than 100 lines were imported. With government encouragement during the 1990s, more successful enterprises started to acquire other companies, forming several large, well-known firms (such as Haier, Kelon, Meiling and Little Swan), reflecting the worldwide trend in consolidation (Zhao, Nichols, and Cam 2005). By 2002, the market share of the top five firms had risen to 60 percent in refrigerators and 68 percent in washing machines. The market for air conditioners also is becoming less crowded. Twenty-seven brands were withdrawn in 2001, leaving 69 by 2005. At the end of 2006, only 20 brands may be left ("Air-conditioners Wilt" 2005). These successful firms also are relying heavily on exports. For example, Galanz exports 65 percent of its microwave ovens and is becoming a major producer of air-conditioning units (Sull and Wang 2005; "An Alpha Delta" 2006). Changhong Electric also is expanding its production of air conditioners ("Telecoms and Technology" 2006). But many of the Chinese producers depend on foreign firms for such key items as compressors.

Haier, now the fourth-largest white goods manufacturer in the world, was the first Chinese manufacturing firm to invest abroad in 1999 ("Haier to Create" 2006).[17] It is also the first Chinese firm to hire an international advertising agency to establish its brand ("Chinese Fridge Magnate" 2005), and now has dozens of factories scattered overseas.

India

India's white goods industry is at an earlier stage of development, relative to China's industry. Exports are insignificant and there is no Indian equivalent to China's Haier prowling international markets. Protectionism, slow-growing demand from the middle class, little FDI until recently, subscale production, and inadequate supplies of electricity have combined to keep India out of the running. Demand from the middle class is picking up now, and the white goods industry has seen double-digit growth in recent years. The market size for white goods is about Rs. 80 billion ($1.76 billion).

MNCs are expanding their manufacturing capacity in India, but the country's slow start means that producers based in India are unlikely to be exporting substantial quantities of finished products for some time. The export of components, however, is feasible. China has established a lead in white and brown goods, and it could be that it will extend its lead over India as MNCs transfer more technology and expand capacity through FDI in China.

Pharmaceuticals

Pharmaceuticals is one of India's brightest prospects and is underpinned by strong entrepreneurship in the private sector; the abundance of skills in chemistry, biology, and chemical engineering; and the long-term mastering of complex process technologies made possible until recently by the absence of intellectual property protection for foreign pharmaceutical products under Indian law (Chaudhuri 2004). Here again China is a close match, although its corporate capability is weaker than India's. India is the fourth-largest producer of pharmaceuticals by volume—the 13th in terms of value—and for several compelling reasons it is likely not only to retain this ranking over the next decade but also to expand its global market share (Grace 2005). China is the

---

17. This investment was in a factory in South Carolina (United States). Haier plans to expand the existing factory with additional investment amounting to $150 million. Furthermore, it plans to invest in an R&D facility in the United States ("Haier to Create" 2006).

second-largest producer of pharmaceutical ingredients and generic drugs in terms of value after the United States (with 5 percent of world output in 2004 valued at $54.4 billion) ("China: Pharmaceuticals Sector" 2005). Remarkably, Chinese firms have shown less initiative in this field than in others, although they exported $4 billion worth of products (including traditional medicines) in 2004 and are beginning to move into the neighboring fields of biotechnology and stem cell research (Fernandez and Underwood 2006).

In addition to graduating 15,000 chemists each year, India has the corporate muscle to invest in R&D and to test and market drugs. Firms such as Ranbaxy, Cipla, Dr. Reddy, Wockhardt, and Nicholas Piramal have the size and the experience to embark on substantial research activities involving drug discovery, a significant departure from their past practice of imitating drugs produced abroad and selling mainly in the market for generics.[18] Indian companies currently account for $8 billion of the $48 billion global market for generic drugs ("Selling Generics" 2006). The presence of these homegrown firms and the many MNCs beginning to locate some of their research in India (such as Novartis and GlaxoSmithKline) is creating a dynamic environment. India's huge size, numerous hospital facilities, and capacity to conduct drug trials involving large and heterogeneous populations are additional advantages over smaller countries like Singapore and Korea, which also are engaged in the development of new drugs and procedures. Developing a drug in India can cost as little as $100 million, compared with a cost of $1 billion or more in the United States. China shares these advantages with India and is beginning to exploit them (see Yusuf and Nabeshima 2006b).

Outside of the United States, India now has the largest number of manufacturing plants approved by the U.S. Food and Drug Administration, and with the newly strengthened intellectual property regime, that is a firm basis for future growth.[19] Again, the competition is likely to be among the advanced countries, China and India, and possibly Brazil, with other countries certain to be squeezed by the presence of the big players in an industry where size matters greatly at several levels.

---

18. Until the revision of intellectual property rights in 2005, Indian firms were able to manufacture generic versions of medicines developed in other countries without waiting for those drugs' patents to expire.

19. It is surprising, however, that a survey by Bain and Company in 2006 found that pharmaceutical executives felt China was the more attractive site for low-cost manufacturing of drugs ("China Looms Large" 2006).

Autos and Parts

Traditionally, automobile firms have tended to prefer local assembly to exporting because of the bulkiness of the finished cars and the need to comply with local regulations that often differ substantially among countries. This is not to say that trade in the automobile sector is insignificant. On the contrary, it is growing at double-digit rates, especially trade of more sophisticated and expensive parts.

In 2004, the Chinese share of automotive products exports was a mere 0.7 percent, and that of India was 0.2 percent (Noble 2006). The Indian production of automobiles (in 2004/05, close to $9 billion) could climb to approximately $40 billion in 2015, with $20–25 billion of that total exported. Production of automobiles in China was $60 billion in 2003. By 2015, China's export of automobiles could be as much as $120 billion (Noble 2006). India seems to have a comparative advantage in exporting small cars.[20] The recent entry of Chinese producers such as Chery and Geely could change the picture, however, as could the strategies of MNCs to use China as a base for producing and exporting small cars, including hybrids (Ma, Ngyuen, and Xu 2006).[21] China and India are modernizing their auto industries through joint ventures with foreign firms. Virtually all the major international auto manufacturers have set up facilities in China and some (for example, Honda, Hyundai, and Toyota) are entering India ("Honda to Invest" 2006). The Indian government partnered with Suzuki in the early 1980s to form a joint venture, Maruti Udyog, and began delicensing the auto components industry (Gokarn and Vaidya 2004).[22] In 1993 India ended the licensing of foreign automobile ventures, and in 2001 it lifted almost all the restrictions on FDI in the automobile industry. Tariffs have remained high, however, at 100 percent on vehicles and 35 percent on their parts. In contrast, tariffs in China declined to 25 percent on vehicles and 10 percent on parts after its accession to the WTO (Noble 2006).

FDI from multinational corporations is spurring the emergence of parts manufacturers in China (some of them foreign affiliates) (Noble 2006; Raws-

---

20. Just seven years after it started production, Tata Motors was making net pretax profits of 10 percent and was the largest group in the Tata business empire ("Today India" 2005).
21. In 2004, 15 percent of the production was exported (Balakrishnan et al. 2006). China was a net exporter of vehicles in 2005, to about 10,000 ("Figures Show China" 2006). Most of the exports were minivans sent mainly to the Middle East, but this is likely to change with increasing exports of sedans.
22. The earliest entry was by General Motors, assembling Chevrolets in India in 1928 (KPMG International 2006).

ki 2006). China is acquiring an edge in the international market for auto parts with exports of $0.3 billion in engines, $3.25 billion in auto parts and bodies, and $1.35 billion in tires, compared with $1.4 billion in 2004/05 for India for these products combined (Balakrishnan et al. 2006). The assemblers and first-tier suppliers (Sutton 2004) in both countries are able to manufacture products of sufficient quality, no matter where they are produced, and are able to export their products.[23] The distribution of observed defects confirms the view that first-tier suppliers to newly arrived carmakers in China and India already are operating close to world-class standards (Balakrishnan et al. 2006). India's auto industry, however, is handicapped by a significant cost disadvantage relative to China: costs are close to 20 percent higher in almost all the parts and component production.

In both China and India, auto assemblers are facing difficult times in procuring parts of sufficient quality from the lower-tier suppliers (Noble 2006). With pressure coming mainly from the MNCs, the Indian automobile parts industry recently has redoubled its efforts to improve quality, to streamline the delivery system (just-in-time delivery), and to improve the efficiency of its factory operations (Balakrishnan et al. 2006).

In its push to raise the level of technology, China is ahead of India. The automobile industry is one of the most R&D-intensive industries.[24] The list of top R&D spenders includes many of the well-known automakers, some of which have transferred a portion of their R&D activities to China. Chinese automakers slowly are increasing their R&D spending as well. For instance, Geely claims to invest more than 10 percent of revenues in R&D (Noble 2006). By comparison, Tata Motors spends approximately 2 percent of revenues on R&D, and Maruti Udyog spends only 0.48 percent.[25] This may change because Indian engineering and metalworking firms, such as Bharat Forge, are gearing up to provide high-value products and services in conjunction with software houses—particularly products with embedded software. In this regard, India may be several steps ahead of China.

Both China and India are beginning to worry about the environmental impact of their rapid motorization, and they share similar concerns about energy

23. Most of India's automotive exports are by the international first-tier suppliers (Balakrishnan et al. 2006).
24. Among the top 10 firms in terms of R&D spending, 5 are automotive firms, led by DaimlerChrysler (United Kingdom 2005).
25. The market share of Maruti Udyog is 54.5 percent in passenger cars, with the capacity to produce 500,000 units annually ("Smooth Drive" 2006).

security and dependence on imported oil. As a result, the Giants may be able to help push the technological frontier for fuel-efficient, small, and clean cars made with predominantly recyclable material and parts, but only if they set and enforce appropriate environmental standards and encourage the formation of closed-loop supply chains (Gallagher 2006; Noble 2006). Toyota recently began assembling its Prius hybrid car in China, a technology well suited for China's cities and a technological direction appropriate for a world in which petroleum consumption threatens to overtake the feasible growth in supplies.[26]

Steel

China's steel production passed 349 million tons in 2005, making it by far the largest producer in the world (with 31 percent of the global share) and the fourth-largest exporter (with sales of 27 million tons approximately on par with imports).[27] The significant developments with portent for the future are China's extremely rapid increases in capacity (25 percent between 2004 and 2005 alone); the increasing concentration of production in large-size modern plants (although many small, antiquated facilities remain); and the growing technological capacity to produce high-quality construction steel, stainless, galvanized, and coated steels, and flat products for burgeoning downstream transport and durable goods industries.[28] These developments point to declining imports and the scope for higher exports.

Compared with China, India's total output and per capita consumption are small. By fiscal 2004/05, India was producing 38 million tons of steel, and its exports of 3.8 million tons approximately balanced imports of 3.2 million tons. As India enlarges its transport, engineering, and white goods industries and modernizes its severely backward infrastructure, the demand is likely to rise as sharply as it has in China. Thus, it is realistic to expect India to produce 55–60 million tons of steel by 2010 and as much as 120–130 million tons by 2015.

The production trends in China and India will have consequences for the rest of the world. One such consequence is that the Giants' capacity expansion will add enormously to the demand for iron ore and coking coal (unless

---

26. Hyundai is planning to market a hybrid version of its Accent in China by 2008 ("Automotive" 2006).
27. In December 2005, China became a net exporter.
28. Closing down small inefficient plants and consolidating production in a few giant firms is a government objective ("Attempting a Steel Revolution" 2005).

production of steel plummets elsewhere) and, to the extent that this demand cannot be met through the development of local mines and associated transport facilities, it will spill over into imports. Second, Indian production still largely consists of mild steels, as does China's to a lesser extent. Only Tata's most modern plant is beginning to meet the needs of the auto industry for hot-rolled steel.[29] A considerable amount of investment, learning, and gains in process technologies might be needed even before China and certainly before India can meet the requirements of their own advancing transport and engineering industries. For the above reasons, India is not likely to emerge as a significant exporter of steel—especially high-tech and specialty steels—during the next decade. It is more likely, if infrastructure, housing, and industrial development take off, that for a time both India and China will be importers of certain types of specialized steels. China, however, is sure to ascend the ranks of steel exporters, edging out the 35 members of the European Union and possibly Russia within five years.

Electronics

Competition, globalization, indigenization, and powerful policy factors have been the forces driving the electronics industries in China and India. Further impetus, at least for China, has come from the outsourcing of manufacturing from Europe, Japan, Taiwan (China), and the United States in the 1990s. However, the development of each country's electronics industry has been shaped by different industrial policies.

India's policy framework has focused on technological self-reliance and has assigned a limited role to foreign investment and to the development of electronic components manufacturing, which has contributed to the success of the industry in Taiwan (China) (Joseph 2004). The Indian Electronics Commission established in 1971 promoted protectionist policy measures to control production capacity, investment, and imports. The strategy channeled development of the industry to the public and small-scale sectors, and regulated the entry and operation of foreign capital and technology. Discontent with the policies emphasizing self-reliance, and with restrictive industrial policies in general has led to a gradual liberalization of the electronics industry (Gokarn, Sen, and Vaidya 2004).

---

29. Tata's earnings before interest, tax, depreciation, and amortization were $293 per ton in 2005, three times the industry average ("Tata Steel Girds" 2006).

By fiscal 2004/05, India produced $11.1 billion of electronics hardware, a third of which was for consumer electronics. The production of color TVs leads the increase in consumer electronics production, with more than 10 million units made in fiscal 2004/05. The production of color TVs gradually is shifting toward flat-screen units (based on tubes), and more advanced liquid-crystal display (LCD) and plasma flat-panel models. This is happening in China, too, although mastering the latest generation of this technology is proving difficult for domestic producers there. Backward links have encouraged investment in some types of component manufacturing. For example, India is the world's third-largest manufacturer of optical storage media, with 18.5 percent of the global market. Approximately 80 percent of the production is exported to 82 countries.

The shipment of personal computers (PCs) in India reached 2.34 million units in the first half of fiscal 2005/06, a 36 percent increase compared with the same period in fiscal 2004/05. The growth of computer production is driven by businesses and various government agencies widely adopting PCs and by the development of affordable broadband connections. There now are 800,000 broadband subscribers, but this number is expected to increase to 10 million by the end of 2007, further fueling the demand for PCs.

China's path to achieving a flourishing electronics sector approximates the development in other newly industrialized economies. For decades China has attached strategic importance to the electronics sector and has developed electronics capability over the course of a succession of "five-year plans" (FYPs). Initially the push was to meet defense needs, those of the industrial sector, and to a lesser degree, those of households for electronic appliances, mainly radios. With increasing consistency the country has compelled foreign investors to transfer technology to local producers, and this strategy gradually is yielding results (Rodrik 2006b). The seventh (1986–90), eighth (1991–95), and ninth FYPs (1996–2000) witnessed a dramatic surge in the production of consumer electronic products, with an average annual growth rate of approximately 66 percent. By the ninth FYP, the output of the electronics sector amounted to $72 billion, and exports had climbed to approximately $35 billion. In addition to its manufacturing capability, China strengthened its technological capacity through investment in R&D, and it was able to develop a number of products, such as very-large-scale integration devices, the Panda ICCAD system, and rewritable compact discs. This period also witnessed the emergence of new companies, such as Changhong Electric, Tsinghua Tongfang, Caihong Electronics, Panda, and Lianxiang, and numerous Taiwanese transplants, all of which have since enabled China to become the leading manufacturer of color TVs, LCDs, laptop computers, PCs, color tubes, program-controlled switchboards, cell phones, display devices, and monitors (Pecht and Chan 2004).[30]

By leveraging its low-cost labor supply and the impetus gained from WTO accession, China has doubled the scale of the electronics industry, which now accounts for more than 8 percent of industrial output. In India the electronics subsector accounts for less than 3 percent of a much smaller industrial sector.

In little more than a decade, China has made the transition from limited production of low-quality electronic items to a place in the global production chain for a wide spectrum of components and finished products (Fernandez and Underwood 2006). Today there are more than 10,000 foreign-invested firms in China, and it is likely that many more foreign component producers will relocate there because of lower labor costs, tax incentives, a large domestic market, and adequate infrastructure.[31] Companies like Intel and Motorola have taken the lead in promoting electronics R&D in China. Intel has opened a test and assembly plant in Chengdu, and Motorola is investing more than half a billion dollars in an R&D facility in Beijing. Leading Taiwanese firms, such as Foxconn Hon Hai Precision and Quanta, are doing the same. Chinese universities, too, have created links with institutes/universities abroad and are attempting to gain access to advanced technologies. The future of China's electronics industry lies in its ability to transform from a still relatively low-skilled, labor-intensive sector toward an IT-enhanced electronics manufacturing sector (Sigurdson 2005).

Conversely, India's shortcomings in both the private and public sectors have been marked by a strong reliance on imported technology and inadequate R&D. A shift from import-induced to R&D-induced technology would

---

30. Although Chinese companies are catching up, the principal exporters of the high-end electronics products, such as laptop computers and digital video discs, are Taiwanese companies (for example, FoxConn, Techfront, and Magnificent Brightness) (Branstetter and Lardy 2006).

31. Yang (2006) has predicted a further expansion of China's processing trade assisted by the International Technology Agreement, a part of the WTO accession. Yang, however, does not anticipate a shift of high-value components to China for some time. Foreign firms in China receive a tax exemption during their first two years and a 50 percent reduction of the full rate for three years due after the first profitable year. This is in contrast to Japan and the United States, where corporate tax rates are 42 percent and 35 percent (federal rate), respectively (Pecht and Chan 2004).

be beneficial for the electronics industry there. India is now, belatedly, attempting to overcome shortcomings by making significant concessions to export-oriented firms, and so has experienced an increase in exports. But liberalization is also leading to competition from imports and to a decline in profits
across industry branches. The Indian electronics industry must now compete
with China to gain a share of the gap left by the newly industrialized countries, all the while maintaining its lead in the export of electronics software.[32]

Concluding Observations

This bird's-eye view of the Giants' industrial capabilities leads us to the following observations on the evolution of global industrial geography. First we
observe that the rapid buildup of industrial capability in China across a wide
range of subsectors is quite remarkable. It shows how the codification of technology; its diffusion through FDI and trade; and its harnessing by investment
in human capital, plant and equipment infrastructure, and organizational
skills have changed the rules of the game. Catching up and leapfrogging have
become easier if countries have the policy determination and the ability to
mobilize capital and build the infrastructure to generate skills. Second, larger
countries do enjoy scale economies and are better placed to attract FDI and
induce MNCs to transfer technology. China has achieved a commanding lead
in major low-, medium-, and high-tech industries that it may be in a position
to consolidate and enlarge over the next 15 years (Lall and Albaladejo 2004;
Roland-Holst and Weiss 2005; and Devlin, Estevadeordal, and Rodríguez-
Clare 2006). Although many complex capital goods, components, and products that are design and research intensive are likely to remain the preserve of
the advanced countries, China's industrial strength could put pressure on
manufacturing industries in middle- and low-income countries and force
them to rethink, narrow, and focus their industrial ambitions. Survival in
those economies will depend on achieving industrial and innovation capability that equals or exceeds China's. Innovation may drive competitiveness, and
other countries must match or exceed China's own investment in its innovation system.

---

32. Signs that India is attracting the MNCs are supported by IBM's announced intention to
invest $6 billion in India and by the investment of $3.9 billion by Microsoft, Intel, and Cisco ("IBM to Build" 2006).

India is likely to be a major force in the software, business processes, and consulting industries (including design and engineering services), competing not so much with such leaders as Germany, Japan, and the United States as with the mid-range and lower-end players (including China, which soon might enjoy an edge in terms of technical skills volume). India is certain to build manufacturing capability but, at least during the coming decade, there is only a slim prospect that it will emerge as a China-scale exporter of mass-produced consumer products in such key industries as electronics, autos, and auto parts. India more likely could become a force in certain kinds of engineering products and services that leverage its skill base, including software skills. India's many institutional bottlenecks, gaps in its infrastructure, and emerging shortages of skills will remain as drags on industrial advance ("India: Poor Infrastructure" 2006).

There is no doubt that China will be a formidable competitor for labor-intensive manufactures that depend on a semiskilled, disciplined, low-wage workforce for at least another decade, and if the domestic and international regulatory environment allows it, India can become a major competitor in this area as well.[33]

The world market of manufactures and business services, however, is not going to be divided between China and India as the main suppliers while the rest of the world specializes in products based on natural resources and arable land. The world has not repealed the theory of comparative advantage. China's success in so many areas of manufacturing points to the forces that gradually are going to change China's competitive position. Wages in the coastal areas of China already are rising to a level sufficient to reduce the country's competitiveness at the labor-intensive end. Moving these plants to areas where wages are still low will postpone the day when China must abandon many of these sectors, but the rapid movement of workers to China's cities will raise incomes in the countryside and thereby will force up wages in the nation's interior as well. With the right policies, Indian low-wage manufacturers (along with those in other low-wage countries) may be major beneficiaries of China's rising wages, just as China benefited from the rapid increase in wages in Korea, Taiwan (China), and Hong Kong (China) over the past 20-plus years. Although India could become a major world exporter on the

---

33. Recent trends also suggest that the Giants could develop significant bilateral trade links as well (Wu and Zhou 2006).

scale of China and, over time, experience rapidly rising wages, that is not a re-alistic prospect in the next 10 years.

Finally, one must be careful not to assume that because China and India can produce hundreds of thousands of scientists and engineers each year, they soon will dominate the high end of all manufactures and services worldwide. Because the Giants are very large countries with rapidly expanding modern industrial and service sectors, they require a large number of engineers and scientists to staff a wide range of domestic activities. China and India will be able to create (and in some cases already have created) world-class research in the more advanced technologies, but they have the qualified personnel to do this in only limited areas.

CHAPTER 3

Competing with Giants
Who Wins, Who Loses?

Betina Dimaranan, Elena Ianchovichina, and Will Martin

The rapid growth of China and India in recent years has raised many questions about the implications for the world economy. Will most countries gain? Or will the outcome be brutal competition in a narrow range of products and consequent declines in the prices of developing-country exports, which will impoverish not just China and India but also other developing economies? If some countries lose from increased competition, as found by Freund and Ozden (2006) and Hanson and Robertson (2006), which countries and which products will face the most serious competition? Will the industrial countries face ever-more-sophisticated Chinese and Indian exports that destroy the jobs of skilled workers in today's advanced economies? Or will the benefits of lower prices from China and India allow real incomes in industrial countries to continue to rise strongly?

Are the pessimists right? Although it is certainly the case that rapid increases in exports of any given product must be accommodated by a decline in its price, three recent developments have the potential at least to attenuate these stark scenarios of relentless competition. One development is the rise of two-way trade in manufactures, which makes the recipient countries the beneficiaries of improvements in efficiency in their trading partners (Martin 1993). Another development is the growth of global production sharing, where part of the production process is undertaken in one economy, and subsequent stages are performed in another (Ando and Kimura 2003). This process, fueled by improvements in transport and trade facilitation and in communications, and frequently involving foreign direct investment links,

67

makes participants beneficiaries rather than victims of improvements in their partners' competitiveness. The third development is recognition that trade expansion by developing countries typically involves expansion in the range of products they export, improvements in product quality, and exporting to additional markets as their exports grow (Evenett and Venables 2002; Hummels and Klenow 2005).

All of these developments have potentially major implications for the growth prospects of China and India, and for the rest of the world. The share of developing-country manufactured exports going to other developing countries has risen in recent years, making developing countries potentially major gainers from improvements in the economic performance of other developing countries. The explosive growth of production sharing in East Asia has meant that many of these economies gained from trade liberalization associated with China's accession to the World Trade Organization (WTO) (Ianchovichina and Martin 2004), despite increased competition in third markets.

Another factor that is likely to make the implications of export expansion from large developing countries, like the Giants, more favorable for each other and for other developing countries is that such export expansion seems to involve sharp increases in the range of products made and in the quality of those goods. Hummels and Klenow (2005) found that two-thirds of the growth of exports comes from expansion in the number of products made, rather than from expansion in the volumes of existing products exported. Where consumers prefer variety in the goods that they consume or use as intermediate inputs, this factor lowers the effective price of these goods. Whether these forces are sufficient to reverse the price-depressing impact of increased exports, however, is ultimately an empirical question whose answer depends on the way in which the growth of China and India evolves.

Much can be learned by examining developments in the trading patterns of these countries. Although both economies have been quite successful in expanding their exports and imports, they have done this in *very* different ways. Broadly, China has relied primarily on exports of manufactures, frequently as part of an East Asian production-sharing network. By contrast, India has concentrated more heavily on services. Within manufactures, China has relied heavily on exports of finished goods, whereas India has focused much more on exports of intermediate inputs. India's exports are frequently of capital and skill-intensive goods, whereas China has emphasized exports of labor-intensive goods—although these goods are increasingly sophisticated (Rodrik 2006b). If the past is a good guide to the pattern of development (as assumed by Kochhar et al. [2005]), the prospect of head-on competition would seem less likely than might be suggested by a simple, aggregate view of competition between labor-intensive exporters of standardized manufactures.

However, there have been major recent reforms in both Giants, whose impact may not have been fully felt. As noted in chapter 2, India now appears to be moving toward deeper integration into systems of global production sharing—partly by following China's earlier pattern of using duty exemptions and free trade areas for the production of exports, and partly by reducing protection in a manner more consistent with China's broader trade liberalization. It seems important to take these changes into account, and doing so may require adjustments by (as well as creating opportunities for) other developing countries.

No analysis of potential future developments can be undertaken reliably without an examination of the current situation, and how that situation came to be. Therefore, this chapter first reviews some key features of China's and India's trade, particularly the recent rapid growth of exports; the changing relative importance of goods and services; and changes in the composition of exports within the broad groups of merchandise and services. With that overview as background, we then use a global economywide modeling approach to take into account all of the potential effects and to complement the industry-focused studies presented in chapter 2. First we will examine the implications of the reforms under way in India to see if they might result in greater competition between China and India. Then we use model-based simulations to generate a baseline for growth and to examine the potential implications of higher-than-expected growth rates in these two economies. From that baseline, we consider first the impact of more rapid economywide growth in China and India. Finally, we examine the implications of two different types of growth—that is, growth focused on the relatively sophisticated products discussed in chapter 2 and growth driven by increased accumulation of physical and human capital.

Developments in Trade

Both China and India have grown relatively rapidly in recent years, and the importance of trade in both economies has risen substantially, relative to gross domestic product (GDP). As is evident in figure 3.1, both of these large, low-income countries had very low export-to-GDP ratios around 1980, when the process of reform was beginning in China. From the mid-1990s, as the export

Figure 3.1 Exports of Goods and Nonfactor Services as a Share of GDP

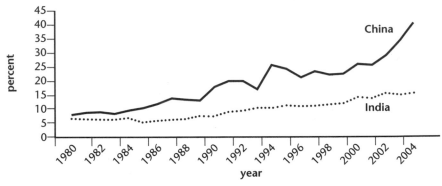

Source: World Bank, *World Development Indicators* database.

processing arrangements were broadened beyond the initial special economic zones in China, the share of exports in China's GDP began to climb sharply.[1] With the sharp devaluation of the official exchange rate in 1994, the share of exports in GDP rose and then stabilized or declined in the mid-1990s. From 2001 to 2004, China's export share rose dramatically (to approximately 40 percent— more than two and a half times India's export share). Even the up-ward GDP revision by 17 percent in 2004, which raised the importance of services relative to goods (see World Bank Office 2006), left China's export share at 31 percent, more than double India's level.

Exports of Services

A striking difference between China and India is in the importance of servic-es relative to merchandise exports (Panagariya 2006). Figure 3.2 shows that the share of commercial services in total exports of goods and services has been much higher in India than in China, not only since the rapid expansion on the export of computing services around 2000 but for the entire period

---

1. The export processing arrangements included duty exemptions on imports used for the production of exports. These exemptions were offered to foreign-invested enterprises that initially were located in special economic zones in the southern coastal regions of China, but subsequently were broadened to a wide range of enterprises (World Bank 1994) that typically did not receive the economically questionable and (now WTO-inconsistent) in-come tax concessions traditionally available in the zones.

Figure 3.2 Share of Commercial Services in Total Exports

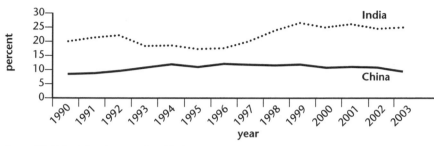

Source: World Bank Development Data Platform.

since 1990 during which comparable estimates are available. The share of services in India's exports began around 20 percent, more than twice as high as China's share. India's share declined until the late 1990s when again it began to rise sharply. Since 2000, services have accounted for more than a quarter of India's exports, whereas the share of services in China's exports has declined to less than 10 percent of total exports (although China's exports of services have been growing rapidly in absolute terms).

There also have been contrasting patterns within exports of services. As is evident in figure 3.3a, the composition of China's exports of services has changed significantly, with the relative importance of transport services declining and the importance of travel services (including tourism) increasing substantially. Travel and tourism services rose to approximately 50 percent in 2002, although they appear to have declined in 2003. The share of communication and computing services rose to nearly 45 percent in 2003. Exports of financial services provided only a small, and declining, share of China's total exports of commercial services.

India's services exports have shown remarkable dynamism (Mattoo, Mishra, and Shingal 2004). The main development evident in our data was a dramatic increase in the importance of communications and computing services, from approximately 40 percent in 1990 to roughly two-thirds in recent years. Mattoo, Mishra, and Shingal pointed out that this rise was associated with a rapid increase in such activities as business process outsourcing and computing services. However, Nikomborirak (2006) showed an explosive growth rate in software services, with these exports growing twelvefold between 1997 and 2003. The importance of both transport and travel services declined, relative to the extremely dynamic communications and computing services. Figure 3.3b shows that financial services also were a small but stable share of services exports (approximately 3 percent of the total).

Figure 3.3 Composition of Services Exports

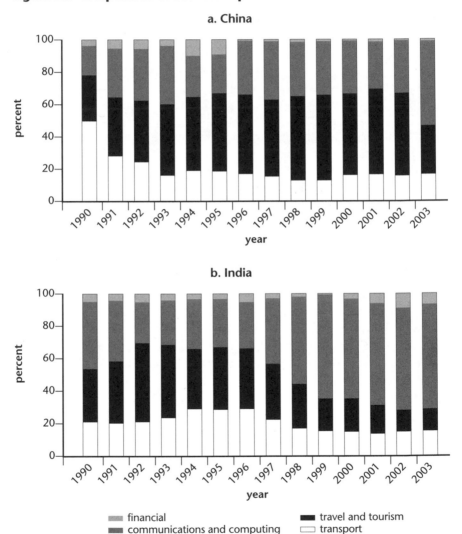

Source: International Monetary Fund balance of payments statistics extracted from the World Bank's Development Data Platform.

Merchandise Trade

The merchandise exports of both China and India are dominated by manufactures (World Bank 2003a). The composition of these manufactures and the approach to their production, however, appear to differ considerably. Table 3.1 presents information on export and import patterns for each country, using data on stage of production from the United Nations' Broad Economic Categories classification system. Because of the very different importance of fuel imports and exports to the two countries, these data are presented only for nonfuel products.

If we look first at the import data for 2004, we find that 63 percent of China's nonfuel imports are of manufactured intermediate inputs, whereas these account for 60 percent of India's imports. Only when we consider imports of parts and components do we see the sharp distinction that we might expect between the two countries, given the discussions on global production sharing. These imports accounted for 31 percent of China's merchandise imports, compared with only 12 percent in India.

On the export side, the importance of final goods in their exports differs greatly between the two Giants. Although 61 percent of China's nonfuel exports are classified as final goods, only 40 percent of India's exports are so clas-

Table 3.1 Composition of Nonfuel Imports and Exports by Broad Economic Classification, 1992 and 2004

	China		India	
	Imports	Exports	Imports	Exports
1992				
Nonfuel primary inputs	8	6	30	6
Intermediate inputs	61	30	55	47
Final goods	31	65	15	47
Total	100	100	100	100
Parts/components	15	5	15	5
2004				
Nonfuel primary inputs	10	1	16	8
Intermediate inputs	63	38	60	52
Final goods	28	61	25	40
Total	100	100	100	100
Parts/components	31	17	12	6

Source: United Nations Commodity Trade Statistics database, accessed via the World Bank's World Integrated Trade Solution (WITS) software.

sified, with 52 percent being intermediate manufactured goods, and 8 percent nonfuel primary products.

Between 1992 and 2004, the major change evident in the data in table 3.1 is the dramatic increase of China's trade in parts and components. In 1992, these items accounted for only 15 percent of nonfuel imports; by 2004, this share rose to 31 percent. In contrast, this share in India declined from 15 to 12 percent over the same period. Although discussions of China's role in production networks tend to focus on its imports of components, there also has been a substantial increase in the importance of parts and components in China's exports, with this share rising from 5 to 17 percent. By contrast, in India this share rose only from 5 percent to 6 percent of total nonfuel exports. These data are consistent with the widespread perception that India remains much less integrated in global production networks than is China, despite the existence of Indian policies to allow duty-free access to imported components for use in the production of exports (World Bank 2004b).

As Hausmann and Rodrik (2003) have emphasized, the exports of different countries reflect a wide range of differences in trade regimes, as well as idiosyncratic factors that lead apparently similar countries to have very different product mixes at the finer levels of disaggregation. Table 3.2 presents the top 25 exports for China and for India at the six-digit level of the original Harmonized System (HS), the so-called 1988–92 version. These exports, which account for 38.4 percent of China's and 58.4 percent of India's merchandise exports, are almost mutually exclusive sets. Only one product—refined petroleum—appears on both lists, accounting for 0.9 percent of China's exports and almost 10 percent of India's exports. A notable feature of China's list is the prominence of computer and electronic equipment products under chapters 84 and 85. These two chapters (which also include nonelectronic equipment) alone accounted for almost 42 percent of China's exports in 2004, up from 16 percent in 1994. In India, three HS products under chapter 71 (diamonds and jewelry) and refined petroleum under chapter 27 likewise accounted for 28 percent of total exports.

Methodology and Simulation Design

The preceding discussion of trade patterns provides valuable background, but does not enable us to assess the implications of higher growth rates in China and India. To do that, we used a modified version of the standard Global

Table 3.2 Top 25 Exports for China and India, 2004

	China			India	
Product	HS code	Share (%)	Product	HS code	Share (%)
Computer parts and accessories	847330	4.0	Diamonds, nonindustrial	710239	12.7
Digital auto data processing machinery	847120	4.0	**Petroleum oils, etc. (excl. crude)**	**271000**	**9.7**
Input or output units	847192	4.2	Articles of jewelry and parts thereof	711319	4.6
Transmission apparatus	852520	3.1	Iron ores and concentrates	260111	4.5
Parts for radio-telephony equipment	852990	2.3	Semi-milled or wholly milled rice	100630	2.6
Monolithic integrated circuits	854211	1.9	Other organic compounds	294200	2.1
Storage units for computers	847193	1.5	Flat-rolled products, zinc-plated	721049	2.0
Video recording equipment (non-tape)	852190	1.5	Medicaments, packed for retail sale	300490	1.9
Optical devices, appliances	901380	1.4	T-shirts, singlets, and other vests	610910	1.4
Video tape recorders	852110	1.2	Women's or girls' blouses or shirts, cotton	620630	1.4
Color television receivers	852810	1.2	Frozen shrimp and prawns	030613	1.5
Cargo containers	860900	1.1	Men's or boys' shirts of cotton	620520	1.3
Electric converters, static	850440	0.9	Imitation jewelry of base metal	711719	1.2
Parts and accessories of apparatus	852290	0.9	Furnishing articles, non-knitted	630492	1.2
Petroleum oils, etc. (excl. crude)	**271000**	**0.9**	Oil-cake and solid soybean residues	230400	1.1
Coke and semi-coke of coal	270400	0.9	Cashew nuts, fresh or dried	080130	1.1
Printed circuits	853400	0.9	Made-up articles (incl. dress patterns)	630790	1.1
Footwear with rubber soles	640399	0.9	Motor vehicle parts and accessories	870899	1.0
Automatic data processing machines	847199	0.9	Polypropylene, in primary forms	390210	0.9
Bituminous coal, not agglomerated	270112	0.8	Copper cathodes and sections	740311	0.9
Rubber footwear	640299	0.8	Agglomerated iron ores and concentrate	260112	0.9
Travel goods of plastic or textiles	420212	0.8	Men's or boys' shirts of cotton, knit	610510	0.9
Digital process units	847191	0.8	Automobiles with reciprocating piston	870321	0.8
Sound reproducing apparatus, such as CDs	851999	0.7	Woven fabrics of high-tenacity yarn	540710	0.8
Jerseys, pullovers of manmade fiber	611030	0.7	Collages and similar decorative plaques	970190	0.8
Total	n.a.	38.3	Total	n.a.	58.4

Source: United Nations Commodity Trade Statistics database, accessed via the World Bank's World Integrated Trade Solution (WITS) software.
Note: CD = compact disc; HS = Harmonized System. Harmonized System codes align with the 1988–92 version; n.a. = not applicable.

Trade Analysis Project (GTAP) model to assess the potential implications of rapid growth and structural change in China and India.[2] Unlike less formal approaches to projection, a global applied general equilibrium model such as GTAP has the advantage of ensuring consistency while including important sectoral detail—each region's exports of particular goods equal total imports of these goods into other regions (less shipping costs); global investment equals the sum of regional savings; regional output determines regional income; global supply and demand for individual goods balance; and demand for a factor in each country/region equals its supply. These accounting relationships and the behavioral links in the model constrain the outcomes in important ways not found in partial equilibrium analyses—increased exports from one country must be accommodated by increased imports by other countries; broad-based increases in productivity that raise competitiveness also raise factor prices and help offset the original increase in competitiveness.

The model emphasizes the role of intersectoral factor mobility in determining sectoral output supply. Product differentiation between imported and domestic goods, and among imports from different regions, allows for two-way trade in each product category, depending on the ease of substitution between products from different regions. Factor inputs of land, capital, skilled and unskilled labor, and a natural resource factor in some sectors are included in the analysis. The model incorporates the explicit treatment of international trade and transport margins, a "global" bank designed to mediate between world savings and investment, and a relatively sophisticated consumer demand system designed to capture differential price and income responsiveness across countries.

The constant returns to scale version of the GTAP model was adjusted to incorporate China's duty exemptions—which have been a key reason for the rapid integration of China into global production networks—and was modified to allow analysis of the impact of an effective system of duty exemptions for inputs used in the production of exports in India. Duty exemptions were incorporated in the GTAP model and database following the methodology developed by Ianchovichina (2004). This duty exemption model allows for two separate activities in each industry. Production of exports is represented as an activity for which imported intermediate inputs are available duty-free. Production for the domestic market uses the same technology but requires

2. This model is documented comprehensively in Hertel (1997) and in the GTAP database documentation (Dimaranan forthcoming).

payment of duties on intermediate inputs. Firms engaging in production for either the domestic market or the export market purchase both imported and domestic intermediate inputs, which are imperfect substitutes following the Armington structure. Ianchovichina (2004) documented the approach used to introduce duty exemptions into the GTAP model and showed that failing to account for duty exemptions introduces bias in trade liberalization outcomes in countries with such a system.

The 57 sectors and 87 regions of the GTAP-6 database were aggregated into 26 sectors and 24 regions, based on the importance of these sectors and regions as China's and India's trade partners—the sectors and regions are shown in various tables below. To start, we used historical and projected growth rates for GDP, skilled labor, unskilled labor, capital, and population to roll the global economy forward to 2005. This presimulation essentially updates the database for 2001 to 2005, the starting point of our projection simulations. It also includes the removal of textiles and apparel quotas on exports to Canada, the European Union, and the United States under the WTO's Agreement on Textiles and Clothing; China's WTO accession commitments, following Ianchovichina and Martin (2004); and the remaining commitments of developing countries under the Uruguay Round using tariff data from Jean, Laborde, and Martin (2005). The efficiency gains in China's motor vehicle sector that resulted from WTO accession reforms are captured using productivity shocks, as in Ianchovichina and Martin (2004).

Although the examination of trade data above suggests that there is surprisingly little overlap in the export mix of China and India, this situation might change with India's move to greater integration in the world economy, including the very large reductions in protection that have been undertaken in India since 2001; the further reductions in manufacturing sector protection that have been foreshadowed by the government; and measures intended to enable Indian manufacturers to participate fully in global production sharing. These measures include more effective duty exemptions for intermediates used in the production of manufactured exports, tariff cuts intended to bring tariffs on manufactured products to around the 7 percent level prevailing in China after accession (Ianchovichina and Martin 2004, p. 11), and 20 percent reduction in international transport costs to and from India.[3]

---

3. The tariff reduction is based on continuation of the rapid liberalization undertaken in India's nonagricultural tariffs in recent years. The reduction in transport costs is based on trade facilitation experts' broad estimates of the potential cost-reducing impacts of trade facilitation measures.

As is evident in table 3.3, this simulation sharply expanded India's exports of manufactures, with particularly large increases in exports of machinery and equipment and of electronics. The expansion in India's exports of products such as textiles and apparel, however, was smaller than the average expansion, thus implying a reduction in their share in India's exports. In figure 3.4, we compare the share of each product represented in the model in China's exports with the share in India's exports before and after the policy reforms. In the graph it does not appear that these reforms will expand greatly India's exports of products in which China has particularly large export shares. In fact, the correlation for overall exports rises modestly, from 0.36 to 0.41. However, the correlation within manufactures falls, from 0.01 to –0.02.

The second simulation explores the strong growth prospects in China and India in the context of world economic expansion over the period 2005–20.[4] This process provides a baseline from which we can assess the impact of an additional annual growth of 2.1 percentage points in China and 1.9 percentage points in India in the period 2005–20. Using the methodology for assessing potential growth effects of reform presented in Ianchovichina and Kacker (2005), we concluded that these were potentially feasible increases relative to the baseline.[5] We implement these growth dividends using favorable, sector-neutral, annual shocks to total factor productivity (TFP) of the same size, focusing purely on productivity increases to isolate these effects from those resulting from increases in the stock of particular factors. These assessments of upside potential may be conservative in that they do not explicitly take into account the potential benefits from reforms of labor market policies in India that are widely believed to have enormous potential for productivity growth and fuller participation in global production chains (Mitra and Ural 2006). Nor do they account fully for the potential benefits of reforms in services trade (Nikomborirak 2006), which Markusen, Rutherford, and Tarr (2005) found to be potentially very large.

---

4. The forecasts of growth rates for real GDP, skilled and unskilled labor inputs, investment and capital accumulation, and population were based on the "central projections" for 2005–15 in the World Bank's Global Economic Prospects database at the time the analysis was undertaken. The methodology for constructing the macroeconomic projections to 2020 (known as the "GTAP baseline") is documented in Walmsley, Dimaranan, and McDougall (2002). The growth rates to 2020 are very close to the World Bank's central projections to 2020, used in chapter 1 of this volume.
5. Ianchovichina and Kacker (2005) presented growth scenarios for all developing countries using a cross-country growth model estimated by Loayza, Fajnzylber, and Calderon (2005).

Table 3.3 Impact of India's Integration with the World Economy, 2020
Percent change

Product	Output	Producer price	Exports	Imports
Rice	1.12	0.50	24.83	15.04
Wheat	0.44	0.23	12.71	2.75
Grains	0.14	0.65	0.98	3.48
Vegetables and fruits	−0.42	0.49	12.15	6.35
Oils and fats	−1.75	0.10	11.18	8.23
Sugar	0.31	0.73	11.34	13.73
Plant fibers	−1.89	−0.07	12.05	1.94
Other crops	−0.10	0.59	8.46	11.46
Livestock and meat	−0.03	0.76	5.23	9.66
Dairy	0.34	1.01	−6.57	13.80
Other processed foods	0.70	0.55	4.37	5.85
Energy	−0.83	−0.87	42.47	−0.20
Textiles	−1.90	−0.83	35.70	234.58
Wearing apparel	12.78	−0.81	26.55	257.38
Leather	11.57	−1.34	48.70	241.71
Wood and paper	−8.85	−0.27	30.17	90.69
Minerals	−3.28	−0.62	38.35	46.31
Chemicals, rubber, and plastics	−8.82	−3.42	90.22	128.04
Metals	−11.76	−3.25	108.29	209.06
Motor vehicles and parts	1.41	−2.31	59.51	30.91
Machinery and equipment	20.98	−4.42	167.71	41.11
Electronics	34.97	−3.64	140.28	3.18
Other manufactures	9.41	−3.19	56.48	82.57
Trade and transport	−0.21	0.43	−1.81	1.51
Commercial services	0.29	0.30	−0.62	1.46
Other services	0.36	0.32	−1.09	1.75
Food	*0.02*	*0.55*	*9.85*	*7.23*
Energy and minerals	*−1.50*	*−0.80*	*39.47*	*6.27*
Manufactures	*−0.49*	*−2.74*	*67.63*	*84.17*
Services	*0.14*	*0.36*	*−0.68*	*1.51*
Total	1.14	−1.08	52.36	50.46
Welfare (EV in $ 2001)		4,989	Per capita utility	0.91
Real returns to	Capital	3.26	Skilled labor	3.88
Real returns to	Land	1.70	Unskilled labor	3.28

Source: Authors' simulations with modified GTAP model; see details in text.

Note: EV = equivalent variation measure of welfare change. The simulation includes introduction of duty drawbacks, a drop in manufacturing tariffs to 7 percent, and a 20 percent reduction in transport costs to and from India.

Figure 3.4 Export Shares in China and India, 2001

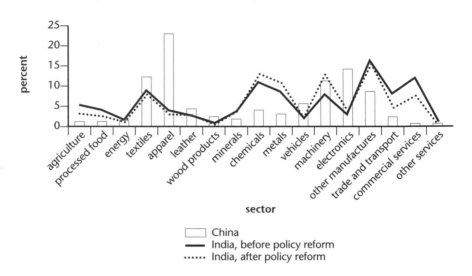

Source: GTAP-6 database and authors' simulation.

We then assess the impact of strong growth on the quality and variety of exports from China and India. Quality improvements in exports recently have been identified as a key influence on the performance of rapidly growing exporters, such as China and India (Hummels and Klenow 2005). We follow Hummels and Klenow (2005), who observed that larger economies export more in absolute terms than do smaller economies and analyzed the extent to which larger economies export higher volumes of each good (intensive margin growth), a wider set of goods (the extensive margin), and improved-quality goods. Their estimates imply that rising quality in existing product lines accounts for *increases* of approximately 0.09 percent in export prices for each 1.00 percent increase in income levels, despite increases of 0.34 percent in the quantities exported. Furthermore, they found that 66 percent of the export growth resulting from an increase in income arises from exports of new products.[6] This specification provides smaller benefits to trading partners from in-

---

6. Hummels and Klenow (2005) found that the contribution of the extensive margin varies with the levels of aggregation. At the six-digit level, exports of new varieties account for 66 percent of the country differences in exports. At the one-digit level, the variety effect accounts for 15 percent of the country differences in exports.

creased variety than Krugman-style new economic geography models (see Puga and Venables 1999), but provides additional gains from improved quality.

In the standard modeling framework in which we operate, the number of goods cannot rise as exports grow. However, both the increase in the number of varieties exported and the improvements in the quality of goods exported result in increases in the demand for goods contained within each of our standard aggregates. We specify these increases in demand as product-augmenting technical changes that increase the effective quantity of each good in the eyes of the purchaser, and correspondingly lower the effective price of the good to the purchaser. Using the price aggregator dual to Hummels and Klenow's (2005) quantity aggregator, we are able to specify the reduction in the effective price associated with their combinations of increases in variety and quality. This price aggregator is

$$P^* = \left[N \cdot (P / \lambda)^{(1-\sigma)} \right]^{(1/(1-\sigma))}, \tag{3.1}$$

where P is the actual price of individual commodity exports, N is the number of varieties, λ is the quality change index, and P^* is the overall effective price of exports. With this formula we can calculate the change in the effective price corresponding to a change in real GDP. We show that when the elasticity of substitution σ is 7.5,[7] the effective price declines corresponding to the cumulative increases in China's and India's real GDP growth in the high-growth scenario relative to the baseline are 9.2 percent and 8.2 percent, respectively. We implement the impact of this effect as a 9.2 percent and an 8.2 percent product-quality-augmenting technical change on imports by other countries of goods from China and India, respectively.

Finally, because we do not know the exact channels through which China and India will grow in the next 15 years, we undertake three simulations that are alternatives to the preceding neutral high-TFP scenarios and that enable us to investigate whether China's and India's export growth might create more competition for developing or industrial countries. We first study the implications of positive productivity shocks of 2 percent per year in the relatively capital- and skill-intensive sectors considered in the case studies presented in chapter 2: metals, electronics, machinery and equipment, automobiles, and commercial services in China and India. Then, we consider shocks that augment the stocks of human and physical capital, and that could be expected to shift the composition of China's exports toward goods more intensive in human

---

7. This is the mid-range value considered in Hummels and Klenow (2005).

and physical capital and so more competitive with the exports of the industrial countries. We first assess the effects of a 2 percent annual increase in the stock of physical capital in China and India. Then we compute the effects of a 2 percent annual increase in the stock of human capital in China and India.

The macroeconomic closure of the simulation model assumes a constant level of employment, with perfect mobility of skilled and unskilled labor between sectors and none between regions. Because we look at long-run trends, we have doubled the elasticity of substitution between imported goods from different sources and between composite imported and domestic goods from the values used in the GTAP-6 database. In all simulations the trade balances as shares of GDP were fixed for our focus countries (China and India) to avoid potentially important changes in welfare resulting from changes in financial inflows from abroad when growth rates in these countries change substantially.[8]

Trade Effects of Global Growth, 2005–20

The projections for such key variables as output, labor force growth, and investment in table 3.4 assume that the world economy will grow in real terms at an average annual rate of 3.1 percent in the period 2005–20. The volume of world trade is projected in these standard model projections to grow only slightly faster (at an average annual rate of 3.7 percent). The small gap between GDP growth rates and the growth of trade reflects the assumptions that productivity grows equally in all sectors, so that no great imbalances are created, and there is no expansion in the range or quality of varieties traded in this scenario. Growth in China, India, and other developing economies in South and East Asia is much higher than the average for the world, which causes their role in the global economy to grow.

The rate of unskilled workforce growth in China and India is projected to slightly outpace population growth rates over the projection period, whereas skilled labor and physical capital are projected to grow at much higher rates than is unskilled labor (table 3.4). Differential rates of factor accumulation and differences in income elasticities of demand for particular goods lead to structural changes rather than a balanced growth path for the world. This augmentation of physical and human capital is expected to have important

---

8. Financial inflows to other countries not experiencing differential growth shocks are much less likely to change substantially and hence create misleading indicators of welfare change.

implications for the structure of output—switching it toward capital-intensive products—and for factor rewards. On the demand side, the consumption
profile changes to reflect the effects of growing per capita incomes coupled
with nonhomothetic preferences, implying declines in the share of expendi-

Table 3.4 Output, Factor Inputs, and Population Projections, 2005–20
Average annual growth rates percent

Trading partner	GDP	Unskilled labor	Skilled labor	Physical capital	Population
Australia and New Zealand	3.5	1.6	0.6	3.8	0.7
China	6.6	0.8	3.9	8.5	0.6
Japan	1.6	0.2	−0.7	2.5	−0.2
Korea, Rep. of	4.7	2.0	5.8	4.9	0.3
Hong Kong and Taiwan (China)	4.3	0.6	3.0	4.9	0.4
Indonesia	5.2	2.7	6.5	4.7	1.1
Malaysia	5.6	−1.4	3.9	5.8	1.4
Philippines	3.5	1.8	4.6	3.5	1.5
Singapore	4.9	0.6	1.1	5.3	0.8
Thailand	4.6	0.1	3.2	3.9	0.5
Vietnam	5.4	1.4	1.9	6.0	1.1
Rest of Southeast Asia	3.1	1.3	3.6	3.6	1.0
India	5.5	1.6	4.0	6.1	1.1
Rest of South Asia	5.0	2.1	3.6	5.1	1.7
Canada	2.6	1.6	0.9	3.2	0.4
United States	3.2	1.5	0.8	3.9	0.7
Mexico	3.8	2.7	4.6	3.3	1.4
Argentina and Brazil	3.6	0.9	3.7	3.1	1.0
Rest of Latin America	3.3	1.6	3.8	3.6	1.3
EU25 and EFTA	2.3	0.3	0.0	2.6	−0.1
Former Soviet Union	3.2	0.3	0.8	3.6	−0.1
Middle East and North Africa	4.1	1.7	3.3	4.1	1.6
Sub-Saharan Africa	3.5	2.6	3.3	3.2	1.9
Rest of the world	3.7	0.7	1.2	2.6	0.5
LICs	*4.7*	*1.7*	*3.1*	*4.2*	*1.5*
MICs	*4.5*	*1.0*	*3.1*	*3.9*	*0.8*
HICs	*2.7*	*0.9*	*0.4*	*3.0*	*0.2*
World	3.1	0.9	0.8	3.2	0.9

Source: World Bank projections to 2015 extrapolated to 2020.
Note: EFTA = European Free Trade Association; EU = European Union; HIC = high-income country; LIC =
low-income country; MIC = middle-income country.

ture on necessities such as food and increases in those on luxuries such as services. These pressures for change from the individual regions contribute to changes in relative world commodity prices that also influence the pattern of structural change worldwide.

Under our initial assumption of sectorally neutral technical change, strong growth in the developing world implies that demand outpaces supply for energy, natural fibers, and farm products (such as wheat, grain, vegetables, fruits, and other crops). Energy prices rise by 41 percent (or 2 percent per year) over the 15 year period considered, in part because of the presence of a fixed resource in the model's representation of this sector and under the assumption that extraction efficiency improves no faster than efficiency in other activities. The prices of mineral products decline, indicating that fixed natural resource factors are a small share of the cost of output in this sector (table 3.5) and the rise in its price is offset by increased productivity in their use. Liberalization of the textiles and apparel markets puts downward pressure on these products' prices. With strong growth in China and India, competition in the manufacturing sectors intensifies, and the prices of manufactured goods and services fall relative to those of food, energy, and minerals. World prices, on average, fall relative to the factor price numeraire in the period 2005–20 (table 3.5) because of increased productivity.

The projected implications of global growth at the country level are presented in table 3.6. China and India are expected to increase their volume of trade at much higher rates than those of other economies in East and South Asia, although exports of other middle- and low-income countries also grow at rapid rates (above 100 percent). In the baseline, both China and India almost triple their export volumes and more than double their import volumes (table 3.6).[9] However, the implications of strong economic performance for per capita income differ significantly for the two countries because India's population grows at twice China's rate.

Impact of Improvement in Growth and Quality of the Giants' Exports

The effects on key variables of higher growth in China and India and of higher growth with and without increased variety and quality of exports are pre-

---

9. The disparity in export and import growth does not imply an increasing trade surplus because prices change, including declines in the price of the Giants' manufactured exports.

sented in table 3.7. These impacts are presented for real incomes (welfare), for export volumes, and for terms-of-trade effects. For each variable, the effect depends on whether the income increases in China and India result in growth of the same exports ("growth"), or whether export growth is accompanied by

Table 3.5 Changes in Key Economic Indicators as a Result of Global Growth, 2005–20

percent

Sector	Output	Exports	World price[a]
Rice	49.5	68.7	−2.3
Wheat	50.2	64.3	8.8
Grains	53.3	52.1	9.7
Vegetables and fruits	38.7	42.0	8.9
Oils and fats	74.0	80.5	−9.4
Sugar	56.6	60.5	−10.1
Plant fibers	88.4	118.3	7.9
Other crops	45.4	53.6	7.6
Livestock and meat	57.1	123.0	−8.6
Dairy	44.9	76.7	−11.6
Other processed foods	43.7	44.9	−12.5
Energy	79.4	110.0	40.6
Textiles	72.6	60.8	−13.7
Wearing apparel	72.3	58.2	−17.4
Leather	58.6	47.0	−13.7
Wood and paper	60.4	58.3	−15.5
Minerals	66.2	66.6	−13.6
Chemicals, rubber, and plastics	52.2	58.2	−11.5
Metals	65.3	68.4	−14.2
Motor vehicles and parts	58.6	62.1	−15.0
Machinery and equipment	65.2	72.1	−15.8
Electronics	92.2	88.9	−17.4
Other manufactures	91.3	77.6	−19.2
Trade and transport	62.1	70.4	−14.1
Commercial services	64.8	65.1	−19.5
Other services	61.9	64.2	−15.9
Food	*49.75*	*66.2*	*−5.82*
Energy and minerals	*76.05*	*101.2*	*26.94*
Manufactures	*68.33*	*69.1*	*−15.19*
Services	*62.87*	*64.7*	*−16.10*
All sectors	66.64	71.7	−11.28

Source: Authors' simulations with modified GTAP model; see details in text.
a. Relative to a numeraire of aggregate factor prices.

Table 3.6 Welfare and Trade Changes as a Result of Global Growth, 2005–20

Trading partner	Welfare		Output (% change)	Exports (% change)	Imports (% change)
	2001 US$ billions	% change			
Australia and New Zealand	285	70.3	66.3	58.2	86.1
China	1,965	146.2	161.9	187.8	167.7
Japan	936	24.5	27.6	87.6	65.8
Korea, Rep. of	421	93.3	99.7	122.4	115.9
Hong Kong and Taiwan (China)	385	83.0	87.3	94.3	94.3
Indonesia	181	116.5	112.8	127.9	137.4
Malaysia	118	126.8	127.8	132.1	136.3
Philippines	47	61.7	68.2	89.7	77.0
Singapore	76	89.4	105.9	156.5	150.5
Thailand	115	93.4	97.2	109.6	110.2
Vietnam	38	111.9	121.1	103.7	104.8
Rest of Southeast Asia	45	60.5	58.2	57.0	88.7
India	631	116.5	124.4	189.9	151.4
Rest of South Asia	161	103.2	109.1	139.8	117.3
Canada	334	48.2	46.7	47.4	51.3
United States	5,838	58.4	60.8	67.1	65.6
Mexico	450	77.5	75.2	59.7	75.9
Argentina and Brazil	526	71.6	68.8	31.3	86.9
Rest of Latin America	382	66.1	63.6	55.5	68.2
EU25 and EFTA	3,191	40.2	41.1	38.6	42.4
Former Soviet Union	340	71.6	59.6	74.1	64.0
Middle East and North Africa	1,028	97.3	82.9	51.5	89.7
Sub-Saharan Africa	251	78.0	68.2	48.5	79.7
Rest of the world	99	72.9	72.5	61.0	76.3
LICs	*1,126*	*99.6*	*101.4*	*115.1*	*113.8*
MICs	*5,249*	*98.1*	*97.3*	*104.3*	*107.5*
HICs	*11,466*	*47.8*	*49.8*	*57.8*	*58.7*
World	17,841	58.5	60.0	71.7	71.7
LICs (excl. India)	*495*	*84.3*	*80.7*	*70.7*	*90.7*
MICs (excl. China)	*3,284*	*81.9*	*75.6*	*73.0*	*87.0*

Source: Authors' simulations with modified GTAP model; see details in text.

Note: EFTA = European Free Trade Association; EU = European Union; HIC = high-income country; LIC = low-income country; MIC = middle-income country.

Table 3.7 Impact of Improved Growth and Quality Exports in China and India, Relative to Base, 2020

Region	Welfare Growth 2001 $ millions	Welfare Growth Percent	Welfare Growth and quality 2001 $ millions	Welfare Growth and quality Percent	Exports Growth (%)	Exports Growth and quality (%)	Terms-of-trade effects Growth (2001 $ millions)	Terms-of-trade effects Growth and quality (2001 $ millions)
Australia and New Zealand	2,743	0.45	5,568	0.91	-0.06	0.72	2,652	5,240
China	1,145,733	39.9	1,253,425	43.6	29.41	55.34	-48,229	38,159
Japan	6,588	0.16	17,276	0.42	2.44	4.80	9,186	18,946
Korea, Rep. of	829	0.11	7,451	1.00	3.45	5.83	-957	4,646
Hong Kong and Taiwan (China)	3,811	0.53	12,749	1.78	1.94	3.78	4,260	13,307
Indonesia	791	0.27	1,822	0.61	0.18	-0.10	723	1,907
Malaysia	1,555	0.87	3,636	2.03	0.27	0.02	1,570	3,698
Philippines	-627	-0.57	-994	-0.89	-0.26	-3.19	-559	-583
Singapore	-2,280	-1.68	-458	-0.34	4.92	6.50	-159	2,019
Thailand	-639	-0.31	492	0.24	1.63	2.33	-857	312
Vietnam	-41	-0.07	166	0.29	-1.10	-2.33	63	468
Rest of Southeast Asia	424	0.41	603	0.58	-2.85	-2.11	382	541
India	361,740	33.7	394,490	36.7	28.89	47.05	-12,379	10,661
Rest of South Asia	-962	-0.35	-159	-0.06	1.60	2.98	-1,110	-517
Canada	2,767	0.32	5,182	0.59	-0.91	-1.43	2,634	4,736
United States	124	0.00	20,262	0.15	0.67	2.87	479	20,671
Mexico	535	0.06	1,000	0.11	-1.33	-2.37	175	489
Argentina and Brazil	1,410	0.13	3,134	0.28	-0.06	0.45	1,072	2,570
Rest of Latin America	3,015	0.36	4,703	0.56	-0.48	-0.26	2,652	4,251
EU25 and EFTA	-4,306	-0.04	16,893	0.18	-0.14	-0.18	3,013	22,183
Former Soviet Union	9,958	1.37	12,914	1.77	1.34	2.34	9,750	12,039
Middle East and North Africa	23,780	1.31	29,108	1.60	-1.50	-1.50	22,592	27,568

continued on next page

Table 3.7, *continued*

Region	Welfare				Exports		Terms-of-trade effects	
	Growth		Growth and quality			Growth and quality (%)	Growth (2001 $ millions)	Growth and quality (2001 $ millions)
	2001 $ millions	Percent	2001 $ millions	Percent	Growth (%)			
Sub-Saharan Africa	4,904	0.96	7,676	1.50	-0.24	0.80	4,004	6,439
Rest of the world	-688	-0.34	-500	-0.24	1.46	2.37	-596	-282
LICs	366,065	17.9	402,775	19.7	14.04	23.44	-9,039	17,592
MICs	1,184,823	13.1	1,308,743	14.5	10.70	20.39	-11,707	90,130
HICs	10,275	0.03	84,923	0.28	0.79	1.73	21,109	91,749
World	1,561,163	3.8	1,796,437	4.3	4.4	8.5	363	199,472
LICs (excl. India)	4,325	0.46	8,286	0.87	-0.07	0.77	3,339	6,931
MICs (excl. China)	39,091	0.61	55,315	0.87	-0.18	-0.16	36,522	51,971

Source: Authors' simulations with modified GTAP model; see details in text..
Note: EFTA = European Free Trade Association; EU = European Union; HIC = high-income country; LIC = low-income country; MIC = middle-income country.

expansion in the range of products exported, and improvements in their quality ("growth and quality"). Increases in real income presented are measures of equivalent variation in 2001 dollars. Export expansion is presented using percentage changes in the volume of exports. The terms-of-trade effect is presented in 2001 dollars.[10]

A positive efficiency gain in China and India resulting in annual growth that is, respectively, 2.1 and 1.9 percentage points higher than in the baseline will translate into a welfare gain in 2020 of $1.15 trillion (40 percent) for China and $362 billion (34 percent) for India, relative to the baseline. The volume of exports increases by 29 percent from both China and India—an increase slightly larger than the corresponding increases in output. However, this export expansion is accompanied by declining export prices and a terms-of-trade loss of approximately $48 billion for China and $12 billion for India. Such a loss is expected in a model using the Armington assumption of national product differentiation.

The welfare changes for other countries are relatively small. Gains for most of China's and India's trading partners in the Asia-Pacific region are modest. High-income countries gain, except for those in the European Union where existing distortions and structural change lead to an allocative efficiency loss. Many countries will benefit from improved terms of trade for their products as China increases its imports from the rest of the world by 23 percent and India increases imports by a similar amount. Some middle- and low-income countries (such as the Philippines, Thailand, and some other countries in South Asia) will lose as competition with China and India negatively affects their terms of trade in third markets.

Whereas the aggregate results suggest that competition from China and India would have a small effect on average real incomes, manufacturing industries in many countries are affected negatively; and for industries in some countries, these effects could be substantial (table 3.8).[11] Improved growth of exports from China and India implies an expansion of their textile industries

---

10. Since the price of relevance to the importer is the effective price, which may fall when quality and variety increase, and the price relevant to the producer is the actual price, which rises when quality and variety increase, it is possible for the terms-of-trade to improve for both importer and exporter.

11. Results of improved growth in China alone are available from the authors on request; they do not differ much from the results of improved growth in China and India, except that India's apparel industry contracts by 12 percent whereas the impact on other industries is negligible.

Table 3.8 Manufacturing Output: Effects of Improved Growth and Quality Exports in China and India, Relative to Base, 2020

percent

Region	Textiles	Apparel	Leather	Wood	Minerals	Chemicals	Metals	Auto	Machinery	Electronics	Other
Australia and New Zealand	-6.9	-8.6	-8.5	-1.3	-1.1	-0.8	-4.1	-2.4	-6.7	-5.9	-8.4
	-15.3	-15.5	-13.7	-1.5	0.2	-3.4	-3.9	-6.3	-13.9	-18.5	-15.3
China	35.5	20.3	39.4	41.6	36.8	42.9	38.5	34.8	37.6	35.8	30.5
	30.0	20.5	45.2	34.7	36.3	39.2	34.8	40.9	40.2	58.2	33.1
Japan	-1.6	-6.0	-5.3	-1.1	-1.0	-2.3	-2.7	-3.9	-6.6	-4.8	-4.2
	15.1	-8.0	-8.1	-1.0	-0.6	-1.4	-1.9	-6.6	-9.0	-10.7	-6.8
Korea, Rep. of	-1.3	-2.1	-1.6	0.4	-0.6	-1.7	1.7	-3.0	-1.9	0.0	-7.7
	10.0	-3.7	10.6	4.1	-0.8	2.7	3.9	-9.2	-7.0	-7.9	-11.7
Hong Kong and Taiwan (China)	-5.9	-7.3	-7.1	-2.2	-1.7	-4.8	-5.0	-3.6	-5.7	-2.9	-15.8
	1.7	-1.0	-4.3	-2.5	-3.9	-2.2	-8.8	-10.0	-10.7	-10.6	-26.3
Indonesia	-9.2	-11.7	-7.7	4.6	-2.6	0.3	-5.9	-0.5	-1.2	-1.4	-10.6
	-15.6	-21.4	-20.0	15.4	-3.4	0.9	-8.9	-2.8	-4.4	-12.0	-19.2
Malaysia	-7.5	-15.8	-5.7	0.6	-1.3	1.9	-1.6	-1.1	-4.6	-0.2	-3.6
	-7.3	-27.4	-4.2	5.1	0.5	4.4	1.2	-2.4	-5.9	-3.5	-5.5
Philippines	-7.4	-15.7	-8.7	-0.2	-0.3	3.9	0.1	0.0	-0.2	-4.0	-6.4
	-14.3	-25.7	-17.0	1.9	1.3	5.5	2.6	0.4	4.0	-13.9	-9.9
Singapore	-8.0	-8.1	-11.2	-0.6	2.1	0.7	2.0	-3.6	-1.8	3.4	-10.9
	-7.9	-16.9	-21.7	1.6	3.9	0.8	5.0	-11.4	-2.5	5.2	-20.3
Thailand	-5.1	-5.0	-6.0	1.5	-0.6	2.0	0.5	0.5	-1.4	4.6	-8.1
	-9.1	-9.5	-13.9	6.5	0.3	3.0	2.2	0.3	-3.7	6.2	-15.5
Vietnam	-8.9	-19.3	-5.6	-0.9	0.3	-1.1	-4.9	-4.7	-7.7	-4.8	-6.6
	-15.6	-35.5	-11.9	-0.1	1.0	2.4	-8.4	-8.0	-12.8	-12.6	-10.4
Rest of South-east Asia	-6.3	-3.6	-3.4	0.7	0.7	-0.5	-1.2	-0.4	-3.5	-0.5	-0.8
	-12.4	-6.2	-5.6	9.1	1.4	-2.4	-2.1	-1.1	-6.0	-2.4	-1.2

India	35.1	23.3	41.4	39.8	30.7	30.6	33.9	30.6	29.2	30.7	23.5
	26.2	11.1	45.5	32.1	33.9	33.1	34.0	30.0	41.5	36.5	15.6
Rest of South Asia	-2.7	-12.4	-1.2	0.7	-1.6	-0.4	3.8	-1.5	-3.2	-0.2	-6.4
	-6.4	-25.5	-6.3	2.3	-1.9	-1.2	10.5	-3.8	-8.1	-8.9	-11.6
Canada	-4.4	-8.3	-3.7	-1.4	-2.4	-4.0	-2.1	0.0	-4.1	-2.2	-12.7
	-5.8	-14.9	-3.7	-1.1	-2.6	-3.8	-4.3	-1.0	-8.5	-11.0	-20.5
United States	-5.4	-8.7	-4.3	-0.2	0.1	0.9	-0.7	-0.2	-2.5	-3.5	-10.5
	-10.5	-15.3	-6.4	0.3	0.2	1.4	-1.0	-0.4	-4.2	-11.0	-16.7
Mexico	-2.1	-2.2	-0.8	0.2	0.1	0.9	-0.3	0.7	-4.1	-3.8	-6.5
	-3.9	-3.6	-1.3	1.2	0.8	1.6	0.4	2.0	-5.7	-13.2	-10.1
Argentina and Brazil	-2.0	-1.1	-6.6	-1.0	-1.0	-2.0	-3.2	-1.8	-4.5	-3.1	-2.9
	-3.4	-1.8	-8.4	-0.9	0.0	-2.8	-4.5	-2.5	-7.4	-8.0	-4.9
Rest of Latin America	-4.5	-4.2	-3.4	-0.5	-0.2	-0.3	-2.8	-1.3	-5.5	-5.3	-8.8
	-9.5	-7.9	-6.1	0.4	1.1	-1.4	-2.6	-2.5	-9.9	-15.1	-14.4
EU25 and EFTA	-5.6	-9.7	-5.0	0.0	-0.4	-1.8	-0.7	-0.4	-2.4	-2.5	-3.9
	-9.9	-16.8	-8.5	0.8	-0.5	-3.0	-1.3	-1.3	-5.0	-11.7	-6.6
Former Soviet Union	-2.6	-4.7	-1.4	-0.5	-1.9	-1.1	-3.3	-0.3	-4.4	-3.1	-3.2
	-5.8	-9.4	-4.2	0.8	-2.2	-1.6	-2.9	0.1	-7.9	-6.6	-5.7
Middle East and North Africa	-3.6	-18.6	-2.6	-0.7	-0.5	-5.8	-6.6	-3.2	-8.3	-7.2	-9.1
	-14.8	-29.4	-3.7	-0.7	0.3	-5.9	-6.5	-4.9	-12.9	-15.9	-13.4
Sub-Saharan Africa	-4.6	-5.5	-4.1	0.0	-0.1	0.3	-2.3	-3.8	-8.4	-7.4	-7.6
	-10.4	-10.3	-7.7	0.6	1.2	-2.0	1.4	-8.5	-16.1	-24.9	-13.3
Rest of the world	-2.9	-7.7	-1.7	1.1	-0.1	0.0	-1.2	-0.3	-1.9	-1.8	-14.3
	-5.3	-12.9	-4.1	2.5	-0.1	-1.4	-2.6	-0.7	-4.7	-7.0	-24.0

Source: Authors' simulations with modified GTAP model; see details in text.

Note: EFTA = European Free Trade Association; EU = European Union. For each region, numbers in the first row are results for the case of improved growth in China and India; numbers in the second row are results for the case of improved growth and quality exports in China and India.

and a contraction of the textile industries in other countries, relative to the baseline. Indonesia and Vietnam experience the largest contractions—9.2 percent and 8.9 percent, respectively. The projected growth of China's and India's apparel industries means sharp contractions in apparel production elsewhere. The apparel industries of Vietnam and the Middle East and North Africa are expected to be hit hardest as their output declines by nearly a fifth (19 percent). Similar declines will affect the light manufacturing industry (leather and other manufactures), although the expected declines are much smaller than the declines in apparel. With the exception of the electronics industry in Singapore and Thailand, competition from China and India leads to contractions of the electronics industries in other countries. Machinery and equipment production also will relocate to China and India, thereby reducing the size of these industries in other countries. The expected expansion of automobile production in China and India has a small negative effect on automobile production in other countries, except in Mexico and Thailand.

But not all news will be bad. The boost in China's and India's wood processing industries has positive spillover effects via increased demand for intermediate wood products from Indonesia, the Republic of Korea, Malaysia, Thailand, and other countries in East and South Asia. Similarly, growth in China and India will fuel demand for chemicals from Malaysia, the Philippines, and Thailand; for mineral products from Vietnam and other Southeast Asian countries; and for metals from some countries in East Asia and South Asia (table 3.8). Moreover, in all countries losing manufacturing output, other sectors (not reported in the table) expand as factors move into the farm and services sectors.

Adding to the growth scenario improvements in the variety and quality of exports from China and India increases the benefits to the world economy from $1.6 trillion to $1.8 trillion (table 3.7). In this case, the volumes of exports from China and India grow by 55 and 47 percent, respectively, with positive terms-of-trade effects in all regions other than the Philippines. Most countries benefit because they can import higher volumes from these two countries at lower effective prices and they can experience greater demand for their exports from China and India. The biggest beneficiaries are China and India, of course, because their welfare gains are increased by 3.7 percent and 5.0 percent of initial income levels by the quality and variety effects, raising their overall gains to 44 percent and 37 percent, respectively. In one case—the Philippines—the welfare loss from higher growth in China and India worsens as the Giants improve the quality of their exports and expand output of electronics, machinery, and equipment. Such an outcome can be explained by the high share of electronics in the Philippines' total exports. Indeed, this share is higher than that of any other country/region in the model. The volume of trade between China and India increases more than does either country's trade with the rest of the world, thereby deepening the trade links between the two Asian Giants. Most countries have increases in exports as a result of the Giants' growth and quality improvements, but some suffer losses (most notably, Mexico, the Philippines, Vietnam, and others in Southeast Asia). Middle-income countries other than China suffer an absolute loss of exports.

Pressure on middle-income developing countries to raise the quality of their manufactures will increase as a result of improved-quality Chinese and Indian exports. Improved-quality exports from fast-growing China and India intensify competition in the markets for different manufactured goods and lead to further contractions of the electronics industry in all regions except Singapore and Thailand; in the machinery and equipment industries in all countries except the Philippines; and in the textiles, apparel, and other light manufacturing sectors in most regions. As China starts producing more sophisticated and new varieties of electronics, machinery, and equipment, it reduces the rate of expansion of its processing industries (wood, minerals, chemicals, and metals), thus leaving space for other countries to expand these industries (table 3.8).

Impact of Variety

Our simulations of growth and quality improvement include most of the broad features of new economic geography models, such as Puga and Venables (1999). Improved variety and quality of exports from China and India raise welfare, and lower production costs in their trading partners, in the same way that increased variety does in the Puga-Venables model—that is, through a reduction in the effective price of imports from the Giants. In our formulation, trading partners also face increased competition in third markets, reducing welfare in their competitors. Induced increases in import demand from China and India improve the terms of trade of their trading partners in our formulation, as in Puga and Venables. One difference is that increases in exports from trading partners do not increase the number of varieties supplied by these countries, and hence do not generate benefits from the preference for variety assumed in the new economic geography models. For trading partners where welfare declines but exports increase (Singapore, the rest of South Asia, and the rest of the world), our formulation omits a positive effect that may reverse the very small estimated overall negative impact. For the Philippines, however, exports decline, so this channel would be unlikely to reverse the adverse welfare impact arising from greater competition in third markets.

Alternative Paths to Improved Growth

A positive productivity shock of 2 percent per year in the five Chinese and Indian sectors considered in chapter 2—metals, electronics, machinery and equipment, motor vehicles, and commercial services—is beneficial to the world and all developing countries, except the Philippines. This efficiency improvement in China and India, however, entails substantial structural change (table 3.9). The Giants become much more powerful players in the favored sectors, and world trade grows much faster than envisaged under the scenario of neutral TFP growth of 2 percent. Exports from China double and exports from India jump by more than 72 percent. World trade expands by 11 percent, as regional trade between China and developed economies in the Asia-Pacific region (Japan, Korea, and the United States), and India and its closest partners in South Asia grow as well. The huge effects on trade arise because the assumed stimulus is to existing export sectors, so it exacerbates imbalances between local supply and demand and, hence, requires increased trade to restore equilibrium.

In this scenario, China and India expand their heavy industry and high-tech manufacturing sectors, leaving space for other countries to increase production of light manufactures, chemicals, and minerals (table 3.9). Still, exports from many developing economies that compete with China and India decline as a result of the improved efficiency of China's and India's heavy industry and high-tech sectors; exports from high-income countries decline marginally. Most notable is the decline of exports from the Philippines (18 percent) and Thailand (10 percent), including declines of 65 percent and 53 percent, respectively, in the electronics sector. All economies experience structural change of a similar magnitude. In the simulation with neutral productivity increases across sectors, the growth and quality scenario created increased competition in a number of sectors, and reduced other countries' output levels relative to the baseline in many cases. In almost all cases, however,

Table 3.9 Industry Effects of Improved Sectoral Productivity Growth in China and India, Relative to Base, 2020

percent

Region	Textiles	Apparel	Leather	Wood	Minerals	Chemicals	Metals	Auto	Machinery	Electronics	Other
Australia and New Zealand	10.4	38.7	9.4	3.1	15.8	-0.9	-42.7	-28.5	-44.0	-61.8	25.6
China	-79.6	-72.8	-63.6	-52.3	-0.6	-45.6	42.7	195.8	95.4	252.1	-58.0
Japan	48.3	36.5	30.5	9.1	16.8	22.5	-19.3	-23.1	-31.6	-43.9	28.2
Korea, Rep. of	61.4	40.5	125.8	51.2	27.4	47.0	-32.2	-29.5	-36.2	-54.5	104.2
Hong Kong and Taiwan (China)	1.6	107.2	28.1	9.6	2.6	8.0	-51.6	-40.0	-56.0	-66.3	94.9
Indonesia	38.7	96.2	-2.0	37.0	-7.5	-1.1	-45.7	-26.8	-38.1	-77.9	37.6
Malaysia	99.2	290.7	63.1	88.9	44.1	53.8	-19.2	-12.4	-23.0	-53.2	44.4
Philippines	71.9	266.3	44.2	22.3	4.2	16.1	-40.6	-25.0	-23.9	-64.7	81.3
Singapore	70.4	36.6	29.4	29.9	51.3	30.6	-31.5	-39.0	-42.0	-35.0	48.5
Thailand	54.2	59.4	26.6	35.6	16.4	8.9	-34.4	-14.8	-39.5	-53.3	69.7
Vietnam	48.9	203.1	-5.1	-0.3	6.0	13.5	-41.7	-39.0	-53.2	-57.9	14.9
Rest of Southeast Asia	20.8	26.4	-5.6	21.1	3.4	-3.0	-23.4	-12.7	-29.1	-28.2	2.9
India	-40.5	-67.5	-88.7	-43.8	-37.8	-41.7	117.5	26.2	156.2	8.7	-71.4
Rest of South Asia	23.3	156.1	5.3	5.0	2.4	2.5	-39.2	-40.0	-48.2	-64.8	20.0
Canada	54.7	94.6	49.7	12.0	3.5	12.4	-30.2	-27.5	-37.6	-60.4	100.6
United States	35.6	81.0	33.7	5.8	6.8	14.8	-14.7	-13.7	-24.2	-56.6	77.3
Mexico	57.0	75.0	20.6	8.0	5.0	13.8	-13.6	-16.0	-33.0	-65.0	70.8
Argentina and Brazil	6.0	4.3	28.6	2.3	13.4	-0.9	-20.6	-20.8	-27.8	-36.3	8.5
Rest of Latin America	22.3	43.8	11.7	4.6	10.7	0.2	-34.7	-27.5	-40.3	-61.6	34.9

continued on next page

Table 3.9, *continued*

percent

Region	Textiles	Apparel	Leather	Wood	Minerals	Chemicals	Metals	Auto	Machinery	Electronics	Other
EU25 and EFTA	72.1	111.4	38.1	9.1	4.9	6.4	−24.5	−28.0	−37.1	−62.2	44.2
Former Soviet Union	16.5	50.2	8.2	17.2	−10.6	5.9	−26.3	−9.9	−26.0	−30.4	10.1
Middle East and North Africa	30.2	173.0	2.9	−1.6	7.1	−2.6	−38.2	−32.8	−47.8	−63.9	38.7
Sub-Saharan Africa	17.0	32.2	12.4	6.6	13.2	7.1	−45.8	−41.1	−50.0	−70.4	30.1
Rest of the world	45.1	155.0	15.2	4.3	−7.0	−3.8	−30.1	−25.3	−31.7	−45.7	125.4

Source: Authors' simulations with modified GTAP model; see details in text.
Note: EFTA = European Free Trade Association; EU = European Union.

output continues to rise strongly, relative to its level in 2005. When technological progress is focused in a few key, trade-oriented sectors, on the other hand, the impacts on output are much more variable, relative to the baseline projection. The electronics sector is the most likely to contract, relative to 2005 levels, with declines in most countries associated with extremely rapid expansion in China and India. Outputs of metals and automobiles are projected to increase in absolute terms in most regions, with noticeable declines, relative to 2005 levels, only in Australia/New Zealand (17 percent) and Hong Kong and Taiwan (China). Output of other machinery is projected to come under downward pressure in sub-Saharan Africa and in the high-income countries, where a decline in output of 21 percent is projected for the European Union, relative to 2005 levels. The results from this experiment show just how strongly the impacts at a sectoral level depend on the sectoral pattern of productivity growth in the Giants.

Improved growth through accelerated accumulation of capital (2 percentage points faster than the baseline in China and India) modestly affects real incomes in other regions. China and India increase their production of all manufactured goods, but the expansion of the capital-intensive sectors is larger than that of other sectors. Because the capital-intensive sectors are experiencing efficiency gains in the previous scenario, the export and sector-specific changes are broadly similar but smaller in absolute value than the ones presented for the case of improved efficiency of China's and India's metals, electronics, machinery and equipment, motor vehicles, and commercial services. In terms of total exports, capital accumulation impinges relatively more heavily on other low-income countries than on other middle-income countries in this exercise than it does in the previous exercise, and high-income countries record gains rather than losses (table 3.10).

Finally, improved growth through accelerated accumulation of human capital (2 percentage points per year higher than the baseline) has a much smaller effect on welfare, exports, and sector outputs than does improved growth through accelerated accumulation of physical capital (table 3.10). This occurs because the share of skilled labor is much lower than the share of capital in total factor endowment. The patterns over countries are similar to those of physical capital accumulation, but they impinge relatively more heavily on middle-income countries.

Table 3.10 Export Volume Changes under Various Scenarios, Relative to Base, 2020

percent

Region	Improved sector productivity in China and India	Improved capital growth in China and India	Improved skilled labor growth in China and India
Australia and New Zealand	–0.01	0.14	0.02
China	96.42	23.93	5.39
Japan	4.40	2.97	0.66
Korea, Rep. of	4.05	3.25	0.82
Hong Kong and Taiwan (China)	–3.88	1.15	0.32
Indonesia	–0.73	0.12	0.05
Malaysia	–6.60	–0.36	–0.04
Philippines	–18.34	–0.82	–0.06
Singapore	–8.56	3.87	1.03
Thailand	–9.77	0.46	0.15
Vietnam	3.23	–0.49	–0.07
Rest of Southeast Asia	14.02	–0.27	–0.16
India	72.90	35.06	6.92
Rest of South Asia	13.40	2.60	0.56
Canada	–6.96	–1.21	–0.27
United States	5.07	1.82	0.38
Mexico	–8.74	–1.39	–0.31
Argentina and Brazil	1.33	0.50	0.08
Rest of Latin America	0.00	–0.23	–0.07
EU25 and EFTA	–2.45	0.00	0.01
Former Soviet Union	4.44	2.27	0.52
Middle East and North Africa	–0.62	–1.40	–0.33
Sub-Saharan Africa	–2.24	–0.59	–0.16
Rest of the world	12.42	3.19	0.75
LICs	*35.50*	*16.51*	*3.25*
MICs	*32.42*	*8.33*	*1.88*
HICs	*-0.43*	*1.01*	*0.24*
World	11.13	3.94	0.88
LICs (excl. India)	*2.61*	*0.13*	*0.01*
MICs (excl. China)	*–2.24*	*–0.11*	*–0.02*

Source: Authors' simulations with modified GTAP model; see details in text.
Note: EFTA = European Free Trade Association; EU = European Union; HIC = high-income country; LIC = low-income country; MIC = middle-income country.

Summary and Conclusions

This study highlights the very sharp differences in the trade patterns of China and India, and assesses the implications of rapid growth and structural change on the trade patterns of those economies and of the rest of the world. The chapter explains that services exports are roughly twice as important for India as for China. Within merchandise trade, both countries are dependent on manufactures, with China much more strongly integrated into production networks through trade in parts and components. However, the Giants' product mixes are radically different, with only one product—refined petroleum—appearing in the top 25 products for both. Each country has undergone quite radical trade reform.

Our baseline projections suggest that there is scope for China and India to expand their exports and imports significantly without hurting each other's development prospects or those of most other economies. Improved growth in China and India will intensify competition in global markets for manufactures, however, and the manufacturing industries in many countries will be affected negatively. Improvement in the range and quality of exports from both countries may create substantial welfare benefits to the world and to the Giants, and may act as a powerful offset to the terms-of-trade losses otherwise associated with rapid export growth. Lacking efforts to keep up with China and India, some countries may see further erosion of their export shares and high-tech manufacturing sectors. As China starts producing more sophisticated and new manufacturing products, there will be opportunities for other countries to expand their processing industries. We take into account increases in the variety and quality of exports from China and India, but, based on the most recent evidence (see Hummels and Klenow 2005), we specify export growth as arising only partially at the extensive margin (that is, through increases in the number of varieties exported). However, we augment these gains with the important Hummels-Klenow finding that the quality of existing exports rises with economic growth. One feature of the new economic geography that we do not take into account is potential gains from increases in output variety in the additional partner exports induced by the growth of these high-growth economies (see, for example, Puga and Venables 1999).

Efficiency improvements in China's and India's high-tech and heavy industries have much stronger trade effects than a uniform efficiency improvement of the same magnitude. This scenario will lead to severe competition in the high-tech sectors and entail substantial structural change, with China and India displacing other countries in markets for high-tech products, but leaving space for other countries to increase production of light manufactures.

Some caveats are important. First, what we have presented here are thought experiments, not predictions. Although they show that China's and India's growth could be beneficial to nearly all other countries, and that the impact on particular countries will depend on those countries' own trade, production, and consumption profiles and on the patterns of growth in China and India, they offer only the broadest indications of probable effects. Likewise, our results strongly suggest that benefiting will depend on adapting to the new opportunities and challenges. By themselves these results cannot dictate the necessary adjustment. They must be supplemented with sector-specific case studies, both to identify the emerging patterns in general and to consider particular products. Our aggregation hides important information on intraindustry trade in components as part of the global production sharing arrangements.

Moreover, note that we have not estimated the adjustment costs of this economic transformation—and these costs could be substantial. Finally, recall that the chapter focuses on the static trade aspects of growth in China and India; it ignores important investment–growth links that may amplify the effects discussed here and may affect the welfare results.

CHAPTER 4

International Financial Integration of China and India

Philip R. Lane and Sergio L. Schmukler

The goal of this chapter is to assess how the increasing economic prominence of China and India is reshaping the international financial system. These countries have grown strongly over the last decade and projections suggest this trend will continue (see chapter 1). Although restrictions remain, both countries gradually have adopted more market-oriented policies and have liberalized both inward and outward capital flows across their borders.

To analyze the implications of the emergence of the Giants for the global financial system, we consider several dimensions of their international financial integration: net foreign asset positions, gross holdings of foreign assets and foreign liabilities, and the equity-debt mix on international balance sheets. We also analyze the importance of domestic developments and policies related to their domestic financial systems for both the current configuration of their external assets and liabilities and the dynamics of the international financial integration of China and India.[1] We thus discuss the effects of three different interrelated domestic factors in each economy: (1) financial

We are grateful to Jose Azar, Agustin Benetrix, Francisco Ceballos, Vahagn Galstyan, Niall McInerney, and Maral Shamloo, who provided excellent research assistance at different stages of this project; and to the Singapore Institute of Policy Studies, the Institute for International Integration Studies, and the World Bank Irish Trust Fund for financial support for this chapter.
1. In the other direction, it is clear that international financial integration fundamentally influences the functioning of the domestic financial system. That relationship, however, is not the focus of this chapter.

liberalization and exchange rate/monetary policies, (2) evolution of the financial sector, and (3) impact of financial reform on savings and investment rates. Finally, we assess the current international financial impact of these countries and probe how their increasing weight in the international financial system will affect the rest of the world over the medium term.

Three salient features emerge from the analysis of China's and India's international financial integration. First, regarding size, China and India still have only a small global share of privately held external assets and liabilities (with the exception of China's foreign direct investment [FDI] liabilities). Second, in terms of composition, these countries' international financial integration is highly asymmetric. On the asset side, they both hold mostly low-yield foreign reserves (that is, by 2004 these countries accounted for 20 percent of global official reserves). Equity instruments feature more prominently on the liability side, primarily taking the form of FDI in China and portfolio equity liabilities in India. Third, although neoclassical models would predict these countries to be net borrowers in the international financial system, given their level of economic development, over the last decade both China and India have reversed their large net liability positions, with China even becoming a net creditor. Their debtor and creditor positions in the world economy are small. We argue that domestic financial developments and policies, including the exchange rate regime, are essential factors in explaining these patterns of integration with the international financial system and in projecting future integration.

Those three characteristics of China's and India's current engagement with the global financial system have offered these countries some important benefits in recent years. Accumulating reserves has insured against the risk of international financial crises and has enabled these countries to maintain stable exchange rates. FDI inflows to China have contributed to technology transfer, and portfolio equity inflows to India have facilitated the rapid expansion of its stock market, while the domestic financial sectors of both countries have been mostly insulated from the potentially destabilizing impact of greater cross-border debt flows. Finally, improving net foreign asset positions may have been a prudent response in the wake of India's crisis in the early 1990s and, more recently, the 1997–98 Asian financial crisis.

The current strategy nonetheless entails considerable opportunity costs in terms of the pattern of net resource flows, the "long-debt, short-equity" financial profile, the constraints on domestic monetary autonomy, and the insulation of the domestic banking sector from external competitive pressures. In particular, the benefits of reserve accumulation come with a cost arising from the return differential; on average, these countries pay more on their liabilities than they earn on their assets. Moreover, as our analysis will highlight, domestic financial development alters the current strategy's cost–benefit ratio because the rationale for financial protectionism declines and the potential gain from a more liberal capital account regime increases.

Looking to the future is a difficult task, and projections on the evolution of China's and India's international financial positions are conditional on changes in their domestic financial systems, among other things. Nevertheless, we project that further progress in domestic financial reform and liberalization of the capital account will lead to a restructuring of these countries' international balance sheets. In particular, further financial liberalization will widen opportunities for foreign investment and expand the international investment alternatives for domestic residents, with the accumulation of external assets and liabilities by the private sectors in these countries likely to grow. With these changes we may expect to see a diminution in the compositional asymmetries of external liabilities, with a greater dispersion of inflows among the FDI, portfolio equity, and debt categories. On the asset side, there should be a marked increase in the acquisition scale of nonreserve foreign assets. With the projected increase in their shares in world gross domestic product (GDP), China and India are set to become major international investing nations.

Although projections about net balances are subject to much uncertainty, institutional reforms and further domestic financial development would put pressure on the emergence of significant current account deficits in both countries in the medium or long term, all else being equal. Accordingly, if taken together with a possible deceleration in their rates of reserve accumulation, the roles of China and India in the global distribution of external imbalances could undergo a substantial shift in the coming years. These changes will have significant implications for other participants in the international financial system.

The analysis in this chapter builds on several strands of the existing literature. A number of recent contributions have highlighted the importance of domestic financial reform for the evolution of these countries' external positions.[2] The roles of China and India in the international financial system

---

2. Among other sources on China, see Blanchard and Giavazzi (2005); Chamon and Prasad (2005); Lim, Spence, and Hausmann (2006); Goodfriend and Prasad (2006); Ju and Wei (2006); and Prasad and Rajan (2006). Among other sources on India, see Kletzer (2005) and Patnaik and Shah (forthcoming).

have been much debated, with opinions divided between those who consider the current role of these countries (together with other emerging Asian economies) as large-scale purchasers of reserve securities to be essentially stable in the medium to long run, and those who believe that the current configuration is a more transitory phenomenon.[3]

Relative to the existing literature, we make a number of contributions. First, we provide a side-by-side examination of China's and India's current degrees of international financial integration, with a focus on the levels and compositions of their international balance sheets. Although we put these countries together in the analysis because of their size and growing economic importance, many differences remain and are highlighted in the chapter. Second, we provide a comparative account of the development of their domestic financial sectors, and we show how distinct policies in the two countries help explain differences in their external capital structures.[4] Third, we conduct a forward-looking assessment of how future reforms in their domestic financial sectors will affect the evolution of international balance sheets, with an emphasis on highlighting the broader impact on the international financial system.

The rest of the chapter is organized as follows. The next section documents the basic stylized facts of the international financial integration of China and India. We then briefly link that to the developments in the countries' domestic financial sectors. The fourth section analyzes the impact of their international integration on the global financial system. The final section offers some concluding remarks.

Basic Stylized Facts

To document the major trends in China's and India's international financial integration, we study the international balance sheet of each country.[5] Bal-

---

3. Dooley, Folkerts-Landau, and Garber (2003) famously dubbed this configuration the "Bretton Woods II" system; Caballero, Farhi, and Gourinchas (2006) provided theoretical support. Although this hypothesis has a broad appeal in explaining the stylized facts of recent imbalances, it remains highly controversial. Other authors (Eichengreen 2004, Aizenman and Lee 2005, Goldstein and Lardy 2005, and Obstfeld and Rogoff 2005) have provided broad-ranging critiques.

4. The analysis here is partly based on Bai (2006), Kuijs (2006), Li (2006), Mishra (2006), Patnaik and Shah (2006), and Zhao (2006).

5. Lane (2006) has provided more details concerning the historical evolution of the international balance sheets of China and India.

ance sheets provide a reasonable measure of international portfolios, where they stand, and how they might shift; and they help us compare stock positions with the evolution of capital flows (with flows responding to stock adjustments).[6] In some places we also discuss recent patterns in capital flows, especially where these patterns signal that the current accumulated positions are undergoing some structural changes toward new portfolio balances.

We start with figure 4.1a, which plots the evolution of the net foreign asset positions of China and India from 1985 to 2004. The figure shows that both countries have followed a similar path—accumulating net liabilities until the mid-1990s but subsequently experiencing a sustained improvement in net foreign asset position. By 2004, China was a net creditor at 8 percent of GDP, whereas Indian net external liabilities had declined from a peak of 35 percent of GDP in 1992 to 10 percent of GDP in 2004. Figures 4.1b and 4.1c show that the net foreign asset positions of other East Asian countries also have improved in the wake of the 1997–98 financial crisis, while the net positions of the countries in the G-7, Eastern Europe, and Latin America have deteriorated. According to the International Monetary Fund's World Economic Outlook database, since 2004 China's current account surplus has continued to increase, reaching 7.2 percent in 2005 and projected at 7.7 percent for 2006–07, thus strengthening their creditor position. In contrast, the Indian current account balance has returned to negative territory with a deficit of 1.5 percent in 2005 and projected deficits of 2.1 and 2.7 percent for 2006 and 2007, respectively, thus deepening their debtor position.

Compared with other developing countries, China and India have net foreign asset positions that are less negative than is typically the case for countries at a similar level of development (Lane and Schmukler 2006). This remains true today. Although some other developing countries have more positive net positions, those typically are resource-rich economies.

In global terms, the imbalances of China and India are relatively small. At the end of 2004, the Chinese creditor position amounted to only 7.4 percent of the level of Japanese net foreign assets, whereas Indian net liabilities were only 2.8 percent of U.S. net external liabilities.[7] Scaled differently, China's net creditor position of $131 billion at the end of 2004 amounted to only 5

---

6. See Lane and Milesi-Ferretti (2006) for a discussion of the advantages of focusing on balance sheets instead of capital flows.

7. Japan is the world's largest creditor nation; the United States is the world's largest debtor nation.

Figure 4.1 Net Foreign Asset Positions, 1985–2004

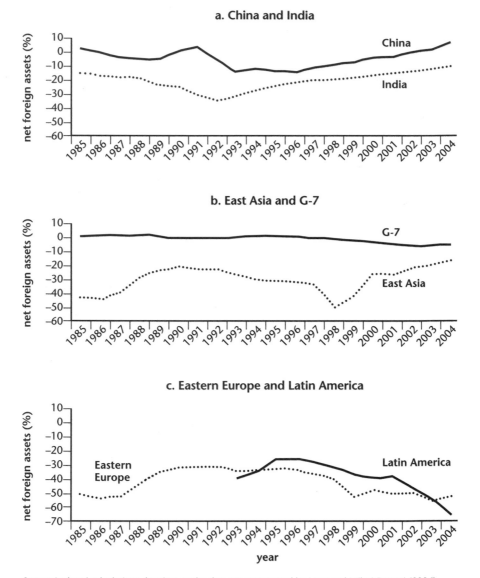

Source: Authors' calculations drawing on the data set constructed by Lane and Milesi-Ferretti (2006).
Note: Net foreign asset position expressed as a ratio to GDP. East Asia is the average of Indonesia, the Republic of Korea, Malaysia, and Thailand. G-7 is the average of Canada, France, Germany, Italy, Japan, the United Kingdom, and the United States. Latin America is the average of Argentina, Brazil, Chile, and Mexico. Eastern Europe is the average of the Czech Republic, Hungary, and Poland. The series for the regions are weighted averages where the weights are the countries' GDPs as a fraction of the region's GDP.

Table 4.1 Composition of Foreign Assets and Liabilities, 2004
Percent of GDP

Component	China		India	
	Assets	Liabilities	Assets	Liabilities
Portfolio equity	0.3	2.9	0.1	9.1
Foreign direct investment	1.9	25.7	1.3	6.4
Private debt	13.3	11.9	2.6	17.0
Reserves	31.8	n.a.	18.3	n.a.
Total	47.3	40.5	22.3	32.5

Source: Authors' calculations, based on data set constructed by Lane and Milesi-Ferretti (2006).
Note: n.a. = not applicable.

percent of the U.S. negative external position of $2.65 trillion.[8,9] China's position, however, is increasingly important on a flow basis: its projected 2006 current account surplus of $184 billion amounts to more than 20 percent of the projected U.S. current account deficit of $869 billion (IMF 2006b).

Underlying these net positions is a significant increase in the scale of China's and India's international balance sheets. Figure 4.2a shows the sum of foreign assets and liabilities (divided by GDP). This indicator of international financial integration has increased sharply for both countries in recent years, although the levels are not high when compared with other regions (figures 4.2b and 4.2c). Whereas the growth in cross-border holdings is substantial, we have shown that the relative pace of financial integration has lagged behind the expansion in trade integration and the growth of China and India's share in global GDP (Lane and Schmukler 2006).

There are significant asymmetries in the composition of the underlying stocks of gross foreign assets and liabilities. Table 4.1 shows the composition of foreign assets and liabilities for China and India. On the assets side, the equity position (portfolio and FDI) is relatively minor for both countries, with a predominant role for external reserve assets that amount to 31.8 percent of GDP for China and 18.3 percent of GDP for India at the end of 2004. On the liabilities side, the table also shows some important differences between the two countries. In particular, equity liabilities primarily take the form of FDI in China, whereas portfolio equity liabilities are predominant for India. External

---

8. A billion is 1,000 millions.
9. These calculations are based on data drawn from Lane and Milesi-Ferretti (2006). In recent years, the major oil exporters plus other Asian economies also have run substantial current account surpluses.

Figure 4.2 International Financial Integration: Sum of Foreign Assets and Liabilities

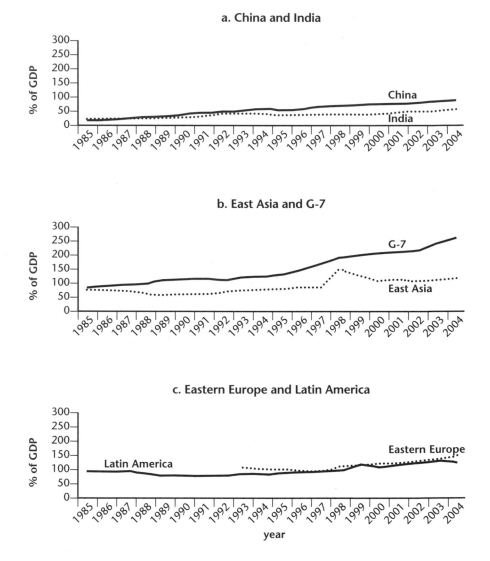

Source: Authors' calculations drawing on the data set constructed by Lane and Milesi-Ferretti (2006).
Note: Net foreign asset position expressed as a ratio to GDP. East Asia is the average of Indonesia, the Republic of Korea, Malaysia, and Thailand. G-7 is the average of Canada, France, Germany, Italy, Japan, the United Kingdom, and the United States. Latin America is the average of Argentina, Brazil, Chile, and Mexico. Eastern Europe is the average of the Czech Republic, Hungary, and Poland. The series for the regions are weighted averages where the weights are the countries' GDPs as a fraction of the region's GDP.

Table 4.2 Asymmetries in the International Balance Sheet, 2004
Percent of GDP

Component	China	India
Net portfolio equity	–2.6	–9.0
Net foreign direct investment	–23.8	–5.0
Net equity	–26.5	–14.1
Net private debt	1.5	–14.6
Reserves	31.8	18.3
Net debt	33.3	3.7

Source: Authors' calculations, based on data set constructed by Lane and Milesi-Ferretti (2006).
Note: Net private debt equals nonreserve debt assets minus debt liabilities.

debt comprises less than one-third of Chinese liabilities but more than one-half in the Indian case.

Table 4.2 considers the net positions in each asset category at the end of 2004. Both China and India are "long in debt, short in equity": they have positive net debt positions and negative net equity positions. As observed by Lane and Milesi-Ferretti (2006), this is currently a common pattern for developing countries. However, the scale of the asymmetry is striking, especially in China's case.

Figure 4.3 shows the relative importance of the different components of China's and India's international balance sheets. Relative to other countries, one of the most notable features of China and India is their low levels of nonreserve foreign assets (also discussed in Lane 2006). According to the data compiled by Lane and Milesi-Ferretti (2006), China's foreign portfolio and FDI assets amounted to $5.7 billion and $35.8 billion, respectively, at the end of 2004, whereas the figures for India were $0.95 billion and $9.6 billion, respectively. Relative to global stocks of foreign portfolio equity and FDI assets ($8.98 trillion and $12.55 trillion, respectively), these correspond to global shares of 0.06 percent (China) and 0.01 percent (India) in terms of foreign portfolio equity assets and 0.29 percent (China) and 0.08 percent (India) in terms of FDI assets. As a benchmark, their shares in global dollar GDP are 4.7 percent and 1.7 percent, respectively, whereas they hold 16.0 percent and 3.3 percent of world reserves.

Regarding global impact, figure 4.3 shows that by the end of 2004, the FDI liabilities of China represented 4.1 percent of global FDI liabilities.[10] Al-

---

10. Some of this FDI represents round-tripping activities, by which domestic residents route investment through offshore entities to benefit from the tax incentives and other advantages provided to foreign investors (see World Bank 2002; Xiao 2004).

Figure 4.3 Top Foreign Asset and Liability Holders, 2004

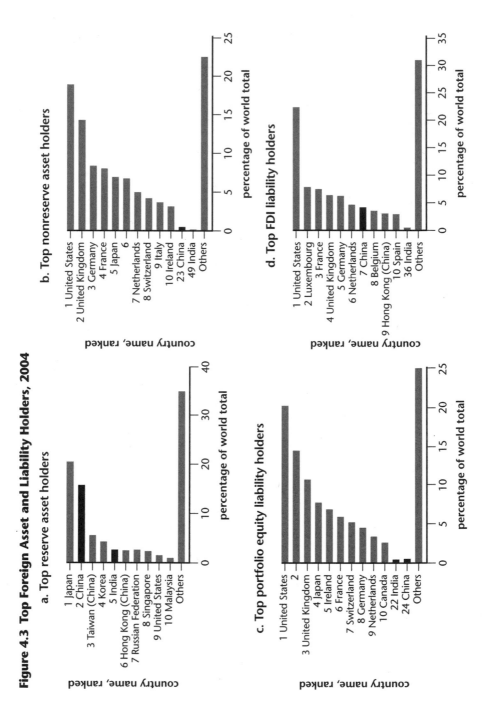

a. Top reserve asset holders

b. Top nonreserve asset holders

c. Top portfolio equity liability holders

d. Top FDI liability holders

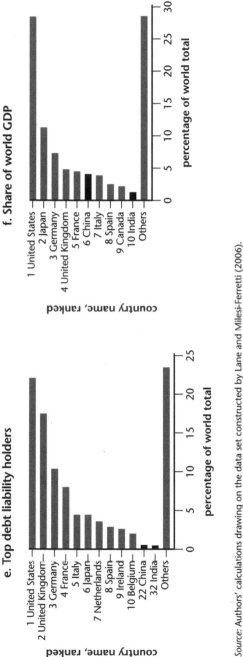

f. Share of world GDP

e. Top debt liability holders

Source: Authors' calculations drawing on the data set constructed by Lane and Milesi-Ferretti (2006).
Note: The figures show the holdings of foreign assets and liabilities, by type of asset and liability, of the ten largest holders, China, India, and the sum of all the other countries, as a percentage of total holdings of that type of asset or liability. They also show the share of world GDP of the ten largest economies and India. Holdings are expressed as a percentage of the sum of the holdings of all the countries in the data set. Numbers next to holdings show position in world ranking.

though this is broadly in line with China's share in world GDP (in dollars), global shares are much lower for the other nonreserve elements of the international balance sheet. In portfolio terms, China and India are "underweight" both as destinations for international investors and as investors in nonreserve foreign assets (Lane 2006).

Domestic Financial Sector

To probe the extent to which the stylized facts above can be explained by developments and policies related to the domestic financial sectors in China and India, we very succinctly summarize the trends in three interrelated aspects of the financial sector: financial liberalization and exchange rate policies, evolution (and state) of the domestic financial sector, and patterns in savings and investment.[11]

As becomes evident when summarizing their evolution, these factors are fundamentally related to cross-border asset trade and the international balance sheets. We conduct the analysis by turning to the particular developments in the financial sectors of each country.

China

China has adopted a gradualist approach to financial liberalization, including the capital account. During the 1980s and 1990s, the main focus was on promoting inward direct investment flows (that is, FDI), which led to a surge of direct investment in China in the 1990s. Investment by foreigners in China's stock markets has been permitted since 1992 through multiple share classes, but access is still restricted and a heavy overhang of state-owned shares limits its attractiveness. Debt inflows have been especially restricted, as have been private capital outflows. This has enabled the state to control the domestic banking sector by setting ceilings on interest rates, for example. These measures are summarized in Lane and Schmukler (2006).

China's financial liberalization policies have been linked intrinsically to its exchange rate regime. Since 1995 the renminbi (RMB) has been de facto pegged to the U.S. dollar, albeit with a limited degree of flexibility since the

---

11. A brief but much more detailed account is provided in appendixes to Lane and Schmukler (2006).

3 percent revaluation in July 2005. A stable value of the exchange rate has been viewed as a domestic nominal anchor and an instrument to promote trade and FDI. The twin goals of maintaining a stable exchange rate and maintaining an autonomous monetary policy have contributed to the ongoing retention of extensive capital controls.

These policies have had a large impact on China's international balance sheet. The capital account restrictions have encouraged significant round-tripping (Lane and Schmukler 2006), with Hong Kong (China) playing a dominant role in channeling investment into China. Moreover, targeting the exchange rate has had a powerful influence on the composition of China's international balance sheet. On the liabilities side, the scale of private capital inflows (at least until the July 2005 regime switch) can be attributed partly to speculative inflows in anticipation of RMB appreciation (Prasad and Wei 2005).[12] To avoid currency appreciation, the counterpart of high capital inflows has been the rapid accumulation of external reserves and expansion in monetary aggregates (see figure 4.4a and Lane and Schmukler [2006]). In turn, the sustainability of reserves accumulation has been facilitated by interest rate regulation that has kept down the cost of sterilization (Bai 2006).

Turning to the domestic financial sector, China's level of domestic financial market development was low at the start of the reform process in 1978. Gradual liberalization of the sector has been accompanied by a sharp deepening of the financial development indicators in China during the last 15 years figure 4.4a and Lane and Schmukler [2006]).

Regarding the banking sector, figure 4.4b shows that bank credit to GDP increased almost twofold, and deposits to GDP rose almost threefold between 1991 and 2004, reaching levels much higher than those in India and other relevant benchmark groups (East Asia, Eastern Europe, Latin America, and the G-7).[13] In terms of size, credit is as high as in the G-7 economies, and deposits are substantially larger than all the other comparators. Despite the apparent financial depth captured by these indicators, however, the banking sector remains excessively focused on lending to state-owned enterprises, and it does not appear to be an adequate provider of credit to private enterprises and households. An interest rate ceiling also distorts the behavior of

---

12. Prasad and Wei (2005) pointed out that unrecorded capital inflows have been growing in recent years as foreign investors seek to evade limits on their ability to acquire RMB assets in anticipation of future currency appreciation.
13. Canada, France, Germany, Italy, Japan, the United Kingdom, and the United States.

Figure 4.4 Selected Financial Sector Indicators

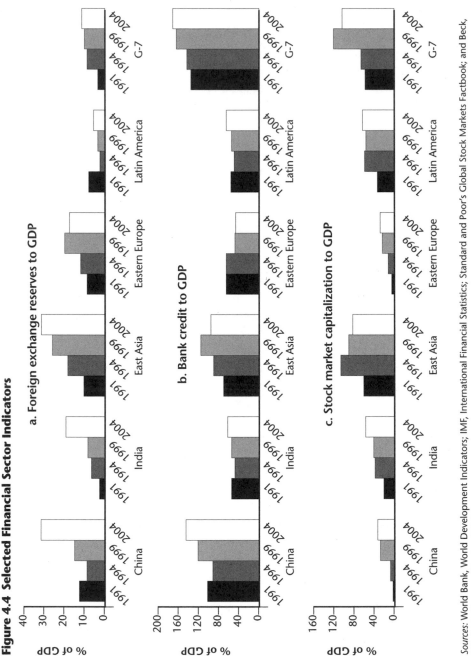

Sources: World Bank, World Development Indicators; IMF, International Financial Statistics; Standard and Poor's Global Stock Markets Factbook; and Beck, Demirgüç-Kunt, and Levine 2006.

Note: For a description of East Asia, G-7, Latin America, and Eastern Europe, see note to figure 4.1.

banks and limits the attractiveness of banks to domestic and foreign investors (Bai 2006).

With respect to domestic capital markets, although the stock market has undergone significant expansion since 1991 (figure 4.4c), the large overhang of government-owned shares implies that tradable shares are only about one-third of total stock market capitalization. In addition, equity pricing is perceived as open to manipulation, with the government regularly intervening in the market in response to political lobbying by the brokerage industry. Furthermore, corporate governance in China remains far from international standards. This contrasts with the focus of the Chinese government on guaranteeing safety for direct investment. The difference in the protection of foreigners' property rights between direct and portfolio investments has made FDI much more attractive than portfolio equity for foreign investors wanting to participate in the Chinese market.

Internal funds have been the main source of investment financing for the Chinese corporate sector.[14] According to Kuijs (2006), enterprises in China saved 20 percent of GDP in 2005. Their level of investment, however, was much higher than that, at 31.3 percent of GDP in 2005. The most important supplier of external finance has been the banking sector. Allen, Qian, and Qian (2005) showed that other important channels of external financing have been FDI (especially for private sector enterprises) and the state budget (for state-owned enterprises).

These features of the domestic financial sector help explain some elements of China's integration into the international financial system. In particular, the problems in the banking system (that is, the concentration of its loan book on state-owned enterprises, the significant number of nonperforming loans, and solvency concerns) have limited the willingness of the authorities to allow Chinese banks to raise external funds or act as brokers for the acquisition of foreign assets by domestic entities (Setser 2005). In addition, the distorted nature of the Chinese stock market means that portfolio equity inflows would have been limited even under a more liberal external account regime. Similarly, the domestic bond market is at a very primitive stage of develop-

---

14. It is important to acknowledge that retained earnings are also a primary source of investment finance in many developed and developing countries (see, for example, Corbett and Jenkinson [1996]). However, the efficiency in deploying internal funds will differ between systems with effective external monitors and those lacking an external disciplinary device to constrain firms' investment decisions.

ment, and the capacity of domestic entities to undertake international bond issues remains heavily circumscribed.

The third channel linking the domestic financial system with the international balance sheet is domestic savings and investment, with the net difference in turn determining the current account balance.

The domestic financial system influences savings rates through myriad channels. Regarding the household sector, Chamon and Prasad (2005) pointed out that the lack of consumer credit means families must accumulate savings to finance the purchase of consumer durables. Moreover, the underdevelopment of social and private insurance requires households to self-insure by accumulating buffer stocks of savings.[15]

Despite these trends at the household level, Kuijs (2005, 2006) showed that the extraordinarily high aggregate savings rate in China is driven primarily by corporate savings.[16] The high level of enterprise savings required to finance high levels of investment has been facilitated by a low-dividend policy. In the extreme case of many state-owned enterprises, there are no dividends at all. In some cases, the reluctance to distribute profits reflects uncertainty about ownership structures and the weak state of corporate governance.[17]

In addition to a low-dividend policy, two more factors help explain high enterprise savings and investment. The first is the high share of the industry sector in GDP, associated with higher savings and investment because of its capital intensity. The second factor is the rising profits of Chinese enterprises in the last 10 years. These enhanced profits can be explained in part by the

---

15. Blanchard and Giavazzi (2005) also emphasized that high household savings in China reflect a strong precautionary motive, in view of the low provision of publicly funded health and education services. Furthermore, Modigliani and Cao (2004) argued that the one-child policy has led to a higher percentage of employment to total population and has undermined the traditional role of family in providing old-age support, thus increasing household savings.

16. In 2005, household savings were similar to those of other developing countries. For instance, although the household savings rate in China may have been higher than rates of Organisation for Economic Co-operation and Development economies, it was actually lower than the rate in India. The government savings rate is also recorded as relatively high in China.

17. However, the recently established State Asset Supervision and Administration Commission is seeking to assert greater control of state-owned enterprises, including a demand for greater dividend payments. Naughton (2006) has provided an analysis of the political struggle over control and income rights in the state-owned sector.

increasing importance of private firms and the increased efficiency of state-owned enterprises (Kuijs 2006).

On the investment side, the reliance on self-financing and the lack of accountability to shareholders plausibly push up the investment rate, with corporate insiders pursuing projects that would not pass the return thresholds demanded by commercial sources of external finance.[18] In addition, for state-owned enterprises, access to directed credit from the banking sector enables these firms to maintain higher investment rates than would otherwise be possible. Furthermore, restrictions on capital outflows mean that enterprise investment largely has been restricted to domestic projects.

In sum, the underdevelopment of the domestic financial system may help explain the high rates of both savings and investment in China. The net impact on the current account is ambiguous in principle because financial development could reduce both savings and investment rates. However, the cross-country empirical evidence indicates that domestic financial deepening lowers the savings rate and increases investment (see IMF 2005b). Especially in combination with an open capital account, it is plausible that higher-quality domestic financial intermediation could place greater downward pressure on savings than investment. In particular, the international capital funneled through domestic banks and domestic financial markets to high-return domestic projects may compensate for a reduction in investment in those inefficient enterprises that are protected by the current financial system. Moreover, a better financial system could stimulate consumption (by providing more credit) and reduce the need for maintaining high savings levels (either for precautionary motives or to finance future consumption).

India

India suffered a severe financial crisis in the early 1990s, and that crisis subsequently led to a broad series of reforms. The goal was to spur Indian growth by fostering trade, FDI, and portfolio equity flows while avoiding debt flows that were perceived as potentially destabilizing. In the subsequent years, India has undergone extensive but selective liberalization (summarized in Lane and Schmukler [2006]).Substantial capital controls, however, do remain in place.

---

18. Moreover, the lack of financial intermediation distorts investment patterns, with young or prenatal firms starved of finance while mature firms inefficiently deploy excess cash flows.

The discouragement of external debt has restricted domestic entities' ability to issue bonds on international markets and the entry of foreign investors to the domestic bond market. Moreover, the restrictions on purchases by foreigners in the corporate and government bond markets are much more strict. Hence, the market for private bonds remains underdeveloped (Lane and Schmukler 2006).

By contrast, the approach to equity inflows has been much more liberal. Restrictions on FDI inflows have been relaxed progressively, although they still do exist and India receives far less direct investment compared with China (Table 4.1). The distinctive characteristic of equity flows into India, however, is the relatively high level of portfolio equity financing. India's broad domestic institutional investor base has aided the entry of foreign institutional investors that are permitted to take partial stakes in equity of quoted Indian enterprises.

Capital outflows also are restricted, although the system is being liberalized (Patnaik and Shah 2006). In particular, Indian banks are not permitted to acquire external assets, but rather are encouraged to hold government bonds, thereby lowering the cost of financing public deficits. Accordingly, current constraints on asset allocation make official reserves the predominant component of foreign assets. As in China, the de facto exchange rate/monetary regime seeks to maintain a stable value of the rupee against the dollar, which provides a nominal anchor and is viewed as promoting trade and investment. The exchange rate regime has been supported by capital controls, which have allowed some degree of monetary autonomy to be combined with the exchange rate target.

Following the crisis of the early 1990s, India initiated a reform of its financial institutions. There were extensive reforms in the equity markets and the banking sector. As figures 4.4b and 4.4c illustrate, the domestic equity market is much more developed in relative terms than is the banking sector (or the bond market, as shown in Lane and Schmukler [2006]). Corporate governance was improved, thus encouraging investment by domestic and foreign minority shareholders. Successful development of the equity market helps explain the shift in the external financing of listed firms from debt to equity (see Lane and Schmukler [2006]).

As mentioned above, the third channel linking the domestic financial system with the international balance sheet is domestic savings and investment. India's current savings rate is similar to that of most other Asian economies (Mishra 2006). Indeed, its household savings rate exceeds the Chinese level. Although corporate saving is on an upward trend, however, it is far below the

Chinese level, and government saving is relatively low despite an uptick since 2002. On the investment side, private investment has risen steadily while public investment has been declining since the 1980s. In comparing investment levels in China and India, Mishra (2006) noted that an important difference is that India's sectoral growth pattern is more oriented toward services and is thereby less intensive in physical capital. Still, Kochhar et al. (2006) noted that the next phase of Indian development may require a higher level of physical investment—an expansion in the manufacturing sector is required to absorb low-skilled labor, and there are significant deficiencies in the quality of public infrastructure.

As in China, it is plausible that further development of India's domestic financial sector may prompt a decline in household and corporate savings rates as the availability of credit from the financial system increases. Even more strongly than in China, further financial development also may stimulate an expansion in investment, in view of the credit constraints faced especially by small- and medium-size enterprises. In addition, financial development accompanied by further capital account liberalization will stimulate a greater level of cross-border asset trade, with the acquisition of foreign assets by domestic households and enterprises and the domestic financial system intermediating international capital flows to domestic entities.

Impact on the Global Financial System

Many important issues have emerged concerning the impact of China and India on the global financial system and they deserve much more attention than we can devote to them here. In our discussion we will try to summarize the main points, which can be expanded in further work. We group these issues into four broad questions that have already captured attention and, where relevant, highlight the differential effect of China and India on developed and developing countries.

How Important Are China and India as Destinations for External Capital?

China and India account for only a small share of global external liabilities (with the exception of Chinese FDI liabilities). In terms of FDI flows, however, China looks rather more important: the country absorbed 7.9 percent of global FDI flows in 2003–04 (India's share was 0.8 percent). These high flows might represent the adjustment to a new portfolio balance in which China captures a higher share of international investment (more in line with its participation in the world economy) after having a very small weighting in foreign portfolios.[19,20]

With respect to portfolio equity liabilities, Lane (2006) and figure 4.3 have shown that China and India each account for just over 0.5 percent of global portfolio equity liabilities. In terms of flows, China received 1.94 percent of global equity flows during 2003–04, and India received 1.79 percent (Lane 2006). Especially in regard to China, this likely understates its impact on the global distribution of equity flows—because of the poor reputation of the Chinese stock market, overseas entities may prefer to build portfolio equity stakes in "proxy" stock markets that are expected to co-move positively with the Chinese economy (most obviously, the Hong Kong [China] equity market can serve this purpose).

Finally, Lane (2006) recorded that both Chinese and Indian shares in global external debt liabilities have sharply declined in recent years—by 2004, only 0.65 percent and 0.35 percent, respectively. The decline is especially noteworthy for India, which was a much more important international debtor (in relative terms) in the early 1990s.

Turning to the future, continued domestic financial reform and external liberalization should produce some evolution in the level and composition of China's and India's external liabilities. As a benchmark, an increasing share of these countries in world GDP and world financial market capitalization naturally should prompt increasing capital inflows to these countries. In addition, we may expect to see some rebalancing in the composition of external liabilities. For China, reform of the domestic banking system and the development of its equity and bond markets may reduce its heavy reliance on FDI inflows as alternative options become more viable. A reduction in the relative importance of FDI also may be supported by moves to limit the generosity of the current incentives offered to foreign direct investors, which would attenuate FDI directly and through its attendant impact on round-tripping activity.[21] Finally, the expansion of domestic capital markets and reform of the

---

19. It is important to stress that some proportion of FDI represents round-tripping.

20. An interesting question is whether FDI inflows to China have been at the expense of other emerging economies. See Lane and Schmukler (2006) for a discussion of current research on this topic.

21. See Lane and Schmukler (2006) for a more detailed discussion.

banking system also would allow foreign-owned firms to draw on domestic funding sources.

With regard to India, recent moves to further liberalize the FDI regime may increase the relative importance of FDI inflows. India's ability to attract FDI, however, also depends on more widespread institutional reforms that improve the investment environment for foreign investors and encourage them to channel FDI into the country. The major barrier regarding the liberalization of debt inflows could be that opening up the capital account may threaten the government's ability to finance its large fiscal deficits at a low interest cost. Under these conditions, further liberalization may be delayed until the domestic fiscal situation is reformed.

How Important Are China and India as International Investors?

As shown in table 4.1, China and India are much less important as external investors in equity assets than as holders of equity liabilities. This is especially the case for portfolio equity assets, which by 2004 were only 0.3 percent and 0.1 percent of GDP for China and India, respectively. Relative to portfolio equity assets, FDI assets in 2004 were much larger—but remain small at 1.9 percent and 1.3 percent of GDP, respectively. In terms of nonreserve foreign debt assets, China had a much larger position in 2004 than did India (13.3 percent versus 2.6 percent of GDP). Nevertheless, even the China position is small in global terms, representing just 0.6 percent of global nonreserve foreign debt assets in 2004 (Lane 2006; figure 4.3).

In view of the relatively low levels of foreign equity assets and nonreserve foreign debt assets, the foreign assets of China and India are highly concentrated in official reserves, which respectively represent 67 percent and 82 percent of their total foreign asset holdings. As noted earlier, these countries rank highly in the global distribution of official reserves—at the end of 2004, China and India were second and sixth, respectively, and together accounted for about 20 percent of global reserve holdings.

On the financial front, the high level of reserves acts as a subsidy that lowers the cost of external finance for the issuers of reserve assets—primarily, the United States. In turn, this helps to keep interest rates lower than otherwise in these economies. For example, a careful empirical study by Warnock and Warnock (2006) estimated that the foreign official flows from East Asia kept U.S. interest rates about 60 basis points below normal levels during 2004–05. This also feeds into higher asset and real estate prices and a reduction in the domestic savings rate, helping explain the large U.S. current account deficit. Regarding the impact on other developing countries, the low global interest rates associated with high reserve holdings also have translated into a compression of spreads on emerging market debt, with the "search for yield" raising the attractiveness of emerging market destinations to international investors (IMF 2006a).

There are several reasons to believe that the pace of reserve accumulation will start to decelerate. First, the accumulation of reserves comes at a significant opportunity cost in terms of alternative uses for these funds. For instance, Summers (2006) estimated that the opportunity costs for the world's 10 largest reserve holders amount to 1.85 percent of GDP; Rodrik (2006a) calculated that the cost is near 1 percent of GDP for developing countries taken as a whole.[22] Because these countries comfortably exceed the reserve levels that are required to cover imports and debt obligations, the opportunity cost may be high relative to the insurance gains from building up reserves as a precaution against financial risks. Second, to the extent that inflows are not sterilized, the increase in domestic liquidity (shown in figure 7 of Lane and Schmukler [2006]) associated with reserve accumulation threatens the possibility of an asset and real estate price boom and misdirected lending in the domestic economy. Third, it is increasingly appreciated in China that rebalancing output growth toward expanding domestic consumption is desirable to raise living standards even faster and avoid the external protectionist pressures that have been building up in Europe and the United States. Fourth, the move to a more flexible exchange rate system might reduce the pressure on the monetary authority to intervene in the foreign exchange market to maintain a de facto fixed currency peg.

A slowing of reserve accumulation would have several ramifications. The removal of the interest rate subsidy would raise the cost of capital for the primary issuers of reserve assets. In turn, depending on the policy response, this might contribute to a reversal in global liquidity conditions, which also might adversely affect the supply of capital to emerging market economies. However, the full impact on the international financial system of changes in reserve accumulation is difficult to estimate and depends on the other changes that occur along with the deceleration in reserve accumulation, the external net

---

22. Summers (2006) assumed that these countries could earn a 6 percent social return on domestic investments; Rodrik (2006a) compared the yield on reserves to the borrowing costs faced by these countries.

positions, and their contribution to global imbalances. For example, looking only at reserves does not take into account the amount of capital absorbed by these countries from the international financial system.

To mitigate the opportunity cost of reserve accumulation, countries also may decide to redirect excess reserves toward a more diversified portfolio of international financial assets, which might include the liberalization of controls on outward investment by other domestic entities.[23] For instance, Genberg et al. (2005) supported the creation of an Asian investment corporation that would pool some of the reserves held by Asian central banks and manage them on a commercial basis, investing in a broader set of assets with varying risk, maturity, and liquidity characteristics. In related fashion, Prasad and Rajan (2005) have proposed a mechanism by which closed-end mutual funds would issue shares in domestic currency, use the proceeds to purchase foreign exchange reserves from the central bank, and then invest the proceeds abroad. In this way, external reserves would be redirected to a more diversified portfolio and domestic residents would gain access to foreign investment opportunities in a controlled fashion. Finally, Summers (2006) suggested that international financial institutions may have a role to play in establishing a global investment fund that would provide a vehicle for the reallocation of excess reserves held by developing countries.

The different strategies for reserve deceleration have varying implications for the rest of the world. First, to the extent that reserves are reallocated toward other foreign assets, there would be a positive impact on those economies that benefit from the shift away from the concentration on the reserve assets supplied by a small number of countries toward a more diversified international portfolio. The capacity of emerging market economies to benefit from such a move (especially those in Asia) depends on the policy response. At a domestic level, economies that made the most progress in developing domestic capital markets and providing an institutional environment that is attractive to direct investors would benefit most.[24]

Second, a slowdown in reserve accumulation associated with a policy package that promotes increased domestic absorption (for example, through high-

---

23. Indeed, some redeployment of reserves has occurred already. For instance, China transferred $60 billion in reserves in 2004–05 to increase the capital base of several state-owned banks. See also the discussion in European Central Bank (2006).

24. As discussed in Eichengreen and Park (2003) and Eichengreen and Luengnaruemitchai (2004), there is also room for regional cooperative policies (for instance, in developing a more integrated Asian bond market).

er domestic consumption in China and higher investment in India) and a re-orientation away from export-led growth would have other spillover effects on the rest of the world economy. In effect, it would increase the overall cost of capital for the world economy. But it is important in this case not to over-state the initial impact of a deterioration in the current account balances of these countries because they hold small current positions in the global distri-bution of external imbalances. However, it is possible to construct scenarios in which these countries become significant net capital importers as their share of world GDP increases and if their medium-term current account deficits settle down in the 2 percent to 5 percent range.

Third, if a shift in reserves accumulation is associated with a shift in ex-change rate policy, a move toward greater currency flexibility also would have spillover effects on other countries. If this shift in exchange rate policy gener-ates less inflows and less reserve accumulation, the effect on the cost of capi-tal in other countries is difficult to predict: it would depend on how the in-flows previously going to these countries become allocated elsewhere, relative to how reserves were invested. In addition, the effective Asian "dollar bloc" that has been formed by individual Asian economies each tracking the U.S. dollar would be weakened by such a move. In its place, and political condi-tions permitting, smaller Asian economies might move to an exchange rate regime that sought to target a currency basket weighted on the Chinese ren-minbi as well as the U.S. dollar. As such, the renminbi might start to play the role of one of the few world reserve currencies in the international financial system, so long as the capital controls are removed and the financial system consolidates. Similarly, the rupee could increase in importance as a partial an-chor for other currencies in South Asia.

Finally, to the extent that tax and other advantages offered to foreign in-vestors may be eliminated in the future through further financial liberaliza-tion, the gross scale of the international balance sheet as currently measured would shrink because round-tripping activities would diminish.

What Is the Contribution of China and India to Global Imbalances?

China's and India's current net foreign asset positions are small in global terms. In 2004, China was the world's 10th largest creditor and India was the 16th largest debtor (Lane and Schmukler 2006). Moreover, both imbalances are relatively small in absolute terms. Although India has returned to running a current account deficit, the Chinese current account surplus has continued to increase.

Based on a combination of a calibrated theoretical model and nonstructural cross-country regressions, Dollar and Kraay (2006) argued that liberalization of the external account and continued progress in economic and institutional reform should result in average current account deficits in China of 2 percent to 5 percent of GDP over the next 20 years, with the net foreign liability position possibly reaching 40 percent of GDP by 2025.[25] Indeed, any general neoclassical approach would predict that China should be a net liability nation because productivity growth and institutional progress in a capital-poor country offering high rates of return should boost investment and reduce savings at the same time. Although there has been no similar study for India, similar reasoning applies—with greater capital account openness and continued reform, India might run persistently higher current account deficits during its convergence process.

It is worth recalling that the development experience of some other Asian nations has involved sustained phases of considerable current account deficits. For instance, the current account deficits of the Republic of Korea and Singapore averaged 5.0 percent and 14.4 percent, respectively during 1970–82, with the net foreign liabilities of the former country peaking at 44.2 percent of GDP in 1982 and those of the latter peaking at 54.2 percent of GDP in 1976 (in those cases, however, the economies were significantly smaller in relative terms than are China and India today). Likewise, in Europe the neoclassical model is performing well with a strong negative correlation between income per capita and the current account balance, driven by large current account deficits in the poorer members of the European Union and the emerging economies of Central and Eastern Europe. More formally, Dollar and Kraay (2006) considered the determinants of net foreign asset positions in a cross-country regression framework that controlled for productivity, institutional quality, and country size, and they found that the China dummy is significantly positive—the Chinese net foreign asset position is too high relative to the predictions of the empirical model. Similarly, along the time-series dimension, Lane and Milesi-Ferretti (2002) found that increases in per

---

25. The natural evolution is that the scale of current account deficits will taper off and, if these countries become rich relative to the rest of the world, this phase may be followed by a period in which they become net lenders to the next wave of emerging economies. See also Summers (2006).

capita output are associated with a decline in the net foreign asset position for developing countries, contrary to the recent Chinese experience.

If the neoclassical predictions about the impact of institutional reform and capital account liberalization in China take hold, the global effect of a sustained current account deficit on the order of 5 percent of GDP per annum soon would become significant. If India also ran a 5 percent deficit and if projections about the superior growth rate of these countries turn out to be true, the combined deficits of China and India would reach 1.23 percent of G-7 GDP by 2015 and 2.16 percent of G-7 GDP by 2025 (Lane 2006).[26] Clearly, the global impact of current account deficits of this absolute magnitude would represent a major call on global net capital flows. Of course, the feasibility of deficits of this magnitude requires that there are countries in the rest of the world willing to take large net creditor positions. If that is not the case, the desired savings and investment trends will translate into higher world interest rates rather than large external imbalances.

Although a neoclassical approach predicts that these countries could run much larger current account deficits, there is substantial disagreement about these predictions. Critics would argue that the neoclassical predictions do not take into account several factors unique to China and India and do not explain the recent past and distinctive nature. More specifically, several studies have suggested that savings rates are likely to remain high in China and India. For instance, Fehr, Jokisch, and Kotlikoff (forthcoming) interpreted China's recent savings behavior as indicative of a low rate of time preference, and they suggested that China will remain a large net saver. Based on household survey data, Chamon and Prasad (2005) made demographic projections and predicted higher household savings rates over the next couple of decades. Finally, Kuijs (2006) has argued that structural factors mean that savings and investment rates in China will decline only mildly in the decades ahead. With respect to India, Mishra (2006) argued that the upward trend of Indian savings rates will continue. For instance, India's working-age population as a percentage of total population is expected to peak in 2035, much later than in other Asian economies.

Although demographic considerations may mean that savings rates are unlikely to plummet, it is plausible that further domestic financial development and capital account liberalization will induce a downward adjustment in the savings rate. For instance, Chamon and Prasad (2005) pointed out that the

---

26. By comparison, the U.S. deficit in 2005 was 2.41 percent of G-7 GDP.

savings rate (especially for younger households) could decline if the growing demand for consumer durables were to be financed through the development of consumer credit. This would be reinforced by the liberalization of controls on capital flows that would provide greater competition in the domestic financial sector and improved opportunities for risk diversification, leading to more lending and less savings. In addition, there are recent indications that China plans a range of policy initiatives to raise the domestic level of consumption.[27] Furthermore, over time, improvements in social insurance systems and provision of public services in both countries would reduce the self-insurance motivation of high savings rates.

To project the net position, it is important also to consider the prospects for the level of investment. In China and India, a combination of an improvement in domestic financial intermediation and capital account liberalization would raise the attractiveness of these countries as a destination for external capital and would enhance the ability of domestic private firms to pursue expansion plans.[28] In the Indian case, a primary driver of larger current account deficits could be a higher rate of public investment, in view of the deficiencies in the current state of its public infrastructure.

In terms of net positions, Dooley, Folkerts-Landau, and Garber (2003) argued that it is possible to rationalize persistent current account surpluses by appealing to the reduction in country risk that may be associated with the maintenance of a net creditor position. However, even if such an externality effect is present, it may not survive a liberalization of controls on capital flows, in view of the powerful private incentives to invest more and save less.

In summary, our projection is that, all else being equal, a combination of further domestic financial development and capital account liberalization will unleash forces that induce larger net resource flows into China and India. Although this projection seems quite robust at a qualitative level, we recognize that different forces may operate in the other direction. In particular, a stalling of the reform process in either country would reduce the impetus for greater net inflows. Moreover, even if market-orientated reform continues, the rela-

---

27. See the media coverage of the March 2006 Congress of the Communist Party of China.
28. In view of the high level of inefficient investment in China, it is plausible that corporate governance reforms and higher dividend payouts (together with domestic financial deepening and external liberalization) could lead to a reduction in the absolute level of investment in tandem with a decline in the level of enterprise savings. With an increase in market-driven investment and a decline in savings, the prediction of an increased current account deficit still would hold.

tive pace of demographic change in China and, at a later date, in India will be an important force toward a more positive net external position. Even in that case, however, the composition of capital flows will be radically different from the current pattern, with the net balance the product of much larger gross inflows and gross outflows.

Do China and India Pose Additional Global Risks?

It is important to acknowledge that integrating China and India into the international financial system is not risk free. Indeed, Prasad et al. (2003) documented that financial globalization is typically associated with an initial increase in consumption volatility for developing countries, and there have been many currency and banking crises in recent decades that may have been compounded in part by external financial liberalization. Of course, these findings do not in themselves represent a blanket argument against international financial integration. In fact, they point out that financial globalization reduces volatility for those countries that exceed a threshold level of domestic financial development, indicating that the source of instability is the interaction of international capital flows with an ill-prepared domestic financial system. Ranciere, Tornell, and Westermann (2005) showed that long-term output growth increases after external liberalization so that the output reversals associated with "bumpiness" are more than offset by a faster underlying growth rate. On the financial front, Kaminsky and Schmukler (2003) showed that although financial markets might become more volatile in the immediate aftermath of liberalization, volatility is diminished in the longer term.

For China, the 1997–98 Asian financial crisis appears to have shaped its approach to external liberalization: it minimizes the risks involved. In the Indian case, its own external debt crisis in the early 1990s strongly has influenced its subsequent strategy. Both countries have sought to limit the accumulation of foreign currency external debt to private creditors, which has been the central vulnerability in most of the financial crises over the last decade. Similarly, the accumulation of large official reserve holdings provides a good measure of self-insurance in the event of a sudden stop in capital inflows.

In the preceding sections, we have documented that China and India represent only a relatively small share of global external liabilities. For this reason, the spillover impact of a reversal in China or India could be somewhat limited in magnitude because the exposure of international investors to these countries remains quite low. This does not mean, however, that these countries pose no risks to the global economy.

First, the banking sectors in both countries are a source of vulnerability. This is of particular concern in China where a history of directed lending to state-owned enterprises, a significant volume of nonperforming loans, and low levels of efficiency mean that the transition to a commercially based system is far from complete. Solvency concerns could lead to banking instability if restrictions on capital outflows were lifted and weaknesses in the banking sector are not addressed before financial liberalization, with depositors opting to deal with better-capitalized international banks.[29] Moreover, credit has expanded in recent years, with the risk that the quality of new loans is too low (Setser 2005). In the Indian case, as emphasized by Kletzer (2005), the assets of the banking sector have been heavily concentrated in domestic government debt—typically carrying a low interest rate and having a relatively long maturity, with attendant exposure to an increase in interest rates. Significant progress has been made in the last couple of years, however, with a decline in the holdings of government securities, an improvement in risk management, lower levels of nonperforming loans and credit risk, and improved profitability.

A second potential vulnerability relates to the effect of greater exchange rate flexibility on the balance sheets of domestic entities. One manifestation is the much-discussed capital losses on China's and India's large dollar reserve holdings in the event of significant currency appreciation against the dollar.[30] Aside from the value of the local currency with respect to the U.S. dollar, fluctuations in international asset prices and exchange rates will be increasingly strong influences on the balance sheets of banks, firms, and households in China and India. The importance of these valuation effects increases with financial globalization, affecting the dynamics of the external positions (Lane and Milesi-Ferretti 2006). The challenge is to ensure that the domestic financial sector has the capacity to manage such balance sheet risks.

Finally, a third concern is the political economy of FDI. Political opposition from local entities may reduce the inward flow of new FDI. Export-oriented FDI may be harmed by the rise of protectionist pressures in destination

---

29. For this reason, Obstfeld (2005) recommended a gradual approach to capital account liberalization and suggested that China could learn from other countries (Chile, Israel) that have strengthened domestic financial systems before fully opening the capital account.

30. Setser (2005) also stressed that, contrary to the norm in other developing economies, many Chinese firms are financially exposed should such currency appreciation occur because they sell in foreign currency and have debts in domestic currency.

markets. Because China is so highly integrated into an Asian manufacturing chain, a disruption in FDI could have adverse upstream spillover effects on other Asian countries.

Concluding Remarks

In this chapter, we have studied the impact of China and India on the international financial system by examining and comparing both countries, analyzing different aspects of their international financial integration, and linking the patterns in their international balance sheets to policies regarding their domestic financial systems. Given the evolution and probable changes in their domestic financial sectors, this analysis is relevant in projecting the future evolution of the international financial system.

The main current international financial impact of India and particularly China has been in their accumulation of unusually high levels of foreign reserves. Another salient aspect of their integration is the asymmetry in the composition of their gross assets and liabilities. Their assets are low-return foreign reserves, which are liquid and protect them against adverse shocks, but they carry a high opportunity cost. Their liabilities are FDI, debt, and portfolio equity, which usually yield a higher rate of return. FDI has been relatively more important in China, with portfolio investment taking a lead role in India. Despite recent attention and concerns regarding their effects on developing countries, China and India do not seem to have been crowding out investment elsewhere and, despite a recent acceleration in activity, are not yet major accumulators of nonreserve foreign assets. A striking aspect of their integration has been the reduction in their net liability positions, defying neoclassical predictions that they should be running large current account deficits, given their levels of development. Whether the shift in their net positions is transient or permanent is a central issue in assessing the future impact of China and India on the international financial system.

We have argued that the effect of China and India on the international financial system fundamentally is linked to the evolution of their domestic financial systems, including their exchange rate and capital account liberalization policies. As both China and India are likely to undergo further financial development and liberalization, these countries are set to have an ever-increasing effect on the international financial system. We project that the nature of their integration with the international financial system is likely to be reshaped. At one level, the composition of the international balance sheet will become less asymmetric—with a greater accumulation of nonreserve foreign assets and a more balanced distribution of foreign liabilities among FDI, portfolio equity, and debt. This rebalancing should be good news for developing countries that may receive a greater share of the outward investment flows from China and India. At another level, there is a strong (but not undisputed) prospect that the Giants might experience a sustained period of substantial current account deficits. In view of their increasing share in global output, the prospective current account deficits of China and India may be a central element in the next phase of the "global imbalances" debate. If this scenario plays out, other potential borrowers will receive smaller net capital flows, will face a higher cost of capital, or will encounter both problems.

As always, future developments are difficult to predict and are conditional on other factors (like distinct demographic trajectories and economic reforms), domestic policy options, and the international environment. Key aspects to monitor when analyzing the possible paths that China and India may follow (and their impact on the international system) include the following elements. First, it is essential to watch what approaches these countries adopt regarding their exchange rate policies, particularly in light of the sustained appreciation pressure from the market and the international political environment. Although significant appreciation may be resisted in the short run by further reserve accumulation, this is increasingly costly and may compromise other policy objectives. Second, a sharp correction in the U.S. dollar relative to other major currencies may act as an external trigger for a switch to greater exchange rate flexibility in China and India because the renminbi and the rupee would become (more) undervalued relative to those major, relevant currencies. Indeed, concerns about such a correction also may prompt these countries to alter the currency composition of reserves, affecting interest rates and possibly exchange rates (at least in the short run). A third key component to monitor is how fast these countries substitute reserve holdings for other assets abroad. To the extent that the international environment remains favorable, it is likely that some of the ideas described above to shift away from traditional reserve holdings will start to materialize. Fourth, a fully fledged liberalization of capital controls remains unlikely in the short to medium term, in view of the outstanding weaknesses in coping with unrestricted debt flows. It is likely, however, that these countries will continue to liberalize their financial sectors, with implications for the composition of their international balance sheets and net foreign asset positions. The exact form of this liberalization process, its timing, and its pace are still to be determined and will remain a subject of attention. For all these reasons, we anticipate that the international financial integration of China and India is set to undergo significant reshaping in the coming years.

CHAPTER 5

Energy and Emissions
Local and Global Effects of the Giants' Rise

Zmarak Shalizi

Sustainability issues normally do not manifest themselves for decades because either population growth rates or per capita income growth rates are relatively slow. But such issues become difficult to ignore when growth rates are not slow—as has been true in China in the last two decades. China's rapid transformation from an agriculture-based economy to the world's manufacturing workshop has been accompanied by a corresponding change in the spatial concentration and location of the population from relatively low-density rural areas to very high-density urban areas. This transformation is having a significant impact on the quantity and quality of natural resources available as inputs to the production process and consumption, and has affected the environment's ability to absorb the waste by-products deposited in the air, water, and soil. The recent acceleration of growth in India is beginning to generate similar problems.

Development strategies targeting high growth in gross domestic product (GDP) by relying on low-cost, low-efficiency, and highly polluting technology are likely to put pressure on available natural resources and natural sinks that absorb pollution and waste over time. Emerging in Asia is a major one-time opportunity to shift efficiently to a path that does not lock in inefficient resource use. This opportunity arises from the massive investments expected

I would like to acknowledge the substantive input and assistance provided by Philippe Ambrosi, Siyan Chen, and Shyam Menon; and the simulation estimates provided by Jean-Charles Hourcade and colleagues Renaud Crassous and Olivier Sassi, with contributions by P. R. Shukla and Jiang Kejun.

in the next 50 years (amounts on the order of trillions of dollars) to urbanize the population (and simultaneously reduce poverty and the backlog of service provision) (World Bank 2003b).

Addressing emerging domestic and local problems will be the primary national motivation for taking action. But there also is likely to be an international dimension to the problem if externalities are generated on international resources and sinks as needs grow beyond domestic capacity. This will generate costs for other countries, and may even provoke conflict, if domestic and international institutions for collective action do not emerge in a timely manner.[1]

Although this statement of the interaction between growth and natural resources applies to a wide range of natural resources and asset management issues in China and India, this chapter focuses exclusively on the issue of managing and meeting energy needs for growth so as to minimize negative consequences for health and the environment locally and globally. The objective of this chapter is to address the following questions:

- What is likely to be the Giants' demand for energy—particularly oil and coal—under a *business-as-usual (BAU)* scenario in 2020 and 2050?
- What are likely to be the associated levels of emissions that could have damaging consequences locally (such as particulate matter), regionally (such as ozone, sulfur, and acid rain), and globally (carbon dioxide [CO_2] in particular)?
- What domestic interventions in developing the energy-producing and energy-using sectors might make a significant difference in the energy path, relative to a BAU scenario?

Level and Composition of Energy Use and Emissions

For many reasons (such as the energy intensity of an economy and so forth), it is sufficient to focus on the level of aggregate energy use. Local and global

---

1. Developing the institutions to identify and enforce appropriate criteria (that take into account the scale and distribution of externalities, as well as the use of option values) for these investments will determine whether the cumulative investment program enhances welfare or not. Because of path dependency, there is the potential of locking into inefficient energy and emissions paths. However, the topic of institutional development is not covered in this chapter.

emissions from energy use, however, are sensitive to the composition of energy used and not simply to its level.

Emerging Concerns

There are many issues involved in managing energy supply and demand in China and India. However, a few broad concerns are emerging that are of particular interest.[2]

The Demand for Fossil Fuel

At the aggregate level, China and India currently account for about 12 and 5 percent of the world's energy use, respectively. In terms of composition, China consumes slightly less coal than it produces, and exports the balance (table 5.1). Its use of petroleum, however, is increasingly larger than its production—and the balance is imported. For most other fuels, domestic consumption and production are roughly in balance. India's domestic production of coal and oil satisfies an even smaller part of its consumption, and the imbalance is growing—particularly in oil (table 5.1). Both countries produce gas, but gas consumption does not yet account for a significant share of energy use.

At present, China is the second-largest energy consumer in the world, following only the United States. Its total energy use, however, is only half the U.S. use, and its per capita consumption levels are about 10 percent of those in the United States.[3] In 1980, China had one of the highest energy intensities in the world, using GDP at market prices (see table 5.2)—almost seven times as high as the United States and almost four times as high as India.[4] Using purchasing power parity figures lowers the relationship relative to the United States from 6.72 to 1.64, but increases it relative to India from 3.8 to

---

2. This review of problems is based primarily on secondary source literature. In the past few years, the International Energy Agency (IEA) in Europe, the U.S. Department of Energy, and others have produced many reports on energy in China and India to identify key drivers of energy and emissions trajectories and the role of different policy strategies.

3. Energy data is taken from the U.S. Energy Information Administration (USEIA) *International Energy Annual 2003* and population data comes from the World Bank's *World Development Indicators* (2005b).

4. *Intensity* is the amount of energy consumed per unit of economic output.

5.0. In fact, by 2003, measured relative to GDP in purchasing power parity, both China and India appear more efficient than the United States. Given that most energy use is in tradable/marketed sectors and considering the evidence of continuing inefficiency in industry (World Energy Council 1999), however, it seems that the scope for and returns to economizing on China's and India's energy use is still large.

Table 5.1 Energy Balance in China and India, 1980–2003

Country	Year	Coal	Oil	Natural gas	Hydro	Biomass and waste	Nuclear	Total
				Production and Stock Change (Mtoe)				
China	1980	316	107	12	5	180	0	620
	1985	405	130	13	8	189	0	745
	1990	545	136	16	11	200	0	908
	1995	691	149	19	16	206	3	1,084
	2000	698	151	28	19	214	4	1,115
	2003	917	169	36	24	219	11	1,376
India	1980	50	11	1	4	148	1	215
	1985	71	31	4	4	162	1	273
	1990	97	35	10	6	176	2	326
	1995	124	39	17	6	189	2	377
	2000	143	37	21	6	202	4	413
	2003	157	39	23	6	211	5	441
				Consumption (Mtoe)				
China	1980	313	89	12	5	180	0	599
	1985	401	93	13	8	189	0	704
	1990	535	110	16	11	200	0	872
	1995	673	158	19	16	206	3	1,075
	2000	664	222	26	19	214	4	1,149
	2003	862	270	35	24	219	11	1,421
India	1980	53	34	1	4	148	1	241
	1985	76	48	4	4	162	1	295
	1990	104	63	10	6	176	2	361
	1995	134	84	17	6	189	2	432
	2000	159	114	21	6	202	4	506
	2003	173	124	23	6	211	5	542

Source: IEA 2005a.
Note: Mtoe = million tons of oil equivalent.

Table 5.2 Changes in Energy Intensity in China, India, and the United States

Factor	Year(s)	Based on GDP at market prices (constant 2000 US$)			Based on GDP at PPP (constant 2000 international $)		
		China	India	U.S.	China	India	U.S.
Energy intensity[a]	1980	101,936	26,805	15,174	24,922	5,051	15,157
	2003	33,175	25,460	9,521	8,076	4,761	9,561
Growth rate (%)	1980–2003	–4.76	–0.22	–2.01	–4.78	–0.26	–1.98
Relative to U.S.	1980	6.72	1.77	n.a.	1.64	0.33	n.a.
	2003	3.48	2.67	n.a.	0.84	0.50	n.a.
Change in ratio	1980–2003	0.52	1.51	n.a.	0.51	1.49	n.a.

Sources: Adapted from USEIA 2005 and World Bank 2005b.
Note: n.a. = not applicable; PPP = purchasing power parity.
a. Total primary energy consumption (Btu) per unit of output.

Change over time is an important aspect of energy intensity in China and India. In the 23-year period from 1980 to 2003, energy intensity in China declined annually by an extraordinary 4.8 percent—more than double the 2 percent annual decline in the United States and almost 24 times faster than the anemic 0.2 percent annual decline in India.[5] As a result, China's energy intensity dropped by half that of the United States, whereas India's increased by 50 percent relative to U.S. intensity. This significant pattern of change over more than two decades (both within the two countries and relative to the United States) is the same whether one uses GDP at market prices or purchasing power parity prices (see last row of table 5.2).

Domestic Energy Resources

China's use of electricity more than doubled in the decade between 1986 and 1995 and then doubled again by 2003 (National Bureau of Statistics 2005). China has the fastest growing electric power industry in the world—fueled primarily by coal. Hydroelectric generating capacity is a particularly important source of electric power only in the central and western regions. Industry is the largest consumer of electricity, followed by the residential sector, and then the agricultural sector.

5. Most of the reduction in energy intensity in China since 1978 is attributed to technological change, not structural shifts from heavy to light industry (Lin 1996).

India has an installed electricity generation capacity of 112,000 megawatts, which is approximately 10 percent the capacity of the United States (USEIA 2005). Approximately 70 percent of India's electricity comes from coal. Unlike China, India does not have a large supply of high-quality coal nor of gas for generating electricity, so more and more coal and gas have to be imported. Industry is the largest consumer of electricity in India, followed by the agricultural sector, and then the residential sector.

As in China, India's power sector continues to face a considerable demand–supply gap and the supply it has is of poor quality (for example, low voltage and grid instability). Peak power shortage is estimated in the range of 13 percent (Government of India 2003)—probably lower than it would have been with more reliable supply. Transmission and distribution losses in some states (such as Maharashtra) amount to approximately 40 percent of total electricity generated centrally.[6]

Transportation

In the last decade, China has committed itself to a strategy of emulating U.S. dependence on motorization as the dominant mode of transportation. This strategy was determined only in part by mobility considerations; industrial policy considerations were the primary drivers.[7] The automobile industry is seen as a potential engine of growth for the economy as a whole because of its multiplier effect through buyer–supplier links.

With this strategy shift, less energy-intensive vehicles like bicycles and pedicabs have been replaced by more energy-intensive vehicles—motorcy-

---

6. The losses can be of a *technical* nature (such as line losses resulting from poor maintenance, overloading, poor equipment standards, low power factors at off-peak hours) or of a *commercial* nature (such as illegal tapping of low-tension lines, faulty energy meters, unmetered supply, and uneven revenue collection). Problems with loss reduction include lack of energy audits, no segregation of losses into technical and commercial categories, and little transparency in meter reading and billing. Available data cited above do not distinguish between the two types of losses even though the commercial losses, such as theft, are a loss to the utility but not to power available for consumption.

7. The 16th Conference of the National Congress of the Communist Party of China and the 8th Conference of the National People's Congress established the automobile industry as a pillar of the country's economy. For details, see the Web site of the Automotive Sub-Council of the China Council for the Promotion of International Trade, http://www.auto-ccpit.org/).

cles, cars, and trucks. The rate of growth of the vehicle fleet—which averaged 5.7 percent each year through 1999—accelerated dramatically to 26.5 percent a year in the last five years, although now there are signs that the growth rate is beginning to moderate. Automobile ownership in China is still only 8 to 10 per 1,000 people, in contrast to approximately 400 per 1,000 in Japan and about 500 per 1,000 in the United States.[8] A tenfold growth in ownership of automobiles over the next 30 years in China is quite conceivable, however, given the expected growth in household incomes and current government policies. The average number of vehicle miles traveled per household and the volume of freight transported by truck traffic is also expected to expand dramatically: within urban areas, as urban sprawl increases and jobs and residences disperse across a larger area, increasing distances between them, and between urban centers, as commercial and industrial entities increasingly rely on the flexibility provided by the growing highway network linking China's cities and connecting the coasts to the hinterlands. The penetration of fuel-efficient hybrid technology in the vehicle fleet is still very low.

Some cities in India, such as Delhi, have exhibited explosive growth in automobile ownership and use that is similar to China's. Overall, however, India's reliance on the road sector for passenger and commercial traffic is still much lower than in China because India started much later. But the recent growth of the middle class there and the government's decision to expand the highway network dramatically are likely to stimulate a growing dependence on the road sector. Both China and India have seen, in addition, an explosive growth in air traffic—a major consumer of oil products.

Energy Use and Emissions, 1980–2004

China is the largest producer of coal in the world. In 2004, its production was almost double that of the United States (2.2 billion short tons versus 1.1 billion short tons) (USEIA 2006). China's estimated total coal resources are second only to the former Soviet Union, although proven reserves ranked third in the world. China is a net exporter of coal and likely to remain so for at least another decade.

---

8. Vehicle ownership figures in Japan and the United States are higher, at 570 per 1,000 people in Japan and 780 per 1,000 people in the United States. Vehicle ownership includes not just automobiles but also buses, pickups, and trucks—but not motorcycles (World Bank 2005b).

In 2003, coal accounted for 67 percent of China's primary energy production of 1,216 million tons of oil equivalent (Mtoe), oil accounted for 12 percent, natural gas for 3 percent, hydroelectric power for 2 percent, and biomass and other waste for 16 percent (table 5.1). China has a growing nuclear power sector, but its output accounted for only 0.8 percent of energy production in 2003. More recently, China has moved aggressively to expand nuclear, wind, and solar power generating capacity, and to pursue new technologies for coal gasification and the like. In final energy consumption, coal also dominates other energy resources, accounting for 72 percent of fossil fuel consumption and 58 percent of total primary energy consumption.

In 2003, India's total primary energy production was estimated at 441 Mtoe, with coal accounting for 36 percent of the supply mix, oil for 9 percent, gas for 5 percent, hydroelectric power for 1 percent, nuclear for 1 percent, and biomass energy and other renewables for 48 percent (table 5.1).[9] The use of commercial fuels, such as coal and oil, is growing rapidly in tandem with the economic expansion (industrialization and growing per capita income). Nonetheless, unlike China, more than 60 percent of Indian households still depend on traditional energy sources such as fuelwood, dung, and crop residue for their energy requirements (TERI 2004).

The increasing use of fossil fuels (particularly coal and oil) in both of the Giants is generating harmful emissions—particulates (with primarily local effects on health in urban areas), sulfur and nitrogen (with primarily regional effects via ozone and acid rain on agriculture and ecosystems), and CO_2 (with primarily global effects in the form of global warming).

Global Externalities

The United States is the world's largest emitter of carbon emissions from energy, but China is expected to overtake it in the next decade-plus. China's carbon emissions are driven by rapid growth in the use of fossil fuels—particularly coal and oil (gas not yet being a significant contributor). CO_2 emissions from India are a quarter of those from China, but also are growing as a result of the

---

9. Thirty years earlier, before the major expansion of commercial electricity production, traditional biomass accounted for 66 percent of India's total primary energy supply. At that time, biomass was also a major source of energy in China—approximately 30 percent (IEA 2005a).

Figure 5.1 Primary Energy Use of Coal and Total CO$_2$ Emissions from Fossil Fuel Consumption, China and India, 1980–2003

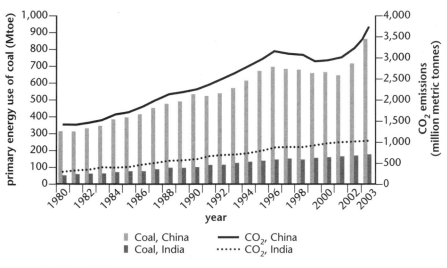

Sources: IEA 2005a, 2005b.
Note: CO$_2$ = carbon dioxide; Mtoe = million tons of oil equivalent.

dependence on fossil fuels, particularly for electricity production. As evident in figure 5.1, CO$_2$ emissions in both countries track coal use quite closely.

What socioeconomic factors are driving CO$_2$ emission changes in China and India? Recent literature covering the period 1980 to 1996/97 has suggested that economic growth was the single largest driver of increased emissions in both countries.[10] Over time the gross emission increases have been offset significantly by improved energy efficiency in China, but in India the offset has been much less sizable. Decarbonization (that is, lowering CO$_2$ emissions by reducing the emission factor through use of better technology and of lower-carbon fuels) was not a significant factor during this two-decade period in either country.[11] However, its importance in India has increased in the 1990s.

10. For China, see Sinton, Levine, and Wang 1998; Van Vuuren et al. 2003; and Zhang 2000. For India, see Paul and Bhattacharya 2004.
11. The emissions factor is calculated as emissions per unit energy.

Local Externalities

As noted earlier, not only is heavy reliance on fossil fuel (particularly coal) associated with the expansion of CO_2; it also is associated with the expansion of various types of local pollutants (such as suspended particulate matter, sulfur/sulfur dioxide, nitrogen oxides, and so forth) that contribute to health problems, particularly in cities, and to ground-level ozone and acid rain that particularly affect rural areas and natural ecosystems.[12]

Sulfur dioxide (SO_2) and soot released by coal combustion are the two major air pollutants that form acid rain, which now falls on approximately 30 percent of China's total land mass (USEIA 2003)—areas also affected by an ozone-generated natural haze. In India, too, acidic precipitation is becoming increasingly common. According to the Environmental Information System of India, soils in the northeast region, parts of Bihar, Orissa, West Bengal, and coastal areas in the south already have low pH values. If immediate mitigative measures are not taken, further aggravation from acid rain may cause these lands to become infertile or unsuitable for agriculture. Studies in India show a 13 to 50 percent decrease in mean wheat yield within 10 kilometers of thermal power stations with capacities of 500 to 2,000 megawatts, respectively (Mitra and Sharma 2002). Similar studies in China have concluded that the deteriorating air quality has reduced optimal yield by 5–30 percent for approximately 70 percent of the crops grown in China (Chameides et al. 1999).[13]

Industrial boilers and furnaces that use coal are the largest single-point sources of urban air pollution, and road transport is the main mobile source of air pollution.[14] Cities in developing countries tend to have higher pollution concentration than cities in industrial countries (see figure 5.2). Depending on what air pollutant one focuses on, a different set of 10–20 cities is among

---

12. Ozone and other photochemical oxidants are formed by the action of ultraviolet light from the sun on nitrogen. Ozone production and concentration is dependent on the presence of nitrogen oxides and ultraviolet light.

13. Assuming sufficient water and nutrients, simulations of the crop-response models demonstrate that atmospheric aerosols lead to lower crop yields through a decrease in total surface solar irradiance, thereby affecting the marginal productivity of other inputs.

14. China's State Environmental Protection Administration estimates that "industrial pollution accounts for over 70 percent of the national total, including 72 percent for sulfur dioxide emissions, and 75 percent for flue dust (a major component of suspended particulates)."

Figure 5.2 Air Quality Comparison, Selected World Cities, 2000
Average annual levels

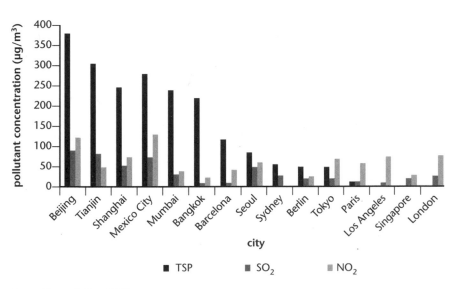

Source: Hao and Wang 2005.
Note: NO₂ = nitrogen dioxide; SO₂ = sodium dioxide; TSP = total suspended particulates.

the most polluted in the world, and many Chinese and Indian cities are listed in these sets.[15]

One can speak meaningfully about pollution in a city, a locality, or a river because assessing pollution per unit area is a function of localized air sheds and watersheds. But there is no equivalent measure for an area as large as a country, so there is no such metric for the average level of pollution in China or India. Instead, it is more useful at the country level to estimate the total number of people exposed to different levels and types of pollution.

In 2003, more than half (58.4 percent) of China's urban population was exposed to average annual amounts of coarse particulate matter in excess of 100 micrograms per cubic meter, which is the Chinese standard (and twice the U.S. standard). Air pollution is estimated to have led to more than 427,000

---

15. Earlier studies include a report released in 1998 by the World Health Organization (WHO).

excess deaths and 300,000 cases of chronic bronchitis in 660 Chinese cities in that year (World Bank 2006a). In the case of India, Cohen et al. (2004) reported an estimate of 107,000 excess deaths in 2000.[16]

Attempts to reduce local emissions in China by curtailing coal production and consumption had some success in reducing SO_2 and other local emissions for a few years in the late 1990s (Hao and Wang 2005). Reduction in SO_2 tracked the apparent dip in coal consumption and CO_2 emissions in China (see figure 5.1). Even though GDP grew by a third (+33.7 percent) in the period 1997–2001, there was almost no increase in CO_2 emissions (+0.2 percent)—in contrast to a 14.0 percent increase that the 1980–97 emissions-to-GDP ratio would have predicted. SO_2 concentrations also dropped by approximately 40 percent. This drop gave rise to much optimism regarding the potential for "decoupling" the growth in emissions and energy requirements from the growth of GDP. Several factors—including faulty statistics—explain this apparent decoupling. The relative weights of these factors are being debated, but the closing of a large number of small and inefficient coal producers was also important (Sinton and Fridley 2000, 2003; Sinton, 2001).

This decoupling, however, could not be sustained. In the presence of low power tariffs, blackouts, and power shortages arising from 9–10 percent annual GDP growth, it has been necessary to use all power-generating capacity, no matter how inefficient. As a result, both SO_2 emissions (particularly in northern cities) and CO_2 emissions have resumed an upward trend.

International Energy Markets

Encouraging more reliance on roads for passenger and freight movements has prompted a surge in the demand for oil (gasoline, diesel, and other oil prod-

---

16. Other partial studies corroborate these findings. In China, the consequences of current air pollution levels are apparent in public health statistics for some cities: "approximately 4,000 people suffer premature death from pollution-related respiratory illness each year in Chongqing; 4,000 in Beijing; and 1,000 in both Shanghai and Shenyang. If current trends persist, Beijing could lose nearly 80,000 people, Chongqing 70,000, and other major cities could suffer tens of thousands in cumulative loss of human life through 2020. With industry expected to maintain rapid growth during the next 20 years, a steep decline in pollution intensity will be necessary just to keep emissions constant"(Dasgupta, Wang, and Wheeler 1997, p. 3). In India, Delhi has been identified as the city having the highest mortality figure—about 7,500 deaths a year (Brandon and Hommann 1995; WHO 2002; World Bank 2005a).

ucts) in both China and India. Oil imports have grown, and with them have come both national implications for balance of payments and energy security, and global implications for world energy markets. This section addresses the latter issue.

Recent growth in energy use by the Giants does account for a significant part of the incremental increase in global energy use, but the annual growth in global use has not been unusual, relative to the past. The Giants' energy use is not the key component in recent oil price surges. Rather, it is the tightening of oil supplies in the context of diminished spare capacity and growing geopolitical uncertainties that has driven up prices in the last couple of years.

Since the late 1980s, nominal oil prices have been relatively stable and flat.[17] There were two exceptions: a momentary spike (reflecting uncertainty) during the Persian Gulf crisis of 1990–91, with prices soaring 50 percent above the average price in the period May 1990–91; and a longer-lasting perturbation during the Asian financial crisis of 1997–98, when per-barrel prices dropped by $12.90 between January 1997 and December 1998. The drop in prices reflected a negative demand shock, caused mostly by the decline in oil demand in Asia and the modest slowdown of economic activity in Europe and Japan. The price drop also reflected a lag in the Organization of the Petroleum Exporting Countries' (OPEC's) downward adjustment of its production. This drop in price was followed during 1999 and 2000 by a symmetrical catch-up in prices under the combined effect of OPEC's successive cuts in production and the renewed growth in global economic activity. Between 2002 and 2004, oil prices entered a period of gradual but sustained increase and, since 2004, oil prices have surged. The time profile and determinants of the recent price trend have nothing in common with the two events in the 1990s, nor with either of the oil shocks in the 1970s (IMF 2005a) that were characterized primarily by abrupt geopolitical supply disruptions.[18]

Buoyant growth in global demand in the context of worldwide economic expansion has driven the more gradual but steady increase of oil prices in the period 2002–04. From 2002 to 2004, global GDP (in constant terms) has exhibited fluctuating but high annual growth rates in the range of 3–4 percent,

---

17. For the purposes of this section (unless otherwise indicated), oil price is to be understood as crude oil spot price, in nominal terms. The (monthly averaged) arithmetic mean of Dubai, Brent, and West Texas Intermediate grades is used.

18. Average annual prices rose by 250 percent between 1973 and 1974 and by 133 percent between 1978 and 1979, in reaction to the abrupt and significant supply restrictions linked to geopolitical events.

with only a slight slowdown in late 2004 and throughout 2005 (World Bank 2006a). Global crude oil use grew from 77.6 million barrels a day (mbd) to 84.2 mbd between the first quarter of 2002 and the fourth quarter of 2004; and despite signs of a slowdown throughout 2005, it continued to increase over 2004 quantities (+1.1 mbd on average), indicating the relative inelasticity of oil use relative to higher prices in the short run (IEA "Oil Market Reports").

Organisation for Economic Co-operation and Development (OECD) countries are responsible for the largest share in crude oil use over this period (relatively steady at approximately 60 percent). China's share grew from 6.06 percent (first quarter of 2002) to 7.87 percent (fourth quarter of 2004) of global crude oil use. As such, it is responsible for the highest increase in global oil use over its early 2001 level, averaging 0.25 mbd initially and then expanding to 2.1 mbd (equivalent to 37 percent of the global increase). Furthermore, although crude oil use in industrial countries was decreasing slightly, parallel to a moderate slowdown of their economic activity in 2001, the Chinese economy's momentum was large enough to offset the decline and generate a net increase in oil use. Since 2005, as the world economy began slowing down (and oil use in industrial countries was levelling off), economic growth in China has continued to sustain some growth in oil use. A similar story applies for India, although it offers much less spectacular figures. India accounts for only 3–4 percent of global use and for 7 percent of the average increase in global oil use since early 2001.

Thus, China and India together account for a large portion (40–50 percent) of *incremental* global oil use this century (see figure 5.3), but they still account for only 9–10 percent of *aggregate* global oil use. In addition, recent growth in oil use in China and India has been offset partially by the deceleration or drop in the use of oil in traditionally oil-dependent countries. As a result, aggregate use of oil has not grown as dramatically in the past few years as it did in the 1990s.[19]

Until early 2005, the supply of oil (and drawdown of inventories) more or less kept up with rising demand. Since that time, however, with OPEC spare production capacity declining, the market has been under pressure, although this eased somewhat toward the end of 2005. All along the supply chain, this tightness has magnified many short-term developments and problems that were not concerns in a period of ample supplies, and has contributed to high

---

19. During the 1990s, overall crude oil demand increased 1.61 percent annually; by contrast, from 2000 to 2005, it increased by less than half that rate (0.74 percent).

Figure 5.3 Increase in Crude Oil Use Relative to First Quarter 2001, Various Countries

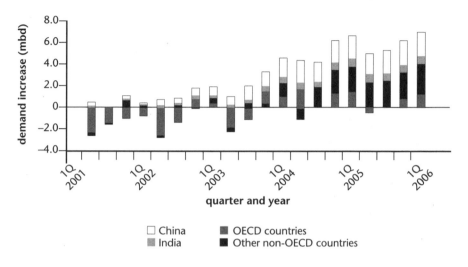

Source: IEA "Oil Market Report," various years.
Note: mbd = million barrels per day; OECD = Organisation for Economic Co-operation and Development.

volatility.[20] Figure 5.4 shows that OPEC spare production capacity started dropping steadily in mid-2002, bringing the market closer to binding constraints on the supply of cheap oil. Since January 2004, this spare capacity has been below 3 mbd. Rough calculations by the International Monetary Fund suggest that a level of spare capacity on the order of 5 mbd may help stabilize the market by halving volatility (IMF 2005a). With geopolitical uncertainties associated with output from Iraq, Nigeria, and the República Bolivariana de Venezuela (see figure 5.4), and underinvestment (both up- and downstream) in the supply chain, the extent of the drop in spare capacity is even higher. As a result, even when demand and supply were roughly in balance between mid-2003 and mid-2004, prices continued to increase significantly. This upward movement of prices has not slowed even after OPEC adopted an accommoda-

---

20. Inadequate investment in refining capacity over the past decade, combined with the refinery damage associated with hurricanes in the Gulf of Mexico, also have constrained the market.

Figure 5.4 OPEC Spare Production Capacity

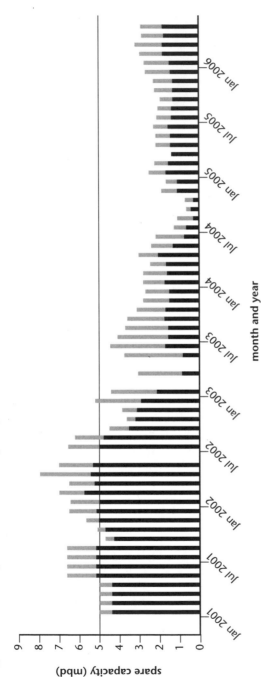

■ Algeria, Indonesia, Islamic Republic of Iran, Kuwait, Libya, Qatar, Saudi Arabia, and United Arab Emirates
▨ Iraq, Nigeria, and República Bolivariana de Venezuela

Source: IEA "Oil Market Report," various years.
Note: mbd = million barrels per day; OPEC = Organization of Petroleum Exporting Countries.

tive stance in mid-2004—to enable OECD commercial crude oil stocks to be replenished fully and to ease the potential fear of supply shortages in the context of a slowdown of non-OPEC production. Thus, supply and demand equilibrium, as captured in the inventory model of the oil market, has ceased to predict crude oil prices fully in the past few years, with market fluctuations in excess demand but a steady rise in prices. The dramatic acceleration in oil prices since 2004 arose because supply was much more inelastic than it was in the past as a result of the decline in spare capacity combined with increased geopolitical uncertainties.

Prices currently are being formed in a setting increasingly driven by expectations of future tightness in a market fueled by concerns about medium-term prospects for cheap energy supplies, such as

- The slowdown of growth in non-OPEC production (despite high oil prices), which is expected to peak in 5–10 years
- The erosion of OPEC spare production capacity, which is already under pressure from increasing social unrest and political developments
- Inadequate spending on exploration and on maintenance of existing oil fields, as well as insufficient spending on appropriate refinery capacities in the context of a respecification of demand, causing extra pressure on demand for lighter products.

Simulation of Energy and Emissions Trajectories to 2050

Both China and India will have to maintain high GDP growth rates for many decades to improve the welfare of their citizens and to generate a steady stream of employment to accommodate the growing labor force. This growth will be fueled by energy. Many analysts of energy use in China and India note that the Giants' own production of fossil fuel energy is not likely to grow at rates equal to their consumption of fossil fuel energy. As a result, they are expected to become increasingly dependent on energy imports. How dependent will be determined by whether they stay with current low-cost but polluting energy options, or move aggressively to adopt a new, more balanced, and diversified energy strategy.

In forecasting energy use in the medium term (over as many as five years), it is common to take GDP growth and its underlying structure as exogenously determined, and use an econometrically estimated elasticity of energy use with respect to GDP to determine likely energy use. This parameter tends to have a value substantially less than unity for most high-income OECD countries. That is especially true since the 1970s when they started shifting to a postindustrial service-based economic structure (in part as a reaction to earlier oil price shocks in the 1970s). The value of the parameter is close to or greater than unity for most developing countries (Zhang 2000; Liu 2004). In the 1990s, however, the value of this parameter dropped to 0.7–0.8 for India—substantially lower than in the 1970s. The parameter has been even less stable for economies undergoing substantial structural changes, such as China, where it has varied from under 0.5 to over 1.0.[21] In fact, reliance on the extra-low numbers for China in the 1990s caused the IEA and other observers of the China scene to underestimate energy demand there dramatically in the post-2000 period (IEA 2002).[22] Based on more recent economic and energy statistics (for 2002–04), China again is exhibiting developing-country patterns of energy demand growth with an energy elasticity of GDP greater than one.[23]

To go beyond estimating aggregate energy needs within a five-year period requires use of more complicated models. To differentiate growth in various energy categories (for example, fossil fuel versus renewables, or subcategories of each), we need a more disaggregated model of the economy that provides structural detail on differential changes within the energy sector and shows how they respond to relative prices, changes in the technology and productivity of different sectors, and so forth. This requires a multisectoral simulation model. Many energy simulation models have a 20- to 30-year horizon because the underlying capital stock for energy production is long lasting and long-term implications of current investments do not show up in shorter time horizons. Even more detailed and longer time horizons are required to analyze the consequence of current investments for future emissions. Different fuels have different emissions coefficients, and fuel switching can affect aggregate emissions significantly even for the same level of energy use. The externalities associated with some energy-related emissions are also a function of the cumu-

21. As noted earlier, the anomaly of elasticities as low as 0.5 has not been explained satisfactorily. It appears to have resulted from a combination of faulty statistics, improved efficiency associated with new industrial technologies, plus some structural change/fuel switching ("low-hanging fruit"), and draconian command economy measures (closing profitable, employment-generating township and village industrial enterprises that were heavily reliant on producing dirty coal).
22. In IEA's 2002 *World Energy Outlook*, the projected total primary energy demand in China for 2010 was 1,302 Mtoe, whereas actual demand reached 1,422 Mtoe by 2003.
23. Elasticity of energy consumption averaged 1.47 over the period 2002–04, according to the National Bureau of Statistics of China (2005).

lative emissions (that is, concentrations of long-lasting pollutants, such as CO_2), not just annual emissions. This requires models with horizons of at least 50 years, which is what we use in this section.[24] It is important to note in analyzing the results of these models that they are neither forecasts nor probability distributions of likely outcomes. Instead, the results are heuristic illustrations of the consequences of selected types of actions. The usefulness of the results depends on the appropriateness of the models and scenarios selected to analyze a given problem.

Choice of Simulation Models

In simulating energy and emissions for individual countries, some analysts rely on top-down, economywide models, whereas others rely on bottom-up, sectoral/technological models. The former tend to generate a lot of trade-offs because they presume that all sectors are operating at their production frontiers, which often is not the case in developing countries. The latter models tend to generate more win-win opportunities, but do not take into adequate account the feedback effects or offsetting effects in the rest of the economy/ energy system. Because of the relative strengths and weaknesses of these two types of approaches, it is increasingly common to use a "system of models" that are "soft-linked"[25] (that is, top-down and general equilibrium economywide models are used in conjunction with bottom-up, partial equilibrium models that have more technological and sectoral detail) to simulate alternate scenarios for country-specific analysis.

Multiregional global models are used to simulate simultaneously the developments in large countries, such as China and India, and to trace the global consequences of these developments for different energy markets as well as global emissions. A number of such multiregional global models are available (such as MERGE, the Mini Climate Assessment Model [Mini-CAM], the Asian Pacific Integrated Model [AIM], and others).[26] This section uses esti-

---

24. Many climate change models operate with five-year increments over a couple of centuries.
25. In a "system of models," the output of one well-calibrated model is fed in as an input into another well-calibrated model instead of establishing a single set of internally consistent equations in a more comprehensive model that is difficult to calibrate.
26. For MERGE, see Kypreos (2000). The Mini-CAM is from the U.S. Pacific Northwest National Laboratory (Edmonds, Wise, and MacCracken 1994; Edmonds, Wise, and Barns 1995). AIM is from Japan's National Institute for Environmental Studies (Morita et al. 1994).

mates generated by the IMACLIM-R model at the International Research Center on Environment and Development.[27]

The IMACLIM-R model is a general equilibrium model with subsector detail on the energy-producing sectors (fossil fuels—coal, oil, and gas—and non-fossil fuels—nuclear, hydro, biomass, and other renewables), the energy-transforming sectors (such as electricity), and key energy-using sectors (such as industry, construction, transportation, and residential). For ease of analysis, the model collapses all other sectors into an aggregate composite sector. Growth is determined partly exogenously (population, savings), and partly endogenously (endogenous productivity growth, variations in the terms of trade, exhaustion of cheap fossil fuel resources, and so forth). Each year a static Walrasian equilibrium is solved and the structural evolution of the economy is endogenized (for example, a scenario in which there is a lot of investment on transportation and in which consumers have a strong preference for mobility will generate different structural growth over time than will a scenario with the opposite assumptions).

Compared with other existing economy–energy models, the IMACLIM-R model has a few advantages:

1. It explicitly incorporates technical information on the demand and supply sides of the energy sectors, including end-use efficiency (often neglected in models using elasticities applied to final energy demand), the ability to simulate "learning by doing," and the incorporation of capital stock vintages for long-lasting investments to trace the path of investment and technological adoption more realistically.
2. It ensures consistency between this technical information and the characteristics of the economic context, including the prevailing set of relative prices.[28]
3. It is based on a modeling compromise between models generating long-term optimal trajectories under perfect foresight (which tend to underestimate the role of social and technical inertia in economic adjustments) and models generating disequilibrium dynamics with a lot of knife-edge pathways and hysterisis.[29] IMACLIM-R is a growth model that allows transitional disequilibrium. The model has the abil-

---

27. For additional detail on this model, see Crassous et al. (2006).
28. In IMACLIM-R, the reaction to prices also depends on technical information, such as the existence of asymptotes in energy efficiency, which is more credible than constant coefficients in the production function, especially when prices move over a large range.
29. Hysterisis entails very slow adjustment and can result in large losses in terms of cumulative GDP.

ity to incorporate shorter-term transitional imbalances (resulting from the interplay of imperfect foresight at a given point in time and the inertia in the economic system) and the ability to adapt (see point [1] in this list). But it also contains all the feedback mechanisms required to enable it structurally to recover over the long run, a Solow-like long-term pathway that results from demographic changes, productivity growth, capital accumulation, and changes in the terms of trade. As such, long-term growth does not depend on intertemporal optimization with rational expectations;[30] rather, it relies on imperfect foresight about future prices and quantities explicitly modeled for investment allocation and technology choices in the electricity sector.

4. It allows international capital flows between regions as a function of the divergence between domestic savings and total desired amount of investments in each of nine global regions (with China and India each representing a separate region). The model is savings driven. A region's (country's) aggregate savings rate is determined exogenously by long-term demographic trends and age structure rather than by short-term interest rate adjustments. All savings are invested. Desired amounts of investment are computed from (imperfectly) expected increases in future demand. There is no reason for the two sides to be balanced within a region. As a result, a region with excess savings becomes a capital exporter, and a region with a deficit of savings to finance its investment needs becomes a capital importer. The international pool gathers the exports of regions with excess savings and reallocates the money to regions with insufficient savings proportional to the total amount of unmet domestic investment needs.[31]

Choice of Scenarios

A reference or base case, designated as the *business-as-usual scenario*, or BAU, is simulated for this chapter.[32] For convenience of exposition, only the results of

---

30. Although the model describes behavior in terms of current prices, this does not necessarily signify the absence of expectations. First, it is assumed that people react to existing prices as the best available information at the time decisions are made. Second, the elasticities that govern these reactions are supposed to mimic real behavior and incorporate implicitly a broader set of parameters, such as inertia, risk aversion, and the like.

31. In simulation, some countries can be modeled as having a fixed predetermined net export of capital.

32. The base year for the projections is 2001, rather than 2005 as used in other models in

this case are described in detail. All others are presented summarily and in relation to the BAU. On average, annual GDP growth rates assumed in the BAU are 6.5–7.5 percent in China over the next decade or two, and 5–6 percent in India with both rates tapering to 3–4 percent a year by 2050. These average growth rates for the future are somewhat lower than recent performance because of presumed institutional and technical constraints within the economies, resulting in inefficiencies in the allocation of resources and limiting their ability to sustain very high growth rates for a prolonged period. However, a variant of the BAU also is simulated. Designated as BAU-H, it assumes annual GDP growth rates that are approximately 1.0–1.5 percentage points higher for both countries (that is, 7.5–9.0 percent for China and 7.0–8.0 percent for India over the next decade or two). These more optimistic growth rates are based on recent performance and extrapolation of government assumptions for upcoming five-year plans. Both the BAU and the BAU-H assume continued heavy reliance on fossil fuels for the next couple of decades, with adverse consequences for local emissions (suspended particulates, sulfur, ozone, and the like) and for global emissions (greenhouse gases, particularly CO_2).

The policy-based *alternate scenarios* (ALTs) are designed to explore the extent to which a package of policies can result in two potential decouplings.[33] The first is decoupling energy growth from GDP growth through reduced energy intensity, either as a result of increased energy efficiency, a structural shift away from energy-intensive manufacturing in economic activity, or both. The second is decoupling emissions growth from energy growth through fuel switching from coal to gas (or clean coal), or from fossil fuels to nuclear energy or renewables (and associated simultaneous improvements in energy efficiency). The decouplings are not policies themselves nor are they totally independent of each other. Rather, they are analytically convenient ways of describing the extent to which policies have been effective in increasing the economy's energy efficiency and reducing its generation of harmful emissions.

Three sets of policy scenarios are simulated:

1. *Demand side scenarios* (designated with a D) that include additional actions geared toward improving end-use efficiency/energy saving,

---

this book. The reason is that IEA data for country-specific energy details (used in the IMACLIM-R simulations) and Global Trade Analysis Project data for all regions are produced with a lag of a couple of years, and it was important to ensure that the economic parameters and energy details used in the simulations were mutually consistent in the base year and tested for a year or two out of sample.

33. For more information on policy options, see Shalizi (2005).

over and above the energy efficiency improvements already incorporated in the BAU case (as described later in the KAYA diagrams in figure 5.6).[34] The additional improvements are (a) a 25 percent improvement in overall energy efficiency in the "composite" sector (including both "pure efficiency" and structural change in the economy with an increase in the share of services in GDP), relative to the base case; (b) an additional 1.1 percent efficiency gain annually in residential/household energy-using equipment, leading to an eventual 60 percent improvement over the base case; and (c) a 50 percent improvement in the fuel efficiency of cars by 2050, compared with the base case.

2. *Supply side scenarios* (designated with an S) that include a higher share of hydroelectric and nuclear power in both China and India than under the BAU cases, which already incorporate some expansion of non-fossil fuels sectors.[35] The additional improvements include (a) a 20 percent increase in hydroelectric capacity, relative to the base case; (b) a 30 percent increase in the share of nuclear power in new investments for power generation; (c) the share of biofuels is increased progressively to 10 percent of the total amount of fuels produced by the Giants. The shares of wind and solar energy increase significantly from a very low base but not enough to offset the reduction in the use of traditional biomass; and (d) energy efficiency is increased by 15 percent in the use of coal for industry and by 8 percent in the use of coal for electricity generation in the new capital stock installed after 2005.

3. *Supply and demand side scenarios* (designated with S&D) that combine efficiency improvements and fuel-switching measures and are in line with Chinese and Indian energy strategies. (Sarma, Margo, and Sachdeva 1998; Liu 2003).

In the working paper version of this chapter, Shalizi (forthcoming), the BAU and ALT scenarios were simulated in two different contexts: (1) the

---

34. The IEA has suggested that end-use efficiency improvements hold the greatest potential for managing energy demand and mitigating CO_2 emissions. Over the 2002–30 period, such improvements could contribute more than 50 percent to reducing emissions for a group of 11 IEA countries (Australia, Denmark, Finland, France, Germany, Italy, Japan, Norway, Sweden, the United Kingdom, and the United States) for which IEA has complete time-series data (see Bradley 2006).

35. Note that fuel switching is often also accompanied by simultaneous improvements in energy efficiency.

base case used here, which assumes that there are no constraints to adjusting to short-term signals on energy·markets; and (2) a context in which there are constraints to timely adjustment in response to growing energy needs either (a) on the deployment of domestic coal supply in China and India, or (b) on the evolution of future oil and gas markets, due to unexpected geopolitical or resource shocks in the global oil markets or to difficulties of the world oil and gas industry (including refineries) in developing the necessary production capacities in time. This introduces a number of refinements to the analysis given here.

These different scenarios generate a series of outcomes that can be compared. The particular outcomes of interest in this study are the energy requirements in the economy, the global emissions associated with these energy requirements (focused on CO_2), the local emissions associated with these energy requirements (focused on SO_2), and investment requirements associated with the different energy trajectories.[36] These simulations also enable us to compare the consequences of accelerated or delayed investments in shifting from the BAU to ALT scenarios, and to explore the potential for self-financing versus additional external financing requirements that might be needed.

Reference Scenarios—BAU and BAU-H

The two base scenarios reflect the rapid energy and emissions growth associated with fast and very fast GDP growth in China and India over the next few decades. These scenarios provide the benchmark energy and emissions trajectories against which the costs and benefits of additional policy interventions can be discussed in the next section.

Country Implications

In China, in terms of key energy-using sectors, industry and services account for the largest share of final energy use over the study period, increasing for the next two decades to more than 60 percent before declining below current

---

36. The variable total suspended particulates, which is used most often in health analysis ex post, is difficult to project ex ante and therefore not included. SO_2 emissions can be projected with the simulation model and are included in the findings. It is not possible, however, to assess their health implications because of the problem discussed earlier in the section on

Table 5.3 Sectoral and Fuel Shares of Energy Consumption in China and India

	China			India		
	2005	2020	2050	2005	2020	2050
Total final consumption (Mtoe)	921.7	1,683.2	2,685.1	400.3	609.4	1,268.1
Sector (%)						
Industry and services	58.5	62.2	54.6	32.7	39.3	48.3
Transportation	10.2	14.4	20.8	10.4	12.3	16.0
Residential use	31.2	23.5	24.6	56.9	48.4	35.7
Fuel mix (%)						
Coal	38.0	37.4	25.5	11.5	13.0	12.0
Refined products	25.0	27.4	27.8	27.5	27.7	25.7
Gas	2.6	3.4	4.4	2.7	3.0	3.3
Electricity	13.3	20.3	35.8	9.9	17.3	37.5
Renewables and biomass	21.1	11.5	6.6	48.3	38.9	21.5
Total primary energy use (Mtoe)	1,223.1	2,483.5	4,436.5	515.6	845.8	2,068.8
Coal (%)	54.3	58.9	62.7	29.2	37.8	57.9
Oil (%)	23.1	22.6	20.5	25.0	22.6	17.7
Natural gas (%)	2.5	3.5	3.4	3.8	5.3	4.5
Nuclear (%)	0.5	0.5	2.4	0.8	0.1	2.1
Hydro (%)	3.7	3.0	3.1	3.7	3.9	1.9
Renewables (%)	15.9	11.5	7.9	37.6	30.3	15.9

Source: Author's calculations based on simulation model.
Note: Mtoe = million tons of oil equivalent.

shares by 2050. The share of residential use also declines from 31 percent to 25 percent, and the share of transportation (relying almost exclusively on refined petroleum products) doubles to 21 percent (see table 5.3). In terms of fuels, electricity represents an increasing proportion of final energy use, with its share almost tripling. The shares of gas and refined petroleum products increase by 2 percentage points each. The shares of coal and traditional biomass drop substantially. The role of coal in final energy use declines as services grow, relative to industry, and the role of traditional biomass in final energy use diminishes as commercial electricity replaces it.

local externalities. Defining the implications requires projecting the spatial distribution of emissions and the density of the population exposed in different localities, and that is not possible at the level of aggregation used in IMACLIM-R.

Though electricity represents only a third of final energy use by 2050, the heavy reliance on coal (80 percent) for generating electric power at midcentury explains why coal retains a prominent share in China's energy balance. By 2050, China's reliance on coal for primary energy use remains high (63 percent in the BAU scenario, 65 percent in the BAU-H scenario). Primary energy use (not final energy use) determines the extent of polluting emissions. In the BAU scenario, primary energy demand in China will double in the 20-year period from 2001 to 2020 and quadruple by 2050.[37] In BAU-H (the higher-growth scenario), the increase in CO_2 emissions will be somewhat greater, at 2.5-fold by 2020 and 5.2-fold by 2050.

In India, final energy demand from industry and services grows from 33 percent to 48 percent, and energy demand for transportation rises from 10 percent to 16 percent. Final energy demand from the residential sector, however, drops from 57 percent to 36 percent (table 5.3).

Similar to the Chinese situation, the switch to electricity in India increases the share of coal in primary energy demand from one-third in 2001 to almost 58 percent in 2050. Coal's share expands relative to hydropower and traditional biomass. In the BAU scenario, there will be a 1.6-fold increase in primary energy demand in India by 2020 and a 3.8-fold increase by 2050.[38] In the BAU-H scenario, the increases will be significantly larger: 2.2-fold and 7.9-fold by 2020 and 2050, respectively.

Global Implications

We look first at oil prices. At present, China accounts for 6 percent of world oil use; this share rises to 10 percent in 2050 in the BAU case. Note that the share of China's oil consumption in total world oil consumption stabilizes after 2030 because oil use in other developing countries grows faster. In the same period, India's global share increases steadily from 3 percent to 5 percent in the BAU scenario (see figure 5.5).

In the base case, the model simulations generate (in 2001 dollars) a price of oil in 2020 of $61.90 (or $62.47 in the BAU-H scenario), which is less than

---

37. These simulations follow official Chinese government estimates for the 11th five-year plan and beyond.
38. These simulations follow official Indian government estimates for the 10th five-year plan and beyond.

Figure 5.5 China's and India's Shares of World Oil Consumption and Trajectory of World Oil Prices, BAU and BAU-H Scenarios

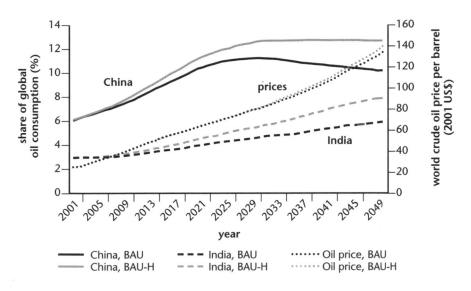

Source: Author's calculations based on simulation model.
Note: BAU = business-as-usual scenario; BAU-H = BAU with high growth.

the actual price prevailing in 2006.[39] However, as noted above, the recent run-up in oil prices does not reflect a steady-state price. Thus, there is a big difference between the high value of oil prices during a short period of time and a steady, permanent high value. The $62 per barrel in 2020 (or the $133 per barrel in 2050, shown in figure 5.5) therefore should be compared with a counterfactual steady-state price independent of the recently observed short-term volatility. This normal price probably would be in the range of $40–$50 per barrel in 2006 (not $75 in July 2006).[40]

By 2050 there is a fivefold increase in crude oil price in the five-decade period between 2001 and 2050 (from $25 to $133 a barrel in 2001 prices). This

39. The conversion ratio from 2001 dollars to 2004 dollars is 1.065, and to 2005 dollars it is 1.092.
40. Oil price formation in IMACLIM-R does not incorporate a risk component (which has been shown recently to play a major role), so crude oil prices in the short run may be lower than prices observed recently on the oil market.

increase is significant but not outlandish relative to historical experience.[41] The price of a barrel of oil in 1970 was only $9.00 in constant 2004 dollars (or $1.80 in nominal prices of 1970) (BP 2006). In 2004, before the recent spike in oil prices resulting from tightness in the oil market and geopolitical uncertainties, the price was $36.40—that is, a fourfold increase in a little more than three decades.[42]

Is it plausible that alternate fuel technologies will not displace demand for oil at such high prices? This question cannot be answered definitively. The growth in oil prices by 2050 is driven by the continuing growth in demand for mobility (particularly road and air transportation) all over the world. This demand generates substantial growth in the use of oil for which there will be few substitutes (unlike in the power sector, where there are many renewable alternatives to fossil fuels). In simulating the model, the market penetration of biofuels or hydrogen as alternatives to oil for transport is assumed to be limited in the time period under review.[43] With the exception of ethanol from sugarcane (and to a lesser extent from corn), all other biofuels are at early stages of research and experimentation. Hydrogen and coal liquefaction are not yet commercially viable technologies and may not be so for another decade or two; it will take another couple of decades before the necessary infrastructure can be put into place to enable a substantial part of the fleet to convert to these alternate fuels. Thus, relying on knowledge of currently practical or likely to be practical technologies within the next two decades, the simulation clearly shows that the upward trend in oil prices will continue, linked to supply conditions.[44]

Because of the adaptation built into the model, a gradual price increase does not generate a significant loss in GDP, whereas a spike in oil prices will generate significant losses in GDP—at least in the short run, when the econ-

---

41. Nor is it outlandish relative to some other projections. The U.S. Department of Energy's projections in its *International Energy Outlook 2006* includes a high scenario with oil prices reaching $96 a barrel (in 2004 prices) by 2030.

42. The 1970 price for Arab light crude was even less—$1.26 in 1970 prices, equivalent to $7 in 2005 prices. In 2003, its price was $40 or almost six times as much (IEA 2006).

43. As noted in the discussion on supply measures implemented in the model, biofuel penetration is assumed to reach 10 percent of fuels in China and India. For the world as a whole, the penetration rate is even lower (3 percent of fuels over the next 50 years, based on *World Energy Outlook* (IEA 2004).

44. Note that this oil price profile already incorporates an increasing role for nonconventional, more expensive petroleum sources.

omy does not have the requisite ability to adjust (Hamilton 2003). Over time, the economy returns to its long-run trajectory. As noted by Manne (1978), if there is either perfect expectation or progressive adaptation over the long run in a world with no erratic shocks, then one cannot expect large GDP variations because energy is a small fraction of the economy. This is no longer the case when there are shocks and surprises.[45] To analyze the behavior of IMACLIM-R in response to a spike in oil prices, a simulation was run assuming a world oil price increase of $35 a barrel over two years, relative to the long-term price trajectory. At the peak, GDP losses reach –3.2 percent in China (–1.6 percent in two consecutive years) and –7.0 percent in India (–3.5 percent in two consecutive years).

Now we turn our attention to emissions. In the BAU case, CO_2 emissions from energy use more than double by 2020, relative to 2005, and quadruple by 2050 to reach 3.6 giga tonnes carbon (GtC) in China. They almost double by 2020 and quintuple by 2050 to reach 1.6 GtC in India. The Giants' combined emissions in 2050 will be 44 percent of world emissions in that year, compared with approximately 20 percent in 2005. SO_2 emissions in both countries follow trajectories very similar to the CO_2 emissions.

The overall conclusion is that the high growth of energy use in China and India is not likely, *alone*, to cause structural imbalances in international energy markets. The main negative outcomes are in terms of local and global (CO_2) emissions (and, beyond 2050, in terms of the accelerated exhaustion of overall conventional and nonconventional oil reserves).

What happens to these variables when GDP growth rates are higher in China and India? In the BAU-H case, China's share in world oil use increases to 14 percent and India's to 8 percent by 2050. The price of oil, however, increases only marginally to $62.47 (relative to $61.90 in the BAU case) by 2020 and to $139.80 (relative to $133 in the BAU case) by 2050.[46] With the higher GDP growth rates in China and India (BAU-H), the rest of the world

---

45. As noted earlier, assuming "no surprise" and "no friction" in the BAU scenarios may not be realistic. However, these scenarios provide a useful benchmark against which to evaluate situations with adjustment problems (rigidity and friction) that prevent prices and quantities from adjusting rapidly and smoothly.

46. In the BAU-H scenario, oil prices are only $6.80 a barrel (+5.1 percent) higher than in the BAU scenario in 2050. This minimal difference is caused by the scenario's assumption that energy policies are deployed in a timely and efficient manner in the coal sectors of China and India to meet their growing energy needs. The rise in transportation demand for oil is significant but not enough to generate drastic imbalances on the oil market.

experiences a 2 percent higher GDP relative to the BAU scenario, induced by the faster economic growth in the Asian Giants.

In the BAU-H scenario, global primary energy requirements will be 16 percent higher by 2050. Carbon emissions, however, will be 19.8 percent higher. The faster growth in carbon emissions relative to primary energy reflects a 5.3 percent increase in the carbon content of the world aggregate energy supply because most of the regions in the world are not able to avoid a higher use of coal and other fossil fuels to meet their higher energy demands. In the higher-growth scenario, China and India's CO_2 emissions in 2020 more than double (to 2.2 GtC and 0.7 GtC, respectively), and by 2050 grow sixfold (to 4.9 GtC) and elevenfold (to 3.2 GtC), respectively. Together, the Giants will account for 60 percent of total world CO_2 emissions by 2050. Thus, comparing the BAU and BAU-H scenarios leads to this not-surprising result: in the absence of alternative policies to accelerate energy efficiency and decarbonization, energy use and CO_2 emissions will be higher, and the rate of GDP growth will be higher.

Because CO_2 persists in the atmosphere for very long periods, it is the cumulative emissions (that is, concentrations) that matter, not the annual emissions[47]—for example, for purposes of analyzing rising temperatures and global warming. It is in analyzing such issues that the advantage of using the 50-year time horizon becomes apparent. If the analysis were restricted only to the period up to 2020, we would see that the higher GDP growth rates in the BAU-H scenarios generate cumulative CO_2 emissions only 9 percent higher in China and 17 percent higher in India, relative to the BAU case. But by 2050 the differences are dramatic: 22 percent higher in China and 79 percent higher in India (or 34 percent higher combined)—and this with only an average 0.75–1.25 percent higher growth rate in GDP annually over the 50-year period 2001–50.[48]

The constrained adjustment scenarios in Shalizi (forthcoming) suggest that, if energy supplies do not expand as expected, GDP will be lower in India (by 8 percent in 2030) and China (by 2 percent) and that world oil prices are likely to be 15 percent higher than projected here. We cannot predict

---

47. This is less the case for SO_2 or other emissions that dissipate more rapidly over time.
48. The 1.0 to 1.5 percent higher growth rates (between the BAU and BAU-H scenarios) cited in the section on business-as-usual simulations refer to the first couple of five-year-plan periods after 2005. The simulation is frontloaded and the growth rates taper off to 3–4 percent by 2050. Thus, over the 50-year period the compound average growth rate (between the BAU and BAU-H scenarios) is only 0.75–1.25 percent.

whether the requisite investments to avoid the constraints will occur, but these results certainly suggest that they are an important element in the effects of Chinese and Indian growth.

Policy Intervention Scenarios—ALT-D, ALT-S, and ALT-S&D

The alternative policy intervention scenarios show that it is possible to increase energy efficiency and reduce emissions substantially without significantly compromising GDP growth.

Country Implications

The ALT (policy-based) scenarios result in a substantial reduction in energy use and CO_2 emissions in both China and India (table 5.4).[49] The combined effect of measures acting on demand and measures acting on supply is much stronger than the effect of either set of measures alone. More important, their positive effects on reducing annual energy use and emissions generated are significant and increase over time with marginal impacts on GDP.

Measuring the Extent of Energy and Emissions Decoupling from GDP Growth

KAYA diagrams provide a convenient way to present the time profile of the extent to which the two decouplings mentioned earlier are achieved. The horizontal axis of a KAYA diagram shows the extent of improvement in energy intensity in an economy (that is, energy used per unit of output) and is read right to left. The vertical axis shows the extent of improvement in carbon intensity (decarbonization) in the economy (that is, carbon emitted per unit of energy) and is read from top to bottom. In the KAYA diagrams presented here (figure 5.6), the lighter line refers to the BAU scenario; the dashed line refers to the scenario induced by measures acting on demand only (ALT-D); the dotted line refers to the scenario induced by measures acting on supply only (ALT-S); and the black line refers to the scenario induced by combining measures acting on supply and demand (ALT-S&D).

In the BAU strategy for China and India there is a strong reduction in energy intensity built in to reflect industry modernization and adoption of new

---

49. Reductions are even more substantial for SO_2 emissions that have local consequences but are not cited in the tables above.

Table 5.4 Summary of ALT scenarios Relative to BAU for China and India, 2005–50

Country and scenario		GDP (2001 US$ trillions)			Primary energy use (Mtoe)			CO_2 emissions (GtC)			Energy investment (2001 US$ billions)		
		2005	2020	2050	2005	2020	2050	2005	2020	2050	2005	2020	2050
China	No change in policy—BAU	1.62	4.46	11.75	1,223.12	2,483.52	4,436.51	0.90	1.96	3.61	71.53	119.68	113.28
	Demand— ALT-D (%)	99.8	99.4	100.8	99.1	90.3	78.8	99.0	88.7	76.7	99.8	96.7	76.0
	Supply— ALT-S (%)	99.9	99.5	99.5	98.7	95.8	98.4	98.5	83.1	79.8	101.2	116.3	121.7
	Supply and demand— ALT-S&D (%)	99.7	98.6	99.2	97.8	86.7	75.9	97.6	72.8	59.9	101.0	114.3	92.2
India	No change in policy—BAU	0.61	1.35	4.59	515.61	845.84	2,068.79	0.26	0.49	1.56	18.44	36.64	74.13
	Demand— ALT-D (%)	99.8	99.4	100.9	99.1	94.1	84.8	99.1	92.8	82.9	99.9	95.2	84.1
	Supply— ALT-S (%)	99.9	99.8	101.4	98.4	93.8	99.3	98.1	77.3	76.4	102.2	113.4	124.9
	Supply and demand— ALT-S&D (%)	99.7	99.0	101.2	97.5	88.7	83.7	97.2	71.6	63.2	102.1	110.5	103.5

Source: Author's calculations based on simulation model.
Note: GtC = giga tonnes carbon; Mtoe = million tons of oil equivalent.

technology. However, carbon intensity increases in both countries—but more significantly in India. China shows a slight improvement in carbon intensity, but only toward the latter part of the 50-year period under review.

Figure 5.6 Extent of Energy and Emission Decoupling in the Case of Final Energy Consumption

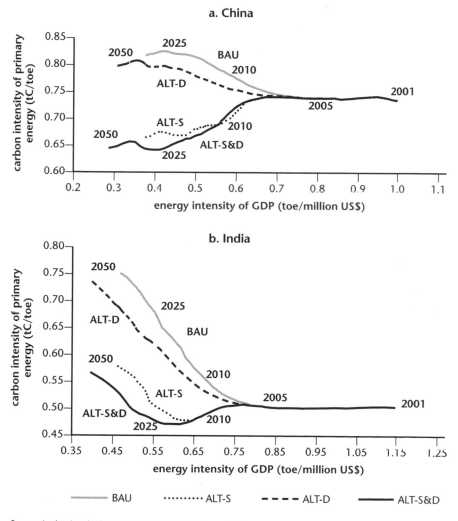

Source: Author's calculations based on simulation model.
Note: tC/toe = tons of carbon to tons of oil equivalent.

Relative to the BAU case, ALT-D measures to reduce demand alone (by increasing energy efficiency), extend the degree to which the energy intensity of GDP is reduced (the line extends farther to the left), and ensure that carbon intensity does not grow as much as it does in the BAU cases. But the time profile of the two decouplings is very similar to the BAU cases in both China and India. In China, demand side policies reduce emissions by 0.84 GtC, relative to the 3.6 GtC of emissions in 2050 (a 23 percent reduction). In India, demand side policies reduce emissions by 0.27 GtC, relative to 1.6 GtC in 2050 (that is, they reduce emissions by 17 percent).

Relative to the BAU case, ALT-S measures to change only supply (that is, the structure of fuels supplied to the economy) do not extend the degree to which energy intensity of GDP is reduced (unlike the demand measures) in either China or India. However, in China they do significantly alter the time profile and the extent to which the carbon intensity is reduced. In India, after an initial shift away from carbon, the carbon intensity starts increasing again (unlike in China) because the share of traditional biomass for household residential use is much higher at the outset of the process in India than in China (48 percent versus 18 percent, respectively). Thus, the greater shift from traditional biomass to commercial electricity for household residential use results in a displacement of less carbon-emitting biomass by more carbon-emitting fossil fuel–based electricity—despite the increased penetration of nuclear and nontraditional renewables, such as wind and solar energy, for producing power. However, supply side policies bring emissions down by 30 percent in India (from 1.56 GtC to 1.19 GtC), a larger reduction than the 20 percent lowering in China (from 3.6 GtC in the BAU case to 2.88 GtC).

Combining demand-reducing measures with fuel-switching measures (ALT-S&D) results in both a lowering of energy intensity and a lowering of carbon intensity, relative to either set of measures alone, and quite significantly relative to the BAU scenario. By 2050, the combined measures reduce energy intensity of GDP by 24 percent in China and 17 percent in India, and reduce carbon intensity of energy by 21 percent in China and 25 percent in India compared with the BAU scenario.

Global Implications

The repercussions of these ALT policy scenarios on world energy prices are mixed. Improvements in transport fuel efficiency in China and India lower global oil prices by a couple of percentage points. The improved efficiency in coal use and the substitution toward nuclear and renewable fuels in generating electricity have a more significant impact on world coal prices, which drop by 5–10 percent by 2050. This has a positive impact on India, which may have to import more coal in the future. These effects are more pronounced in the scenarios with rigidity/friction.[50]

The ALT scenarios have a much more significant impact on emissions, and the effect grows over time and extends beyond 2050. In cumulative terms, however, even by 2050, demand side policies in China reduce CO_2 emissions by approximately 15 percent (18 GtC) and supply side policies produce reductions of approximately 18 percent (21 GtC). The combination of supply and demand policies reduces emissions by 32 percent (36 GtC) or almost one-third, compared with the 116 GtC cumulative CO_2 emissions in the baseline scenario. The overall impact of policies on CO_2 emissions in India is of similar relative magnitude. In cumulative terms, demand side policies in India reduce CO_2 emissions by approximately 12 percent (4.5 GtC) and supply side policies reduce them by about 22 percent (8 GtC). The combination of supply and demand policies reduces emissions by 31 percent (11 GtC) or almost one-third, compared with the 37 GtC cumulative CO_2 emissions in the baseline scenario.

Additional Investment and Financing Requirements

As noted earlier in the section on ALT scenario energy and emissions trajectories, implementing either demand side or supply side measures reduces energy and emissions, compared with the BAU case. The measures do not offset each other so implementing both sets of measures reduces energy and emissions substantially more than implementing either one alone. And this reduction continues throughout the period up to and beyond 2050. This is not the case for energy investments (see the final block in table 5.4).

Implementing measures only to reduce the demand for energy lowers investment requirements in all periods, relative to the BAU case, whereas measures to change only the structure of the fuel supply increase investment requirements substantially, relative to BAU. Combining the two sets of measures, however, results in an intermediate time profile of investment requirements that, in aggregate, are higher in the early period and lower in the

---

50. Note that the impact of the ALT scenarios relative to the BAU reference case is much lower than the effect of scenarios with rigidity/friction.

later period than is true in the BAU case.[51] That is, the requirement for additional energy investments drops by 2050 (and in China they drop to a level below the BAU equivalent). The reason for this drop is that a smaller amount of investment is required in fuel switching when demand is lower.[52]

A key point in this analysis is that net capital flows are fixed exogenously. Thus, the increases in investment in the energy sector must be financed either by reducing net capital outflows or by diverting other domestic investment. Our simulations assume the former for India, which permits its GDP growth relative to BAU, but at the expense of a deterioration in net assets—the welfare implications of which the model ignores. For the sake of illustration, we make the opposite assumption for China: investment is diverted and GDP falls marginally compared with BAU, but asset accumulation proceeds unchecked. The moral is that although the need for the extra investment in the ALT runs is real, the results given for GDP are very poor indicators of likely welfare consequences. The latter depend on the decline in output, on the decline in net assets, and, of course, on the benefits of curtailing emissions.

From a country perspective, the higher initial cost of investment in alternatives to fossil fuels is a concern, so the standard response is to delay adopting cutting-edge technologies until additional technological innovations reduce their costs.[53] Accordingly, another scenario was simulated to explore the consequences of delaying interventions (which is reported in the longer working paper version of this chapter). This shows that delaying policy interventions will save money now but will generate higher investment requirements in the future to reach a given target emissions level by a specified period. However, even these higher investment requirements will be more affordable because they will represent a lower share of a larger GDP, given the intervening growth in the economy. This supports the initial intuition regarding the economic benefits of delaying interventions. The downside of delaying interventions, however, is that the environmental benefits of these policies also will be delayed. What the scenarios show is that the latter never quite fully

51. Investment requirements are 114 percent higher in China in 2020 (equivalent to an additional $13 billion in 2001 prices) and 110 percent higher in India in 2020 (approximately equivalent to an additional $4 billion in 2001 prices).
52. When friction and rigidities are introduced, the aggregate energy investment required in the BAU-f case also is lower than in the BAU case because GDP is lower.
53. In the IMACLIM-R model used for the simulations in this chapter, "learning by doing" is built in; therefore, earlier investments in novel technologies will speed up the rate at which one moves down the cost curve and thus reduce the aggregate financial burden.

catch up with the benefits generated by implementing policy interventions earlier. Even though the costs of investment and the benefits of emissions reduction are both shifted into the future, the net present value of the two policies is not the same. There is a price of carbon for which the two streams of costs and benefits will be equivalent. With early action, the implicit price will be lower than that currently observed ($10–12 per tonne of CO_2) in the project-based segment of the carbon market (Clean Development Mechanism)—which means there is no reason to delay. Delaying action by a decade, however, requires a higher price of carbon today to generate the same returns. This higher carbon price will be above current market prices, and therefore will not be cost effective. As a result, the cumulative "financial cost-reducing" benefit of delaying investments does not offset fully the increased cumulative emissions cost associated with prolonged reliance on fossil fuels.[54,55]

Conclusions

This chapter has made a number of important points on the effects of Chinese and Indian growth on energy markets and emissions. Even at present, demand for electricity is growing very rapidly in both countries, and there are limited low-cost domestic energy resources other than coal for producing this electricity.

Demand for oil also is growing rapidly in response to the growing demand for mobility/transportation. This growing fossil fuel use is generating harmful emissions of greenhouse gas and increasing public health costs from severe local air pollution. The Giants, however, were not the principal drivers of high oil prices in 2006.

Turning to the future, energy externalities (local, regional, and global) are likely to worsen significantly, especially if there is no shift in China's and India's energy strategies.

Many developing countries worry that high energy demand from China and India will hurt their growth by forcing higher prices on international energy markets. This effect is likely to be small and to be offset partially or fully by the "growth-stimulating" effects of the larger markets in China and India.

---

54. This chapter does not evaluate the extent of international carbon trading that might evolve post-Kyoto.
55. Fuller details of this example are available in Shalizi (2006).

The Giants themselves worry that shifting their energy strategies to fuels with lower emissions will reduce externalities and the pressure on world energy prices in world energy markets—but at the expense of their growth in incomes. In fact, the evidence suggests that improved efficiency leaves plenty of opportunities to reduce energy growth without adversely affecting GDP growth. Some of these entail extra costs, but the financing needs are well within the compass of domestic and world capital markets. Making these investments will have both global and local benefits.

Further research is required to link new generation multiregional global models with endogenous growth (such as IMACLIM-R) to more disaggregated models currently being developed or augmented in China and India. This will provide a richer framework to test specific policies tailored to the unique opportunities and constraints in each country. It also will enable analysis of equity issues as well as spatial consequences of different types of interventions.

Annex

Table 5A.1 Energy Balance, 1980–2003

a. China

	Production and stock change (Mtoe)						
Year	Coal	Oil	Natural gas	Hydro	Biomass and waste	Nuclear	Total
1980	316	107	12	5	180	0	620
1981	315	103	11	6	182	0	616
1982	332	104	10	6	184	0	636
1983	352	106	10	7	186	0	661
1984	387	116	11	7	187	0	708
1985	405	130	13	8	189	0	744
1986	423	131	14	8	191	0	767
1987	454	135	14	9	193	0	805
1988	488	140	15	9	195	0	847
1989	495	139	16	10	198	0	857
1990	545	136	16	11	200	0	908
1991	535	140	17	11	202	0	906
1992	555	143	16	11	203	0	929
1993	588	138	17	13	205	0	961
1994	630	144	18	14	205	4	1,015

Table 5A.1, *continued*

Year	Coal	Oil	Natural gas	Hydro	Biomass and waste	Nuclear	Total
1995	691	149	19	16	206	3	1,084
1996	722	158	21	16	207	4	1,128
1997	707	156	21	17	208	4	1,113
1998	698	156	24	18	209	4	1,109
1999	685	161	26	18	213	4	1,106
2000	698	151	28	19	214	4	1,115
2001	705	161	31	24	216	5	1,142
2002	765	168	34	25	217	7	1,216
2003	917	169	36	24	219	11	1,377

			Consumption (Mtoe)				
Year	Coal	Oil	Natural gas	Hydro	Biomass and waste	Nuclear	Total
1980	313	89	12	5	180	0	599
1981	311	84	11	6	182	0	594
1982	329	83	10	6	184	0	613
1983	348	85	10	7	186	0	637
1984	384	88	11	7	187	0	676
1985	401	93	13	8	189	0	704
1986	418	98	14	8	191	0	729
1987	446	105	14	9	193	0	767
1988	478	112	15	9	195	0	809
1989	486	116	16	10	198	0	826
1990	535	110	16	11	200	0	872
1991	523	121	17	11	202	0	874
1992	541	132	16	11	203	0	904
1993	576	146	17	13	205	0	957
1994	615	145	18	14	205	4	1,002
1995	673	158	19	16	206	3	1,075
1996	700	172	19	16	207	4	1,119
1997	685	191	19	17	208	4	1,124
1998	678	188	22	18	209	4	1,119
1999	661	205	24	18	213	4	1,124
2000	664	222	26	19	214	4	1,149
2001	648	227	29	24	216	5	1,149
2002	716	244	32	25	217	7	1,241
2003	862	270	35	24	219	11	1,422

continued on next page

Table 5A.1, *continued*

Year	Coal	Oil	Natural gas	Hydro	Biomass and waste	Nuclear	Total
			Net export (Mtoe)				
1980	3	18	0	0	0	0	21
1981	3	19	0	0	0	0	22
1982	3	20	0	0	0	0	23
1983	3	21	0	0	0	0	24
1984	3	29	0	0	0	0	32
1985	4	37	0	0	0	0	41
1986	5	33	0	0	0	0	38
1987	8	31	0	0	0	0	38
1988	9	28	0	0	0	0	37
1989	9	22	0	0	0	0	31
1990	10	26	0	0	0	0	36
1991	12	19	0	0	0	0	32
1992	14	11	0	0	0	0	25
1993	12	–8	0	0	0	0	4
1994	15	–2	0	0	0	0	13
1995	18	–9	0	0	0	0	9
1996	22	–14	1	0	0	0	9
1997	22	–35	2	0	0	0	–11
1998	20	–31	2	0	0	0	–9
1999	23	–43	2	0	0	0	–18
2000	35	–71	2	0	0	0	–34
2001	57	–66	2	0	0	0	–6
2002	49	–76	2	0	0	0	–25
2003	55	–101	1	0	0	0	–45

b. India

Year	Coal	Oil	Natural gas	Hydro	Biomass and waste	Nuclear	Total
			Production and stock change (Mtoe)				
1980	50	11	1	4	148	1	215
1981	56	17	2	4	151	1	230
1982	58	22	2	4	154	1	241
1983	63	27	3	4	156	1	254
1984	68	30	3	5	160	1	266
1985	71	31	4	4	162	1	274
1986	77	32	5	5	165	1	285
1987	82	32	6	4	169	1	294
1988	89	34	7	5	171	2	307

Table 5A.1, *continued*

Year	Coal	Oil	Natural gas	Hydro	Biomass and waste	Nuclear	Total
1989	92	36	9	5	173	1	316
1990	97	35	10	6	176	2	326
1991	106	34	11	6	180	1	338
1992	111	30	13	6	182	2	344
1993	115	30	13	6	185	1	351
1994	118	36	13	7	187	1	362
1995	124	39	17	6	189	2	377
1996	131	37	18	6	190	2	384
1997	134	38	20	6	193	3	394
1998	131	37	21	7	195	3	395
1999	138	37	20	7	198	3	404
2000	143	37	21	6	202	4	414
2001	148	37	21	6	205	5	422
2002	151	38	23	6	208	5	431
2003	157	39	23	6	211	5	441

Consumption (Mtoe)

Year	Coal	Oil	Natural gas	Hydro	Biomass and waste	Nuclear	Total
1980	53	34	1	4	148	1	241
1981	60	36	2	4	151	1	253
1982	62	39	2	4	154	1	261
1983	66	40	3	4	156	1	271
1984	71	42	3	5	160	1	281
1985	76	48	4	4	162	1	296
1986	80	48	5	5	165	1	305
1987	86	50	6	4	169	1	317
1988	94	55	7	5	171	2	334
1989	97	60	9	5	173	1	346
1990	104	63	10	6	176	2	360
1991	112	65	11	6	180	1	375
1992	118	68	13	6	182	2	388
1993	123	70	13	6	185	1	398
1994	127	74	13	7	187	1	410
1995	134	84	17	6	189	2	432
1996	142	89	18	6	190	2	447
1997	147	94	20	6	193	3	463
1998	144	101	21	7	195	3	472
1999	152	113	20	7	198	3	494

continued on next page

Table 5A.1, *continued*

Year	Coal	Oil	Natural gas	Hydro	Biomass and waste	Nuclear	Total
2000	159	114	21	6	202	4	506
2001	162	115	21	6	205	5	514
2002	168	119	23	6	208	5	527
2003	173	124	23	6	211	5	542

			Net export (Mtoe)				
Year	Coal	Oil	Natural gas	Hydro	Biomass and waste	Nuclear	Total
1980	−3	−23	0	0	0	0	−26
1981	−3	−20	0	0	0	0	−23
1982	−4	−17	0	0	0	0	−20
1983	−3	−13	0	0	0	0	−16
1984	−3	−12	0	0	0	0	−15
1985	−4	−17	0	0	0	0	−21
1986	−4	−16	0	0	0	0	−20
1987	−5	−18	0	0	0	0	−23
1988	−5	−22	0	0	0	0	−27
1989	−6	−24	0	0	0	0	−29
1990	−7	−27	0	0	0	0	−34
1991	−6	−31	0	0	0	0	−37
1992	−7	−38	0	0	0	0	−45
1993	−7	−40	0	0	0	0	−47
1994	−9	−39	0	0	0	0	−48
1995	−10	−45	0	0	0	0	−55
1996	−11	−52	0	0	0	0	−63
1997	−14	−56	0	0	0	0	−69
1998	−13	−64	0	0	0	0	−77
1999	−15	−75	0	0	0	0	−90
2000	−15	−77	0	0	0	0	−93
2001	−14	−78	0	0	0	0	−92
2002	−16	−80	0	0	0	0	−97
2003	−15	−85	0	0	0	0	−100

Source: IEA 2005a.
Note: Mtoe = million tons of oil equivalent.

CHAPTER 6

Partially Awakened Giants
Uneven Growth in China and India

Shubham Chaudhuri and Martin Ravallion

The emergence of China and India on the global economic stage has been the subject of much discussion in international media and business and policy circles. The nearly 9 percent annual rate of real per capita gross domestic product (GDP) growth that China has averaged over the last quarter-century is unprecedented; and with an average per capita GDP growth rate of nearly 4 percent a year since 1981, India's takeoff seems less than spectacular only in comparison with that of China.

In both countries, this growth has been accompanied by substantial—in the case of China, dramatic—reductions in the aggregate incidence of absolute poverty measured in terms of income or consumption. Figure 6.1 displays these two trends for the two countries over the period from 1981 to 2003.[1] The headcount rates of poverty are calculated on as comparable a basis as is currently feasible. The poverty line is the World Bank's dollar-a-day global standard of $32.74 a month at 1993 purchasing power parity. China started this period with the higher poverty rate, but soon overtook India.

Concerns are being expressed about the distributional impacts of the growth processes in both countries. The domestic debate about growth-promoting reforms has become increasingly contentious. It is widely felt that the

---

1. At the time of writing, only preliminary data were available for India for fiscal 2004/05, and this data point is not plotted in figure 6.1. The preliminary data suggest that the overall Indian poverty rate trend shown in figure 6.1 has been maintained, although it has not accelerated (in percentage points per year) since the early 1990s.

Figure 6.1 Growth and Poverty Reduction, 1981–2003

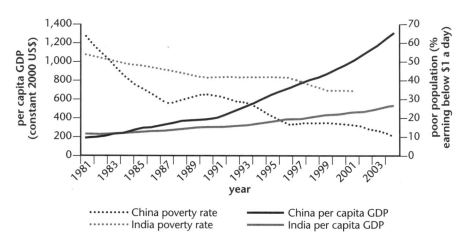

Source: Poverty measures from Chen and Ravallion (2004); GDP from national accounts.

gains from growth have been spread too unevenly, with some segments of the population left behind in relative and even absolute terms. Yes, the Giants are awakening from their economic slumber, but they still are only partially awake in that segments of their societies remain (relatively and absolutely) dormant. This unevenness has shown up as rising income inequality by conventional measures in both countries. These developments in turn have led some observers to question the sustainability of growth.

What is one to make of this? In what ways has growth been uneven? Can we believe the data suggesting rising inequality? If so, should we be concerned that segments of the population appear to have been left behind (at least in relative terms)? And does this pose a risk to the sustainability of growth and poverty reduction?

In this chapter, we try to shed some light on these questions. Certainly of undeniable interest in both countries, these questions also merit attention elsewhere because the impact that the rise of China and India is going to have on the rest of the world depends very much on whether the Giants are able to sustain the growth rates they have achieved over the last quarter-century. And that sustainability hinges on whether concerns about the unevenness of growth thus far are legitimate and whether that unevenness poses a risk to future growth.

After noting a number of data issues, the chapter examines the ways in which growth has been uneven in China and India, and what that unevenness has meant for inequality and poverty. Drawing on analyses based on existing household survey data and aggregate data from official sources, we show that growth has been uneven—geographically, sectorally, and at the household level—and that this has meant uneven progress against poverty, less poverty reduction than might have been achieved had growth been more balanced, and increased income inequality. We then turn to why growth has been uneven and why this should be of concern. Because of the complexity of the underlying issues and the difficulties of settling them in an empirically rigorous manner, the discussion is necessarily somewhat more speculative. We structure the discussion around the idea that there are both "good" and "bad" inequalities—drivers and dimensions of inequality and uneven growth that are good or bad in terms of what they imply for both equity and long-term growth and development.

We argue that the Giants' development paths have been influenced by, and have generated, both types of inequalities. Although good inequalities—most notably, those that reflect the role of economic incentives—have been critical to the growth experience thus far, there is a risk that bad inequalities—those that prevent individuals from connecting to markets and limit investment and accumulation of human and physical capital—may undermine the sustainability of growth in the coming years. We argue that policies are needed to preserve the good inequalities—continued incentives for innovation and investment—but reduce the scope for bad ones, notably through investments in human capital and rural infrastructure that help rural poor people connect to markets.

Clarifying Data Issues

There are always reasons to be skeptical about economic statistics, and measures of inequality and poverty are no exceptions. The issues are rather different between these two countries.

A number of data problems have clouded past assessments of what has been happening to poverty and inequality in China. Some of these problems are common to other countries; others seem unique to China. An unusual feature of China's data is that the National Bureau of Statistics (NBS) uses different annual survey instruments for urban and rural areas, namely the Rural Household Survey and the annual Urban Household Survey; whereas NBS makes some efforts to ensure comparability, problems remain. For the rural survey, there are also comparability problems over time, as discussed in Ravallion and Chen (forthcoming). One of the more serious problems is that, in 1990, there was a change in valuation methods for consumption of own-farm production in the Rural Household Survey: public procurement prices (held below market prices) were replaced by local selling prices.[2] For 1990 (the only year for which the two methods can be compared), Ravallion and Chen (forthcoming) showed that the new valuation method generates slightly lower inequality; for 1990, the aggregate Gini index for rural China drops from 31.5 percent to 29.9 percent, and the rural headcount index of poverty drops substantially from 37.6 percent to 29.9 percent. These effects reflect the high share of consumption from own-farm product among China's poor population.

Another problem in past work has been the failure to adjust for spatial cost-of-living differences. This failure can affect distributional comparisons over space and time. The extent of urban-rural disparities drops appreciably when one corrects for the higher urban cost of living (Ravallion and Chen forthcoming). Also, the positive trend in urban–rural inequality since around 1980 (noted by many authors in the literature) vanishes when one allows for higher inflation rates in urban areas than in rural areas, although a marked positive trend in urban–rural inequality since the mid-1990s is still evident (Ravallion and Chen forthcoming).

Lack of public access to the micro data for China as a whole has restricted researchers' ability to address the data concerns. However, micro data for some selected provinces and time periods have been available. Ravallion and Chen (1999) used the micro data for four provinces of southern China to correct poverty and inequality measures for problems in both the valuation methods for consumption of own product and the deflators. The corrections to the original survey data tend to reduce measured inequality and to attenuate its rate of increase over time.

Not all the likely data problems mean a lower true level of inequality or a lower rate of increase over time. For example, if we could correct for selective

---

2. Until the mid-1990s, public procurement prices for grain were held below market prices. Using these prices to value own consumption overestimates the true extent of both poverty and inequality. This practice largely was abandoned from the 1990s onward in favor of using local selling prices for valuation.

compliance (whereby people who are relatively well off are less well represented in surveys), then we might find higher inequality.[3] We currently have no basis for correcting for this possible problem in China, however; we suspect the compliance problem is of greater concern in urban China than in rural areas.

Poverty monitoring in India since the 1960s has been based mainly on the household expenditure surveys done as part of the National Sample Surveys. The salient features are that household consumption expenditure per person is used as the individual welfare indicator, and the poverty line that is intended to have a fixed real value across time and space (urban and rural areas of states) is determined by combined geographic and intertemporal deflators. The main data issue is that assessing what has been happening to poverty and inequality in India during the 1990s has been clouded by a comparability problem between the two main surveys available for the 1990s (Deaton 2001; Sen and Hiamnshu 2004a, 2004b).[4]

There are concerns about how well surveys measure incomes or consumptions. Survey-based income and consumption aggregates for nationally representative samples typically do not match the aggregates obtained from national accounts. This is to be expected for GDP, which includes nonhousehold sources of domestic absorption. Possibly more surprising are the discrepancies found with both the levels and growth rates of private consumption in the national accounts aggregates; Ravallion (2003) provides evidence. The discrepancies between levels and growth rates of consumption as measured by India's National Sample Survey and national accounts have been of particular concern, but here, too, it should be noted that (as measured in practice) private consumption in the national accounts includes sizable and rapidly growing

---

3. This is not necessarily the case, but there is supportive evidence for the United States (Korinek, Mistiaen, and Ravallion 2006).
4. Since the National Sample Survey began in the 1950s, it has used 30-day recall for consumption. This changed in 1999/2000 with the 55th round for which food consumption (on average, approximately 60 percent of total consumption) was obtained by both 7- and 30-day recall for the same set of households, with the question about the last 7 days' consumption of each commodity coming before the question about the last 30 days' consumption. (The columns for 7- and 30-day recall appear side by side on the same page in the questionnaire.) By contrast, spending on low-frequency nonfood consumption items (about 20 percent of the average total consumption) was obtained using a one-year recall period, unlike earlier rounds. The 30-day recall period was used only for high-frequency nonfood items.

components typically missing from surveys (Deaton 2005).[5] Aside from differences in what is being measured, however, surveys do encounter problems of underreporting (particularly for incomes; the problem appears to be less serious for consumption) and selective nonresponse.[6]

There are also a number of data problems in making comparisons between China and India. China has traditionally used household income (per capita) as the ranking variable whereas India has used consumption expenditure (per capita). Also, the available data on spatial differences in the cost of living are still rather weak in both countries. Furthermore, purchasing power comparisons between the countries are confounded by a number of concerns about the underlying price data and standard index-number problems.[7]

One data-related issue that should be flagged, however, is how well conventional inequality measures capture the significance that is often attached to *between-group* inequalities. Naturally, any conventional inequality measure puts weight on such differences, but it is far from obvious that those weights accord well with the significance attached to between-group inequalities, as argued by Kanbur (2001). Although this issue raises a number of deeper questions about individualism and the role of group identities that are beyond our present scope, we will note the extra significance attached to certain between-group disparities in both China and India.

Ways in Which Growth Has Been Uneven

Growth in China and India over the last quarter-century has indeed been uneven. This unevenness has been apparent in several (related) dimensions, with implications for inequality, poverty reduction, and human development in the two countries. This section makes four claims:

---

5. Deaton and Kozel (2005) provided a useful compilation of papers on this and related issues of poverty measurement in India.

6. In measuring poverty, some researchers have replaced the survey mean by the mean from the national accounts (GDP or consumption per capita); for example, see Bhalla (2002) and Sala-i-Martin (2002). This replacement assumes that the discrepancy is distribution neutral, which is unlikely to be the case; for example, selective nonresponse to surveys can generate highly nonneutral errors (Korinek, Mistiaen, and Ravallion 2006). For further discussion in the context of poverty measurement in India, see Ravallion (2000).

7. We will largely ignore these data problems in this chapter, not because we think them unimportant but because this is not the place to dwell on them.

1. Uneven growth across states in India and provinces in China has meant uneven progress against poverty.
2. Growth has been sectorally uneven, with primary sector growth rates lagging behind growth rates in the secondary and tertiary sectors in both of the Giants, and with rural incomes growing more slowly than urban incomes.
3. Growth has been uneven at the household level. In particular, incomes at the top of the distribution increased much faster than those at the bottom in both countries. That fact has meant rising inequality—dramatically so in the case of China.
4. Because the more rapid growth of both countries has been so uneven in these dimensions, it sometimes has brought disappointing outcomes in terms of progress against poverty and other ("nonincome") dimensions of well-being.

Geographically Uneven Growth Has Produced Uneven Progress against Poverty

The aggregate growth performances of China and India mask considerable unevenness of growth at the subnational level. Chinese provincial GDP growth rates (between 1978 and 2004) ranged from a low of 5.9 percent in Qinghai to a high of 13.3 percent in Zhejiang. In India, growth rates of state domestic product between 1980 and 2004 ranged from a low of 1.7 percent in Jammu and Kashmir to a high of 8.7 percent in Goa. Among India's 16 major states, Bihar (including the newly created state of Jharkand) had the lowest growth rate—namely, 2.2 percent—and Karnataka had the highest—7.2 percent.

Province- and state-level growth rates have been higher and less volatile since around 1980 in China and 1990 in India.[8] Nonetheless, the sustained geographic differences in growth rates have generated some marked regional disparities in both countries. In India, the states that initially were poorer have grown more slowly, resulting in unconditional divergence in both absolute and relative terms.[9] This is apparent in figure 6.2, which plots the average annual growth rate of real per capita state GDP against a state's initial per

---

8. In India, as an example, except for the Green Revolution states of Punjab and Haryana and the state of Maharashtra, annual growth rates before the 1980s were, at most, 2 percent.
9. See Ghosh (2006) for econometric tests indicating more marked growth divergence for India in the postreform period

Figure 6.2 Growth Rates at the Subnational Level

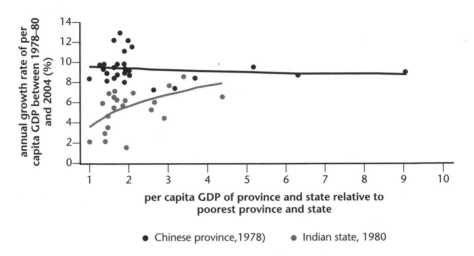

Source: National Bureau of Statistics of China, *China Statistical Yearbook,* various years; Government of India Central Survey Organization.
Note: The lines of best fit are semi-log least-squares regression lines.

capita GDP relative to the poorest state. India's poorer states are experiencing positive growth, but the high growth rates, postreform, have been elsewhere.

In China, provinces that initially were poorer have managed to keep pace with the initially wealthier provinces in terms of aggregate growth rates (figure 6.2). Keeping pace has meant no divergence in relative terms, but absolute differences across provinces have increased. Also, there have been signs of divergence regionally between the coastal and inland areas of China (see Chen and Fleisher 1996; Jian, Sachs, and Warner 1996; Sun and Dutta 1997; Raiser 1998; and Kanbur and Zhang 1999).

The spatial unevenness of growth has contributed in two ways to uneven progress against poverty. First, because household income growth has been associated closely with poverty reduction at the subnational level in both China and India, geographically uneven growth has meant that progress against poverty was uneven as well, with some provinces and states seeing far more rapid reduction in poverty than others.[10] In China, the coastal areas fared better than inland areas; the trend rate of decline in the poverty rate between

10. This is clearly documented for India by Datt and Ravallion (2002) and Deaton and Drèze (2002), and for China by Ravallion and Chen (forthcoming).

1981 and 2001 was 8 percent a year for inland provinces, versus 17 percent for the coastal provinces. In India, most of the western and southern states—peninsular India (with the exception of Andhra Pradesh)—did comparatively well, while the more backward states of Bihar, Madhya Pradesh, Rajasthan, and Uttar Pradesh, along with states in the eastern region, achieved relatively little poverty reduction between 1993/94 and 1999/2000.

Second, the most rapid growth did not occur where it would have had the most impact on poverty. This is evident if one compares growth rates across provinces with the growth elasticities of poverty reduction weighted by the initial shares of total poverty. (The weights ensure that this gives the impact on national poverty of growth in a given province.) Had the pattern of growth favored provinces where growth would have had the greatest impact on poverty, we would find a negative correlation between the growth rate and the share-weighted elasticity. However, for neither country does one find any relationship, one way or the other (see Ravallion and Chen [forthcoming] for China and Datt and Ravallion [2002] for India).

Sectorally Uneven Growth Has Increased the Urban–Rural Income Gap and Suppressed Poverty Reduction

A second dimension of uneven growth in both countries is found across sectors. Growth rates in the primary sector (agriculture) not only have lagged behind those in the secondary (industry) and tertiary (services) sectors, but also actually have declined since 1980 (figure 6.3).

In nominal terms, urban incomes and expenditures clearly have increased faster than rural incomes over the past quarter-century in both countries. For India, this has been reflected in a steady increase in the ratio of urban-to-rural mean real consumption levels, from just below 1.4 in 1983 to approximately 1.7 in 2000. Even in 1981, the urban-to-rural ratio of nominal mean incomes in China was approximately 2.5—much higher than it ever has been in India. And since then, although there have been periods when the ratio of urban-to-rural mean incomes fell, the overall trend has been upward.

Adjusting for cost-of-living differences clouds these trends somewhat. For China, the urban rate of inflation has been higher than the rural rate; and when one allows for this fact, there is no trend increase over time in the ratio of the urban mean to the rural mean (Ravallion and Chen forthcoming).[11]

---

11. There are other data problems with ambiguous implications for urban–rural disparities. The undercounting of rural migrants in China's urban areas is likely to lead to an overesti-

Figure 6.3 Sectoral GDP Growth Rates, 1980–2005

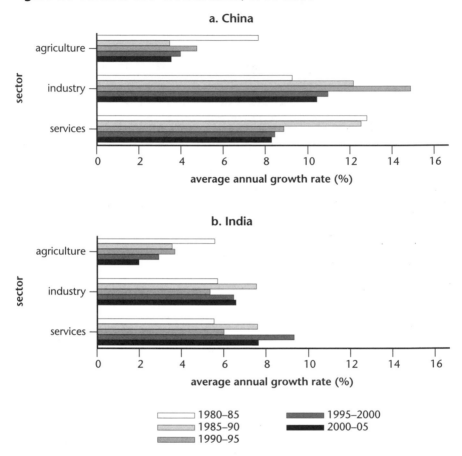

Sources: National Bureau of Statistics of China, *China Statistical Yearbook,* various years; Government of India Central Survey Organization.

There have been subperiods, however, including the period from 1997 to the present, during which the relative urban–rural disparity has risen. Moreover, even allowing for cost-of-living differences, the absolute gap be-

---

mation of the level and growth rate in the ratio of the urban mean to the rural mean. Against this effect, urban survey response rates tend to be lower than in rural areas, and it may be assumed safely that the rich tend to have lower response rates. Our discussions with the staff of the National Bureau of Statistics of China suggest that this problem is growing over time in China.

Table 6.1 Poverty Reduction and the Sectoral Composition of Growth

Growth rate or components	China			India	
	(1)	(2)	(3)	·(4)	(5)
Growth rate of GDP per capita	−2.60 (−2.16)			−0.99 (−3.38)	
Primary sector (share weighted)		−8.07 (−3.97)	−7.85 (−4.09)		−1.16 (−2.96)
Secondary sector (share weighted)		−1.75 (−1.21)			3.41 (1.84)
Tertiary sector (share weighted)		−3.08 (−1.24)			−3.42 (−2.74)
Secondary + tertiary sectors			−2.25 (−2.20)		
R^2	0.21	0.43	0.42		0.75

Sources: Ravallion and Chen forthcoming (China, 1981–2001); Ravallion and Datt 1996 (India 1951–91).
Note: t-ratios appear in parentheses.

tween rural and urban incomes has increased appreciably. This is also true for India.

The sectoral composition of growth has mattered for poverty reduction in both countries over recent decades. This can be seen in table 6.1, which provides regressions of the rate of change in poverty over time (that is, the difference in the log of the headcount rate of poverty) on both the overall rate of per capita GDP growth (that is, the change in the log of GDP per capita) and the share-weighted rates of GDP growth in each of the three sectors. The sector-specific growth rates are share weighted to allow for the fact that sectors growing at the same rate are unlikely to have the same aggregate impacts if one accounts for a much smaller share of aggregate income than the other. When rates are share weighted, one obtains a straightforward, testable hypothesis for whether the composition of growth matters—namely, that the regression coefficients across growth components would be roughly equal (Ravallion and Datt 1996). Note that these regressions are best viewed as decomposition tools rather than causal models of poverty reduction. Deeper explanations must endogenize growth rates and their composition; and Ravallion and Chen (forthcoming) have provided models of poverty reduction in China that try to make some progress in that direction.

For China, the overall elasticity of the headcount index to GDP growth was an impressive −2.6, meaning that a 10 percent growth rate brought (on average) a 26 percent reduction in the proportion of people living in poverty. When growth is decomposed by sector, it is clear that its composition mattered greatly to the rate of poverty reduction. The impact of growth in the primary sector was far higher than for growth in either the secondary or tertiary sector. The effects of the latter two sectors are similar.

The overall growth elasticity of poverty reduction is appreciably lower in India than in China (column 4). For India, too, the sectoral composition of growth was important, although growth in the tertiary sector was relatively more important than in China.[12] This probably reflects the difference between the two countries in the distribution of agricultural land. In rural China, starting conditions at the outset of the reform process entailed relatively low levels of inequality in access to land. The de-collectivization process that started in the late 1970s achieved a relatively equal allocation of access to agricultural land, at least within communes. (Between communes, the only way to equalize land allocation would have been to allow mobility of people, which was not considered a desirable option.) This meant that agricultural growth was a powerful instrument against poverty and inequality in China (Ravallion and Chen forthcoming). The distribution of agricultural land was and is clearly more unequal in India, and that naturally attenuates the impact of agricultural growth on poverty relative to that found in China.

Increases in rural incomes, whether from agricultural growth or (particularly in the case of China) from increased rural nonfarm employment, also turn out to have been critical for overall poverty reduction. Table 6.2 gives regressions of the rate of change in poverty over time (difference in the log headcount index) on the share-weighted growth rates of rural and urban mean incomes and a term capturing the effect of any shifts in population from rural to urban areas. It can be seen that, in both countries, growth in rural incomes is the only statistically significant correlate of poverty reduction. Ravallion and Chen (forthcoming) also reported an alternative decomposition for China, which confirms the quantitative importance of rural economic growth. Approximately 72 percent of the reduction in the headcount index that occurred in China between 1981 and 2001 is attributable to rural poverty reduction, versus 5 percent attributable to urban poverty reduction and 23 percent resulting from the population shift from rural to urban areas.

---

12. Note that the coefficients on growth in the secondary and tertiary sectors for India are of approximately equal size but opposite sign (table 6.1). This suggests that the (share-weighted) difference in growth rates is picking up a distributional effect on poverty reduction.

Table 6.2 Poverty Reduction and the Urban–Rural Composition of Growth

Growth rate or population shift effect	China	India
Growth rate of mean rural income (share weighted)	–2.56 (–8.43)	–1.46 (12.64)
Growth rate of mean urban income (share weighted)	0.09 (0.20)	–0.55 (–1.37)
Population shift effect	0.74 (0.16)	–4.46 (–1.31)
R^2	0.82	0.90

Sources: Ravallion and Datt 1996 (India); Ravallion and Chen forthcoming (China).
Note: t-ratios appear in parentheses.

The results shown in tables 6.1 and 6.2 imply that the particular form of sectorally uneven growth experienced by China and India—primary sector growth rates lagging behind growth rates in the secondary and tertiary sectors, and rural incomes growing more slowly than urban incomes—has meant less poverty reduction than might have been the case otherwise. We can gain a sense of how much extra poverty reduction might have been achieved from a more balanced growth path through counterfactual simulations in which it is assumed that all three sectors grow equally—meaning that the sector shares of GDP in 1981 would have remained constant over time. The estimates from table 6.1 are used to calculate the implied rate of poverty reduction under different assumptions about the overall (common) rate of GDP growth. So, for instance, had it been possible to achieve a balanced growth path while maintaining the GDP growth rates China actually achieved between 1981 and 2001, the mean rate of poverty reduction would have been 16.3 percent a year, rather than 9.5 percent. Instead of 20 years to bring the headcount index down from 53 percent to 8 percent, it would have taken approximately 10 years.

Of course, one can question whether a more sectorally balanced growth path could have been achieved without lowering the overall growth rate, and so this exercise should be viewed as an upper bound on what might have been possible. And there appear to be signs of a sectoral trade-off in that the correlation between China's primary sector growth rates and the combined growth rate of the secondary and tertiary sectors was –0.414 over this period, thus implying that a more balanced growth path in which the growth rate of the primary sector was higher might have meant less growth overall. It is worth noting, however, that the negative correlation is statistically quite weak—a significance level of 6 percent—and that there were subperiods (1983–84, 1987–88, and 1994–96) in which both primary sector growth and combined growth in the secondary and tertiary sectors were above average.

A similar exercise for India suggests that, were it not for the sectoral and geographic imbalance of growth, the national rate of growth since reforms began in full force in the early 1990s would have generated a rate of poverty reduction that was double India's historical trend rate (Datt and Ravallion 2002). The evidence also suggests that states with relatively low levels of initial rural development and human capital development experienced lower elasticities of poverty reduction to economic growth (Ravallion and Datt 2002).

Uneven Growth across Households Has Led to Rising Inequality

The unevenness of economic growth across households at different levels of living can be seen clearly in the growth incidence curve (GIC), which gives the annualized rate of growth over the relevant time period at each percentile of the distribution (ranked by income or consumption per person).[13] Figure 6.4 displays the Chinese and Indian GICs for the periods 1990–99 and 1993–99, respectively. In both cases, growth rates at the bottom of the distribution were lower than those at the top. The gradient is less steep for India.[14] Growth rates in China in the 1990s rise sharply as we move up the income ladder, with the annual rate of growth in the 1990s increasing from approximately 3 percent for the poorest percentile to more than 10 percent for the richest. Although the growth rate in the overall mean was 6.2 percent, the mean growth rate for the poorest 20 percent (roughly according with China's "$1 a day" poverty rate in 1995) was 4.0 percent. The GIC for India for the 1990s shows a slight U shape, with the lowest growth rates—approximately

---

13. See Ravallion and Chen (2003) on the precise definition and properties of the GIC.

14. The shape of India's expenditure GIC for the 1990s depends critically on what adjustment is made for the comparability problems between the 1999/2000 survey and earlier surveys. The GIC shown in figure 6.4 is based on estimates produced by Sundaram and Tendulkar (2003), who resolved the comparability problem by estimating consumption expenditures based on a common "mixed reference period" for categories of consumption. The rural and urban distributions were then aggregated, assuming urban–rural cost-of-living differentials of 33 percent and 38 percent for 1993/94 and 1999/2000, respectively, based on updated poverty lines as used in Ravallion and Datt (2002). This roughly matches the GIC implied by estimates Deaton (2001) obtained using an alternative method, based on a "common reference period," to make the surveys comparable. If no attempt is made to correct for the comparability problem, however, and one simply uses the "unadjusted" primary estimates from each of the surveys, the GIC suggests a much more pro-poor pattern of growth, with growth rates declining from more than 2 percent for the poorest percentile to approximately 1 percent at the top of the distribution (Ravallion 2004b).

Figure 6.4 Growth Incidence Curves for China (1990–99) and India (1993–99)

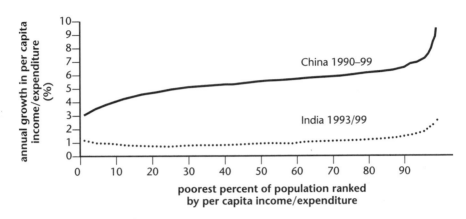

Sources: Ravallion and Chen 2003 (China, using household income); Ravallion 2004a (India, using household expenditure on consumption).

1 percent—for people around the 10th percentile, and a smaller difference between growth rates at the top (close to 2 percent) and those at the bottom (just over 1 percent) than was the case for China.

As we have noted, even large-sample, nationally representative surveys (such as used to construct figure 6.4) typically do not pick up what is happening at the extreme upper tails of the distribution. In the case of India, evidence from other sources indicates that incomes at the top end have risen dramatically. For instance, based on a study of tax returns, Banerjee and Piketty (2003) reported that the super-rich population in India—that is, those at the 99.99th percentile—experienced income growth greater than 285 percent between 1987/88 and 1999/2000.

Figure 6.5 displays the trends in income inequality for the two countries. From a cross-country perspective, India remains a relatively low-income inequality country (World Bank 2005c, 2006), but this is no longer true of China. The Gini index of income inequality for China rose from 28 percent in 1981 to 41 percent in 2003 (although not continuously) and more in some periods and provinces.[15]

---

15. Note that the latter figure is somewhat lower than past estimates for China because corrections have been made for changes in survey-valuation methods (as discussed above) and

Figure 6.5 Trends in Income Inequality, 1978–2003

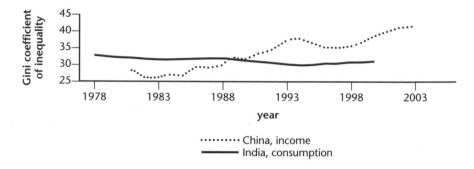

Sources: Authors' calculations (India); Ravallion and Chen forthcoming (China).

The fact that the inequality measures for China use income whereas those for India use consumption (per capita) does not account for the difference in measured inequality, as in figure 6.5. For a few years it is possible to measure inequality using consumption for China. When one does this, the consumption-based inequality measure is only slightly lower than that based on incomes, and it is still appreciably higher than for India (Chen and Ravallion 2006).

In the case of India, one finds that the Gini index rose in the 1990s, although the increase was less pronounced than in China (figure 6.5).[16] It is too early, however, to say if India is undergoing a trend increase in inequality similar to what China has experienced. As can be seen in figure 6.5, looking back over time, rising inequality in India is a recent phenomenon.[17] Indeed, there is no statistically significant trend increase in consumption inequality in India up to the early 1990s (Bruno, Ravallion, and Squire 1998).[18]

---

urban–rural cost-of-living differences, which have tended to rise over time because of higher inflation in urban areas (as price controls and subsidies were progressively removed on certain goods, including housing). Without these corrections, the estimate of the Gini index for 2003 rises to more than 45 percent, instead of 41 percent.

16. Figure 6.5 uses the National Sample Survey "thick samples" only. The thin samples for the 1990s also confirm the increase in inequality (Ravallion 2000).

17. Note that comparisons over the longer term are possible only using the uniform recall period data, using the Deaton method of correcting for the comparability problem in the 1999/2000 data.

18. At the time of writing, the 61st round of the National Sample Survey, for 2004/05, has not been released. Only preliminary tabulated results were available to us at the time of

Perceptions "on the ground" that inequality is rising markedly in India do not appear to sit easily with the impression given by figure 6.5. Popular opinion can be mistaken, but data are not perfect either. As we have noted, the survey-based numbers may well understate the relative gains to the rich, and that is consistent with the evidence from tax returns. The visible changes in consumption patterns and lifestyles that the rich have achieved may not be reflected properly in the survey-based inequality measures. Also, and possibly more important, the perception of sharply rising inequality in India also may reflect rising *absolute inequality*, as reflected in the absolute gaps between the rich and the poor, as distinct from the proportionate gaps (Ravallion 2004a). There is evidence that many people view inequality in absolute rather than relative terms (Amiel and Cowell 1999).

Sectoral and Geographic Unevenness of Growth Has Contributed to Rising Inequality

Because both Giants started their reform periods with sizable urban–rural gaps in mean living standards, the unevenness of the subsequent growth process in which urban incomes increased faster than rural incomes, is likely to have put upward pressure on aggregate inequality. The time-series data and regressions presented in Ravallion and Chen (forthcoming) provide direct evidence of this for China. Controlling for growth in rural and urban incomes, the rising urban population share has had no significant effect on aggregate inequality, and the periods when the urban–rural disparity in mean income rose (fell) were the periods when overall inequality rose (fell). But it also would seem that the rising urban–rural gap now has a salience in popular and government circles that far exceeds its likely contribution to a conventional inequality or poverty metric. This salience appears to stem in part from the (plausible) belief that the urban–rural divergence reflects (in part at least) urban biases in the reform processes and complementary public spending choices. This is reinforced by actual or perceived abuses of local political powers at the expense of poor farmers or the landless rural poor (the recurrent land disputes of land contracts and land-use conversions in rural China are examples).

Similarly, regional inequality concerns loom large in both countries, although the quantitative importance of increasing disparities across regions

writing, but they suggest that the inequality increase in India since the early 1990s that is evident in figure 6.5 has continued through to 2005, and well may have accelerated, although this should be investigated more thoroughly when the micro data become available.

(provinces and states) appears to be greater in India. Although these between-group inequalities have carried weight in policy discussions, it is important to note that growing inequality *within* both urban and rural areas have been a major component of the increase in overall inequality; for China, rising inequality within rural areas has been an important dynamic in overall inequality, whereas inequality in India has risen more within urban areas than rural areas.

The sectoral composition of GDP growth—cutting across the urban and rural divide—is also a significant predictor of changes in inequality. For instance, regressions of the sort reported in table 6.1, with share-weighted sectoral GDP growth rates as covariates, but with the change in inequality (change in the log of the Gini index) as the dependent variable, indicate that primary sector growth in China has been associated with lower inequality overall, whereas there is no correlation with growth in either the secondary or tertiary sector (Ravallion and Chen forthcoming). The regression coefficient of the change in log Gini index on the growth rate in primary sector GDP (without share weighting) is –0.478, with a t-ratio of –2.76. There is also a strong positive trend in inequality (of approximately 5 percent a year), independent of the rate of private sector growth.

How much higher would the rate of primary sector growth need to have been to stem the rise in aggregate inequality? A moving-average annual growth rate of 7.0 percent would be needed to avoid rising inequality, whereas the mean primary sector annual growth rate was under 5.0 percent between 1981 and 2001. Only in two periods (the early 1980s and the mid-1990s) were agricultural growth rates high enough to prevent rising inequality. The divergence between the actual growth rates in the primary sector GDP and the minimum needed to prevent rising inequality is particularly striking in the most recent period. The recent composition of economic growth in China clearly has been increasing inequality.

It is too early to say with confidence that India's (more recent) rise in inequality stems from similar factors. Nonetheless, we can be reasonably sure that the "urban bias" in India's growth process since reforms began has put upward pressure on overall inequality.

Why Growth Was Uneven and Why This Matters

Why was growth uneven—in the aggregate as well as sectorally and geographically—over recent decades and what are we to make of this unevenness?

Should we be concerned that segments of the population in both China and India appear to have been left behind (at least thus far)? And should we worry that inequality has risen?

These questions are more easily posed than answered because of the multiple complex processes through which uneven growth and inequality are generated and reproduced. Policies play a role, but so do initial conditions in the form of history (for example, inherited institutions) and geography (as a determinant of access to markets and public services). Economic forces undoubtedly are important, but so too are political and social factors. Answering these questions in a rigorous fashion is beyond the scope of this chapter. What we can do, however, is provide an assessment based on our interpretation of the evidence from various sources.

We will structure the discussion around a distinction between *good* and *bad* inequalities—drivers and dimensions of uneven growth that are good or bad in terms of what they imply for how the living standards of poor people evolve over time. We will argue that the Giants' postreform development paths have been influenced by and have generated both types of inequalities.

Good Inequalities

Good inequalities reflect and reinforce market-based incentives that are needed to foster innovation, entrepreneurship, and growth. Scattered evidence suggests that the rise in inequality with the introduction of market reforms in China and India at least partially reflects newly unleashed market-based incentives at work, in contrast with the earlier period of artificially low levels of inequality brought about by regulatory distortions and interventions that suppressed incentives for individual effort and innovation.

Perhaps the leading example of the role that good inequalities (and the economic incentives that underlie them) have played in China's growth is the stimulus to agricultural production in the early 1980s provided by the Household Responsibility System. Under this system, rural households were assigned plots of land and became the residual claimants on the output from that land, significantly enhancing the incentives for production. Prior to that system, land had been farmed collectively, with all members sharing the output more or less equally. Incentives for individual effort in this setting were naturally very weak, and the reforms to this system were critical in stimulating rural economic growth at the early stages of China's transition (Fan 1991; Lin 1992). Initially, these reforms were likely to have been inequality reducing because they raised rural incomes relative to incomes in urban areas. Soon, however, some farm households did better than others, depending on their farming acumen, agroclimatic conditions, and access to markets—and that put upward pressure on inequality within rural areas.

Another piece of evidence is provided by Park et al. (2004) in their analysis of the substantial increase in urban wage dispersion in China since the reform period that started around 1980. At the outset of that period, urban China had a system of fixed wage scales, allocation of labor by government, and resulting low returns to schooling (Fleisher and Wang 2004). There were few incentives for work performance or skill acquisition. From this legacy of wage compression and low labor mobility, China moved gradually in the 1990s to a market-based system featuring a dynamic nonstate sector and an increasingly open labor market. With reforms that expanded the scope for employment in a growing private sector and the emergence of a competitive labor market, wage dispersion within skill categories and experience cohorts has increased considerably, and returns to schooling have risen (Heckman and Li 2004; Park et al. 2004). Looking forward, a further implication of the emergence of a more convex structure of returns to education in postreform China (whereby the increase in returns to education has tended to be at higher levels of schooling) is that generalized increases in the level of schooling will put upward pressure on aggregate inequality, though they probably will be poverty reducing.

In India, too, there was growing wage inequality in the 1990s that was partly attributable to increasing wage disparities within educational attainment categories, and those disparities, in turn, reflected increasingly competitive product and labor markets (Dutta 2005). Another example of increasing disparities reflecting the growth-enhancing role of incentives comes from considering the increasing disparities in growth performance across Indian states during the 1990s, when some states significantly accelerated their growth and others lagged behind. Both Ahluwalia (2000) and Kohli (2006) have suggested that at least part of the increase can be attributed to the greater responsiveness of private investment flows to differences in the investment climate in various states. As Kohli (2006) noted, that responsiveness appears to have encouraged state leaders to adopt measures that would improve the business environment and woo private investment—of course, subject to the constraints imposed by state-level political considerations and capacity. This stands in contrast to earlier periods when the share of public investment in total investment was much larger.

There is evidence in India that the impact of incentives was magnified by the presence of agglomeration economies in industrial activity. Lall and Chakravorty (2005) showed that industrial diversity (which is higher in metropolitan and mixed industrial regions) produces cost-reducing effects through agglomeration economies. Therefore, private industrial units favored locating in existing high-density industrial areas, thus increasing the degree of industrial clustering. Conversely, the location decisions of state-owned industry appeared to have been much less driven by these cost considerations and may have been motivated by a desire for greater regional balance. The conclusion that Lall and Chakravorty drew is that the reforms and the scaling back of public investments, and the emergence of the private sector as the primary source of new industrial investments, contributed to higher levels of spatial inequality in industrial activity.

Bad Inequalities

The processes underway in China and India are almost certainly less benign and less automatic than the account above suggests. Geographic poverty traps, patterns of social exclusion, inadequate levels of human capital, lack of access to credit and insurance, corruption, and uneven influence simultaneously can fuel rising inequality and prevent certain segments of the population from moving out of traditional low-productivity activities. Credit market failures often lie at the root of the problem; it is poor people who tend to be most constrained in financing lumpy investments in human and physical capital. These bad inequalities—rooted in market failures, coordination failures, and governance failures—prevent individuals from connecting to markets and limit investment in human and physical capital.[19]

Here we focus on two dimensions of bad inequalities. The first relates to location in the presence of externalities, impediments to mobility, and heavy dependence of local states on local resources. These features can generate geographic poverty traps—that is, a poor household situated in a well-endowed area eventually can escape poverty, whereas an otherwise identical household living in a poor area faces stagnation or decline. This is one possible reason

---

19. World Bank (2005c, ch. 5) provided a useful overview of the arguments and evidence on how certain inequalities can be inefficient, notably when they entail unequal opportunities for advancement. Also see the excellent overview of the theoretical arguments in Aghion, Caroli, and Garcia-Peñalosa (1999).

Figure 6.6 Growth Rates at the Subnational Level Plotted against Initial Poverty Rate

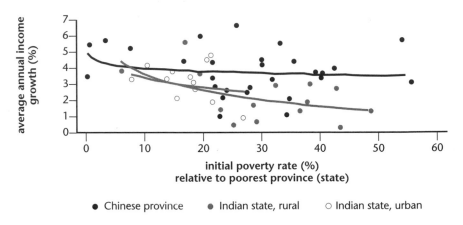

Sources: National Bureau of Statistics of China, *China Statistical Yearbook,* various years; Government of India Central Survey Organization.
Note: The lines of best fit are semi-log least-squares regression lines.

why initially poorer provinces often have seen lower subsequent growth (figure 6.6).

Although these observations from aggregate data suggest that such traps exist, they hardly are conclusive. More rigorous micro evidence of the geographic externalities that underlie such traps can be found in Jalan and Ravallion (2002) and Ravallion (2005), using farm household panel data for rural China. The geographic attributes conducive to an individual's prospects for escaping poverty include both publicly controlled endowments (such as the density of rural roads) and largely private ones (such as the extent of local agricultural development).

The second dimension of undoubted importance relates to inequalities in human resource development—often linked to credit market failures on the demand side but also reflecting governmental failures in service delivery. We argued above that the rising returns to schooling and increasing dispersion of wages represent "good" inequalities because they reflect freer labor markets with increased incentives for work and for skill acquisition. But, naturally, those with relatively little schooling and few assets or little access to credit are less able to respond to these incentives and are less well positioned to take advantage of the new opportunities unleashed by market-oriented reforms. Thus, inequalities in opportunities to accumulate human capital are "bad" inequalities in that they have retarded poverty reduction through growth in both countries.[20]

Basic schooling was far more widespread in China at the outset of the reform period than in India, and China has achieved close to universal primary education. But inequalities in educational attainment beyond primary school remain, and these have become an increasingly important source of disadvantage because a junior high school education (and, in some instances, a senior high school education) has become a de facto prerequisite for accessing nonfarm work, particularly in urban areas where wages far exceed the shadow wages in farming. Thus, lack of schooling is now a very important constraint on prospects of escaping poverty in China, as elsewhere.

India's schooling inequalities clearly have been and are larger than those of China (both at the beginning of the reform period and since) (World Bank 2005c). Unequal attainment of education has inhibited pro-poor growth. The differences we have seen in the effects of nonfarm economic growth on poverty reflect inequalities in a number of dimensions; low farm productivity, low rural living standards relative to urban areas, and poor basic education all keep poor people from participating in nonfarm sector growth (Ravallion and Datt 2002). Interstate differences in initial levels of schooling appear to have been the dominant explanation for the subsequent effects of nonfarm economic growth on poverty. As was true in China, little schooling, few assets, or little access to credit dampened people's prospects to benefit from market-based reforms.

Policy Impediments, Biases, and Neglect

Policy errors of both omission and commission have contributed to the unevenness of growth in the Giants and to the failure of growth to translate into larger positive effects on poverty and human development. These errors have been one of three forms: first, policies that impede the market function; second, policies biased in favor of particular regions or industries; and, third, policies that neglect certain spheres of activity where public intervention is necessary.

---

20. Note that the claim that inequalities in human capital are "bad" is consistent with our earlier point that certain inequalities in outcomes (reflected, for instance, in increasing wage dispersion) are "good." The latter stem from variation in returns that reflect differences in effort. The former arise from differences in endowments that are the results of both supply side governmental failures and demand side market failures (especially credit-market failures).

It has been argued that India's restrictive labor regulations and widespread preferences for small-scale industries are impediments to more broad-based growth. Although ostensibly motivated by distributive considerations, these policies instead have restricted firm growth, dampened job creation, and hindered the movement of labor out of agriculture (World Bank 2006). In a country of 1 billion people, only 8 million Indian workers are protected by such legislation, According to the World Bank (2006), "Current labor regulations seem to be protecting workers in jobs by 'protecting' other workers from having jobs" (p. 17). These regulations probably have not promoted labor absorption, and may have helped keep a much larger share of the Indian labor force in agriculture than is the case in other countries with similar shares of agricultural value added (Virmani 2005). And despite the increase in GDP growth, in recent years the rate of job creation in India has failed to keep up with increases in the size of the labor force, which has led some authors to characterize India's growth experience as jobless growth (Mehta 2003). Although these observations are suggestive, the costs of these policies to the poor remain to be quantified rigorously.

In China, impediments to the movement of labor out of agriculture through internal migration have come in part from government restrictions under the *hukou* system, by which a person must have an official registration to reside in an urban area and use its facilities. Those people born with an agricultural registration historically have had a hard time obtaining urban registration.[21] Other costs of migration facing rural households include the risk of losing one's administratively allocated land and various forms of discrimination rural migrants face in urban areas. A rough estimate of the magnitude of these policy-induced costs of migration is provided by Shi, Sicular, and Zhao (2004) who reported that even after controlling for worker characteristics and cost-of-living differences, urban wages are about 50 percent higher than rural wages. The high costs of migration underlying these gaps probably have been both poverty and inequality increasing. There are also similar restrictions on within-rural and within-urban migration.

Sizable aggregate output losses from these inequality-increasing restrictions on migration are likely. Not only is labor misallocated across sectors, but the restrictions also make it harder for China to realize agglomeration economies

---

21. Despite these migration impediments, China has had a more rapid rate of urbanization than has India. China's urban population share rose from 19 percent in 1980 to 39 percent in 2002. In India, with no such restrictions, the urban share of the population rose from 23 percent to 28 percent over the same period.

(Au and Henderson 2006). Under the (plausible) assumption that these costs of migration lower earnings in the poorer (labor-surplus) sector, they will increase poverty and inequality. Other policy biases against the poor have included public spending and industrial policies that have favored China's coastal areas over the (poorer) inland regions.

Service delivery has been an important area of policy neglect in both countries. The deficiencies of India's education system are well known, and not only from the point of view of poor people (Drèze and Sen 1995; PROBE 1999). Issues of service quality loom large in these concerns (World Bank 2006). Whereas it started from a position of greater equity in service delivery (although with large gaps between urban and rural areas), China also has experienced growing inequalities in access to health and education (Zhang and Kanbur 2005). The weaknesses and interregional disparities in service delivery in both countries can be traced, at least in part, to the large and rising disparities in public spending per capita between rich and poor areas, with rather weak fiscal redistribution and (hence) heavy dependence of local governments on local resources. We return to this point when we discuss policies.

Dynamics: How Good Inequalities Can Turn into Bad Ones

Without the appropriate institutional checks and balances, rising inequality, even if it is initially of the "good" variety, can engender phenomena such as corruption, crony capitalism, rent seeking, or efforts by those who benefit initially from the new opportunities to restrict the access of others to those opportunities or to alter the rules of the game to preserve their initial advantages.[22] Thus, bad inequalities emerge over time.

The growth and subsequent performance of China's township and village enterprises (TVEs) exemplify this dynamic at work. The emergence and growth of TVEs in various parts of China, starting in the mid-1980s, often is cited as a successful example of the country's strategy of incremental institutional innovation—in this case, economic decentralization under which local governments were given the right to establish TVEs and retain the profits generated by them (Oi 1999). The implied autonomy and control, combined with a hard budget constraint imposed from above, provided, at the outset, exactly the right incentives to invest and operate efficiently. The resultant in-

---

22. Antecedents to this argument can be found in the writings of North (1990) and Hellman (1998).

crease in rural nonfarm output and employment was spatially uneven, but probably was inequality reducing overall (given the rural base for this innovation) and likely contributed to China's growth until the mid-1990s.

However, with the proliferation of TVEs and the increased competition in various product categories, pressures emerged for local and provincial governments to increase the protection provided for the (local) markets of the TVEs under their control. These resulted in increasing impediments to interjurisdictional trade and to entry by outside firms, leading to the fragmentation of China's domestic product and factor markets and a deterioration in the investment climate in many localities (World Bank 2005c).

Perceptions and Tolerance for Inequality: The "Bad" Can Drive Out the "Good"

Bad inequalities are doubly harmful. First, they directly reduce the potential for growth because segments of the population are left behind, lacking the opportunity to connect with and contribute to the growth process. Second, persistent bad inequalities in a setting of heightened aspirations can yield negative perceptions about the benefits of reform. Because it is difficult for citizens to disentangle the sources of aggregate inequality in observed outcomes—to determine whether the underlying drivers are good or bad—societal intolerance for inequality of *any* kind emerges. That intolerance can trigger social unrest or harden resistance to further needed reforms, thereby indirectly threatening the sustainability of growth. In effect, the persistence of bad inequalities drives out the good ones.

Han and Whyte (2006) reported results of a survey of more than 3,000 Chinese adults interviewed in 2004. The survey found that 40 percent of respondents "strongly agreed" that inequality in the country as a whole is "too large," and another 32 percent "agreed somewhat" with this view. An astonishing 80 percent favored "governmental leveling" to ensure a "minimum standard of living" (split roughly equally between "strongly agree" and "agree somewhat"). Interestingly, the correlates of perceptions of unfair inequalities did not suggest that the concern was greatest among people who were most disadvantaged, such as farmers or migrants from rural areas. Also notable is that most respondents believed that education, ability, and effort were rewarded in China.

Such high levels of concern about inequality do not imply dissatisfaction with the distributive outcomes of economic reforms. But there are signs that perceptions of (or direct experience with) bad inequalities are translating into growing dissatisfaction with reforms in both China and India. Social protests about various perceived injustices are becoming common in China. In a poll conducted by the Chinese Academy of Social Sciences in 2002, 60 percent of the 15,000 respondents thought that party and government officials had benefited most from reforms, whereas other polls (cited in Pei 2006) consistently rank corruption as one of the most serious problems facing China. In examining the economic underpinnings of social unrest in China, Keidel (2005) made the point that dissatisfaction with the economic dislocations caused by reforms, which are a necessary part of engendering good inequalities, have been amplified by corruption and malfeasance within state-owned enterprises and local governments. Police records reported in official bulletins cited by Gill (2006) indicate that the number of collective protests, violent confrontations, and demonstrations deemed to be incidents of social unrest has risen nearly tenfold, from 8,300 in 1993 to almost 80,000 in 2005. Pei (2006) argued that these indications of social discontent have made it that much more difficult for China to undertake the reforms needed to address remaining structural weaknesses, notably in the financial system—reforms that a study by the International Monetary Fund (Tseng and Rodlauer 2003) suggests might be critical to sustaining growth. Thus, Pei (2006) wrote of China's "trapped transition" (p. 2).

In India, the political failure of the Bharatiya Janata Party's "Shining India" electoral campaign in 2004 has been widely attributed to its neglect of the emerging inequalities in the wake of pro-growth reforms. Such attributions often are questionable, but there is evidence from attitudinal surveys suggesting that rising inequality is a popular concern in India. In a 2004 National Election Survey, three-quarters of the respondents indicated that the reforms of the past 15 years had benefited only the rich (Suri 2004). Within India's democratic polity, such sentiments have resulted in political pressures forcing the government to postpone needed reforms (Bardhan 2005). For instance, in 2005 the government had to withdraw plans to privatize 13 leading industrial public sector undertakings. The concerns about rising inequality and slow progress against poverty also have led to various new antipoverty programs.

Preserving the Good Inequalities and Reducing the Bad Ones

Putting in place the right mix of policies and institutions to ensure that growth is sustained *and* broad-based is now high on both Giants' policy agendas. Although inequality has been prominent in the rhetoric of Indian politics for decades, it is a relatively new concern in China, only having emerged as a major concern in recent years.[23]

Should policy makers be so worried about rising inequality? Possibly it is inevitable to some degree. More than five decades ago, W. Arthur Lewis (1954) observed that the defining feature of structural transformation in economies with large pools of surplus labor is the gradual transfer of surplus labor from "traditional" low-productivity activities to "modern" high-productivity activities. He argued that this process inevitably is accompanied at first by rising levels of inequality while some people make the transition and others, at least temporarily, are left behind.[24] As Lewis put it: "Development must be inegalitarian because it does not start in every part of the economy at the same time."

If indeed what we are witnessing in China and India is such a process of structural transformation, it may only be a matter of time before people left behind catch up. Then the rise in inequality would be a transitional phenomenon—although inequality might continue to rise for several more years because the transition is occurring on a decadal scale (even for a rapidly changing society and economy such as China's). And even when the transition is complete, almost certainly there will be an increase in the steady-state inequality relative to that in the prereform period because of the good drivers of inequality set in motion by the reforms.

However, as we have argued here, there are also a number of reasons to believe that policy makers concerned with ensuring rising absolute levels of living, especially for the poor, should be concerned about the bad inequalities. In this section, we try to provide a simple conceptual framework for thinking about what Chinese and Indian policy makers should do about rising inequality, and review some of the policy options, including those recently implemented in both countries.

---

23. Han and Whyte (2006) quoted results of a 2004 survey of senior public officials, conducted by the Communist Party's Central Party School, that found income inequality to be the highest expressed concern, dominating all other issues.

24. The dimensions along which this productivity divide are manifested—rural versus urban, traditional versus modern agriculture, agriculture versus industry, and so forth—naturally will vary from context to context, even within a country. And which dimensions are most relevant clearly will matter for thinking about policy. The larger point, however, is that there is some axis along which the dualism is manifested.

Defining the Challenge and Avoiding Misdiagnoses

We take it to be self-evident that the objective is sustainable growth that benefits poor people so as to bring large and lasting reductions in the extent of absolute poverty.[25] Efforts to attenuate the bad inequalities should not undermine the drivers of good inequality to the point where the longer-term living standards of poor people are threatened. The challenge will be to identify the mix of policies that directly target the bad inequalities without undermining the good ones.

From that starting point, it is clear that we should not accept redistributive policies that come at the expense of lower longer-term living standards for poor people. Accepting that there is no aggregate trade-off between mean income and inequality does not suggest that there are no trade-offs at the level of specific policies. Reducing inequality by adding further distortions to an economy may have ambiguous effects on growth and poverty reduction. But we should not presume that there will be such a trade-off with all redistributive policies. The potential for win-win policies—promoting growth with equity—stems from the fact that some of the factors that impede growth also entail that the poor share less than is possible in the opportunities unleashed by growth. More rapid poverty reduction requires a combination of more growth, a more pro-poor pattern of growth, and success in reducing the antecedent inequalities that limit the prospects for poor people to share in the opportunities unleashed by a growth economy.

Learning from the Past: Avoiding False Trade-offs

The experience of China and India over the past quarter-century offers important lessons regarding the broad policy directions that are necessary and possible. One lesson is that an aggregate trade-off between growth and equity is often, although not always, a false one. As we have argued above, the trade-off exists for certain inequalities but not others. The right combination of policies can yield win-win-win combinations of growth, reduction in poverty, and declining (or at least nonincreasing) inequality.

---

25. On this definition of "pro-poor growth" and alternatives in the literature, see Ravallion (2004b).

Testing for the existence of an aggregate growth-equity trade-off poses a number of analytic problems. In the case of China, it is at least suggestive that on comparing growth rates with changes in inequality over time we find no sign that higher inequality has been the price of China's high growth. The correlation between the growth rate of GDP and log difference in the Gini index is only –0.05; the regression coefficient has a t-ratio of only 0.22. This test does not suggest that higher growth per se meant a steeper rise in inequality. Although the level of inequality rose at the same time that average income rose, this reflects their common time trends rather than genuine co-movement. The periods of more rapid growth did not bring more rapid increases in inequality; indeed, the periods of *falling* inequality (1981–85 and 1995–98) had the highest growth in average household income. Also, the subperiods of highest growth in the primary sector (1983–84, 1987–88, and 1994–96) did not come with lower growth in other sectors (Ravallion and Chen forthcoming). Nor do we find that the provinces with more rapid rural income growth experienced a steeper increase in inequality; if anything, the opposite was true.

The sources of higher primary sector growth rates in China were probably very different between the early 1980s and the mid-1990s. In the former period, agricultural growth was stimulated (in large part, we expect) by the much-enhanced incentives for production achieved by the introduction of the Household Responsibility System, whereby farmers became the residual claimants on farm output.[26] In the second period (the mid-1990s), the higher agricultural incomes appear to have come from a substantial reduction in implicit taxation of the sector. From the early 1980s to the mid-1990s, the government operated a domestic food grain procurement policy by which farmers were obliged to sell fixed quotas to the government at prices typically below the local market price (but they were free to sell the remainder at market prices). For some farmers this was an inframarginal tax, given that they produced more food grains than their assigned quota, but for others it affected production decisions at the margin. Ravallion and Chen (forthcoming) have provided evidence that the reduction in this implicit tax brought substantial income gains to the rural economy and especially to the poor.

---

26. The literature has pointed to the importance of the reform to this system in stimulating rural economic growth at the early stages of China's transition (Fan 1991; Lin 1992).

Helping the Rural Poor Connect to Markets

Attenuating the rise in inequality and ensuring more rapid poverty reduction will require raising incomes in the lagging rural areas of both countries, and this will require improved access to markets. The question of how this should be done often is framed as a choice between investing in poor-area development (jobs to people) or facilitating out-migration (people to jobs). Posing the choice this way almost certainly oversimplifies the problem. Migration to urban areas is likely to be pro-poor in both countries. However, out-migration often will not be feasible for poor rural households without the right sort of investments in poor areas, especially in human resource development. Conversely, although there may be scope for further increases in agricultural incomes (for example, through diversification into higher-value crops) or for promoting rural nonfarm employment, the share of agriculture in GDP is bound to decline in both countries, and geography and remoteness limit the possibilities of nonagricultural economic activity in poorer regions.

We instead frame the question in terms of identifying and correcting the underlying market and governmental failures and redressing the asset inequalities that lock the poor out of profitable opportunities for self-advancement. From this perspective, in both countries there are three priorities.

First, rural infrastructure should have a high priority. China started its reform period with very poor rural infrastructure. Fiscal and borrowing constraints meant that it was some 10 years before it was feasible to embark on a massive expansion of infrastructure, such as the roads program that started around 1990. The differences in rural infrastructure across counties have strong explanatory power for subsequent consumption growth at the farm-household level in rural China (Jalan and Ravallion 2002). Quite reasonable rates of return are possible from well-designed programs for developing infrastructure in poor rural areas (Ravallion and Chen 2005).

In India, the poor quality of rural infrastructure is widely acknowledged as an impediment to growth and poverty reduction. It is believed that there are high returns in terms of achieving more equitable growth from better rural finance and infrastructure in India, although this is not simply a matter of building facilities; instead, it raises deeper issues about the need for reforming existing institutional arrangements and provider incentives (World Bank 2006).

Second, better policies are needed for delivering quality health and education services to poor people. And third, policies are needed that allow key product and factor markets (for land, labor, and credit) to work better from the point of view of poor people. In India this includes further deregulation of formal-sector labor markets. In the case of China, reducing the policy impediments to migration and instituting legal reforms to allow a market in land-use rights in rural China (giving farmers title over land-use rights that they can sell, mortgage, or pass on to their children) are priorities. China has resisted embarking on agricultural land market reform. Neighboring Vietnam did take this step in the 1990s, and the available evidence suggests that, on balance, this reform has helped in reducing poverty (Ravallion and van de Walle 2006).

Public spending and fiscal policy will play important roles in realizing these priorities. But much depends on fiscal resource mobilization and exactly how that spending is done. Removing biases against the poor in taxation and spending policies will be essential. As we have noted, reducing the government's implicit taxation of farmers through food grain procurement quotas has been a powerful instrument against poverty in China. From this point of view, China's recent policy to give tax breaks to farmers in poor regions is surely welcome, although, without alternative revenue sources in poor areas, one can expect either a decline in the local public investments and services needed for poverty reduction or further poorly compensated expropriations of farmland by local authorities aiming to profit by selling the land to nonfarm activities.

Another continuing issue in both countries is how to enhance local-level fiscal resources in poor areas. The priority both countries now give to the decentralization of social spending will have limited impact on poverty and human development outcomes unless it comes with central efforts to ensure greater fiscal redistribution to poor regions from better-off—and increasingly better-off—regions.

Recent Initiatives

Policy makers and political leaders in both countries clearly are trying to find ways to help the rural poor connect to the process of growth. In China, the reduction and progressive elimination of agricultural taxes and fees and the limited introduction of subsidies for primary education in poor counties during the latter half of the 10th five-year plan were early indications of a significant shift in the government's priorities toward a greater emphasis on improving welfare in the countryside.[27] A key component of the plan is a package of measures aimed at what the leadership has termed "building a new socialist countryside."[28] The package calls for a systemic elimination of all agricultural taxes, but eliminating these taxes and fees raises new concerns. As we have noted, for many rural local governments, particularly in interior provinces and poorer areas, these taxes and fees have been the main source of revenues from which to finance local public services, notably health and education. This policy potentially jeopardizes not only access to and quality of health and education services, given the huge disparities in the revenue bases of local governments, but also has implications for consumption poverty. China has been relatively unique in the high savings rates found among the poor. Although a complete and detailed analysis of this question is yet to be done, common sense and conventional wisdom suggest that (apart from any intrinsic cultural proclivities for thrift) precautionary saving for uninsured health (and other) shocks, saving to finance educational costs, and life-cycle saving to fund old-age living expenses all play an important role in explaining why China's poor save so much.

The government appears to be well aware of the concerns about poor services in rural areas, and a large part of the increased spending under the "building a new socialist countryside" strategy is to be directed toward education and health services in the countryside. Among the initiatives mentioned are plans to provide several billion yuan of transfers from the central government for tens of millions of poor primary and junior middle-school students and to offer free nine-year compulsory education to rural students. The central government also plans to double its subsidies for farmers if they join a state-backed medical cooperative fund designed to reduce their financial burdens. Other elements of the plan include increased subsidy payments for farmers and further government investment in rural public works.

The Minimum Livelihood Guarantee Scheme, popularly known as *dibao*, has been the government's main response to the new challenges of social pro-

27. First announced at the meeting of the Central Party Committee of the Chinese Communist Party in October 2005, the reorientation in policy has been written into the 11th five-year plan formally adopted by the National People's Congress in its 2006 annual session.
28. According to the budget tabled at the National People's Congress, the Chinese government planned to spend 340 billion yuan ($42 billion) on agriculture, rural areas, and farmers in 2006. That amount is 14 percent more than the previous year, and represents 22 percent of the increase in government spending from levels in 2005.

tection in the more market-based economy. This scheme is intended to guarantee a minimum income in urban areas by filling the gap between actual income and a locally established "*dibao* line." In theory, this would eliminate *dibao* poverty, but the practice appears to fall well short of that goal, largely because of imperfect coverage of the target group (Chen, Ravallion, and Wang 2006). Reforming the program and expanding coverage—including to (risk-prone) rural areas—pose a number of challenges. If these plans are implemented effectively and targeted to poorer areas and poorer households in rural China, however, the prospects are promising for poverty reduction, especially in the number of consumption-poor people, during the 11th five-year plan.

There also have been a number of new initiatives in India. The Rural Employment Guarantee Act of 2005 guarantees 100 days of work a year at the minimum agricultural wage rate to at least one member of every family. This is expected to have a large impact on rural poverty. It is far from obvious that the scheme is the most cost-effective option for this purpose, however, if we consider all of the costs involved, including the forgone incomes of program participants (Murgai and Ravallion 2005). The government's 2006/07 budget also calls for substantially increased spending on rural infrastructure, job creation, health services, and education. New programs include the *Bharat Nirman* (Building India) project to provide electricity, all-weather road connectivity, and safe drinking water to all of India's villages; and *Sarva Siksha Abhiyan*, which aims to ensure a minimum standard of elementary education. These programs are not targeted explicitly to poor areas, but that is likely to be the outcome because villages that lack these services tend to be poor.

Conclusions

Aggregate economic growth is rarely balanced across regions or sectors of a developing economy, and neither China nor India is an exception. We have seen that the postreform pattern of growth has not been particularly pro-poor in either country. In China, growth in the primary sector (mostly agriculture) did more to reduce poverty and inequality than growth in either the secondary or tertiary sectors. In India, with higher initial inequality in access to land than China, agricultural growth was less important to poverty reduction than tertiary-sector growth. In both countries, there has been a marked geographic unevenness in the growth process, with numerous lagging regions, including some of those that started off among the poorest. In recent times, overall inequality has been rising in both countries.

India's poor did not start the current reform period with the same advantages as did China's poor, in terms of access to land and education. Persistent inequalities in human resource development and access to essential infrastructure within both countries, but probably more so in India, are impeding the prospects for poor people to share in the aggregate economic gains spurred by reforms. The geographic dimensions of their inequalities and the associated disparities in fiscal resources and government capabilities loom large as policy concerns for the future in both countries.

In the future, high and rising inequality will make it harder for either country to maintain its past rate of progress against poverty. However, it is not particularly useful to talk about "inequality" as a homogeneous entity when discussing appropriate policy responses. Policy needs to focus on the specific dimensions of inequality that create or preserve unequal opportunities for participating in the gains from economic growth. Arguably both countries are seeing a rise in these bad inequalities over time as the good inequalities (conducive to efficient growth) turn into bad ones, and the bad inequalities drive out the good ones.

Although both countries need to be concerned about the bad inequalities we have pointed to, we suspect that China bears the greater near-term risk that rising inequality will jeopardize growth. The Chinese authorities have been able to compensate for rising inequality by achieving high growth rates; arguably, it is the rising inequality that fuels growth in China, through the political economy of maintaining "social stability." The catch is that the emerging bad inequalities in China will make it harder to promote the growth needed to compensate for those inequalities. Maintaining sufficient growth will require even greater efficacy of the policy levers used to promote growth.

Whether the problem of rising inequality is or is not addressed successfully, there are likely to be implications for the rest of the world. If the problem is not addressed then there is a risk that the high growth rates will become much harder to maintain, with spillover effects for trade and growth elsewhere. If it is addressed, and depending on exactly how this is done, there may be some short-term costs to growth, although redressing the bad inequalities would be good for growth. There also may be consequences for the pattern of trade, such as through a change in the sectoral composition of growth; for example, in both countries there appears to be potential for cash crop expansion, which would attenuate one important source of concern about rising inequality, and it can be expected that a non-negligible share of this expansion in domestic cash crop output would be exported.

The new initiatives under way in both countries are probably steps in the right direction, although continuous evaluative research will be needed on the efficacy of these approaches, relative to alternative strategies. There are important but poorly resolved issues concerning the appropriate balance between different types of interventions. But an even harder challenge remains: to improve governance—capacity, accountability, and responsiveness—notably (but not only) at the local level. If this challenge is left unmet, the ultimate efficacy of any of the initiatives described here will be questionable.

CHAPTER 7

Governance and Economic Growth

Philip Keefer

China and India highlight the profound importance for economic growth and poverty reduction of allowing private firms to compete in markets from which they previously were barred and of providing the complementary government services, such as infrastructure, that promote economic productivity. Earlier chapters in this volume have made that clear. This chapter identifies a second lesson that has received less attention: the experience of these two large, but strikingly different, countries underlines the importance of the governance environment for growth and development. In addition, although the political underpinnings of secure governance apparently are very different across the two countries, they share an important characteristic: checks and balances at the top levels of government.

One common definition of governance focuses on outcomes—the extent to which governments enact and implement policies in the interests of all citizens. Another definition focuses on the extent to which governments have incentives to adopt and enforce policies in the interests of all citizens, based on the political institutions and dynamics that determine governance outcomes. One set of governance indicators covering the period 1996 through 2004—that of the World Bank (Kaufmann, Kraay, and Mastruzzi 2005)—embraces both definitions. The indicators *voice and accountability* and *political instability and violence* are related more closely to the political conditions that determine governance outcomes. India scores significantly higher than China on the voice measure and significantly lower on the political stability measure, both scores reflecting the existence of competitive elections in India.[1]

---

1. For example, India is above the 50th percentile and China is below the 25th percentile of all countries on the voice measure.

The governance indicators also include four outcome measures: (1) government effectiveness, (2) regulatory quality, (3) the rule of law, and (4) control of corruption. These outcomes affect development in numerous ways. This chapter addresses their effects on the security of property rights, which is a key driver of economic growth and most often is represented by variables such as government effectiveness, the rule of law, and corruption control. China has ranked consistently higher than India with regard to government effectiveness and, in 2004, with respect to corruption control, but consistently lower than India with respect to the rule of law. Despite the significant differences between China and India with respect to voice, however, none of these outcome differences is statistically significant.

Two puzzles occupy the analysis here. First, what has enabled the Giants to grow rapidly despite the presence of quite average governance outcomes? Fast growth, and extraordinary growth in China, has been accompanied by strictly average governance indicators (right around the 50th percentile, according to the World Bank governance indicators). Poor countries might infer from these experiences that countries can fall considerably short of achieving good governance and still grow rapidly. The analysis below indicates that this conclusion is incorrect. Governance outcomes in China and India, although only average overall, were better than average when compared with those of other poor countries. The difference had a material effect on the Giants' growth, relative to other such economies. Moreover, China and India have benefited from large markets and an abundance of low-cost labor that attracted investment despite merely average governance outcomes. Countries with smaller markets are likely to require significantly more aggressive measures to improve their policy and governance environment to achieve similar growth. Finally, growth in both countries did not occur until meaningful improvements in governance occurred in the late 1970s and early 1980s.

The second puzzle addressed here is why China and India exhibit similar governance outcomes but entirely distinct political institutions and forms of competition? Poor countries might infer from this that political institutions are irrelevant for good governance. The evidence presented below suggests that this inference also is incorrect. At the same time as the two countries pursued policy changes that are widely and correctly credited with triggering growth, they experienced broadly similar political changes, particularly the introduction of greater political checks and balances on the top leadership. These political checks, though comprising vastly different formal institutions, limited the discretion of leaders and laid the groundwork for improved governance.

Fast Growth and Average Governance: Governance Still Matters

Growth took off in both China and India in the early 1980s. In China, per capita growth was approximately 8.0 percent a year in the 1980s, twice that of the 1970s. India's growth accelerated by a similar margin, rising from close to zero in the 1970s to 3.5 percent in the 1980s. India grew approximately twice as fast as the median country, and China grew approximately *five* times faster than the median country. On the surface, it is difficult to discern the role of governance in these growth explosions. It is not possible to use the World Bank governance indicators to examine country-level governance and growth because they go back only to 1996. Instead, we can employ a widely used and closely related index of governance outcomes from Political Risk Services' *International Country Risk Guide* (ICRG) to compare China and India with other countries (see Knack and Keefer 1995).

That index is the sum of *bureaucratic quality*, *rule of law*, and *corruption*, which correspond to the World Bank governance indicators of government effectiveness, the rule of law, and control of corruption. The maximum score on the index is 18. At the beginning of the 1980s, the governance index calculated from ICRG was 9.0 for India and 9.3 for the world as a whole. At the beginning of the 1990s, the index stood at 9.6 for the world, at 10.0 for China, and at 7.1 for India.

Microeconomic evidence from China reinforces the conclusion that growth has proceeded despite a merely average governance environment. Cai, Fang, and Xu (2005) found that firms make large payments to government officials (allocated to the budget item "entertainment and traveling costs" in company accounts) to offset bureaucratic burdens and the threat of opportunistic behavior by governments. Political intervention is a concern for firm managers and it affects business decisions. Nee and Opper (2006) analyzed a survey of 72 firms listed on the Shanghai Stock Exchange, asking about involvement either by government agencies or officials of the Communist Party of China (CPC) in 63 different firm decisions, ranging from finance and investment to personnel and external relationships. On average, firms reported some involvement in all of these decisions. They also presented evidence that the power of government bureaucrats and party authorities over firm decisions is associated negatively with firm return on assets and equity.

At the same time, good relations with the government are essential to credit access. Using data from the World Bank's 2003 investment climate survey of China, Nee and Opper (2006) found a striking reliance on the government's administrative assistance in the loan process. More than 40 percent of state-owned enterprises, collectively owned firms, private firms, and individually owned firms that received government assistance also had a bank loan; only 15 percent of those that did not report assistance had a loan. Similarly, 32 percent of private firms with chief executive officers who held official positions in the CPC received credit, compared with 17 percent of the firms lacking this status.

Similar evidence is not available to document the effects of specific governance lapses on firm behavior in India, although it is clear that access to basic economic inputs often is unrelated to market forces. For example, firm access to credit from state-owned banks, which control the lion's share of credit in India, seems largely unrelated to firm profitability or to changes in firm profitability (Banerjee, Cole, and Duflo 2003).[2]

Although Chinese and Indian governance outcomes were only average, their experience gives other poor nations three reasons to redouble efforts to improve governance outcomes. First, China and India achieved better governance outcomes than did most other poor countries. On a scale running from zero to 18, actual governance levels in China and India exceeded those of countries with similar incomes per capita by roughly 3 and 2 points in 1985 and 1990, respectively.[3]

Second, as is well known, governance outcomes matter for growth. Reiterating this amply documented conclusion, table 7.1 offers the results of regressions that examine the correlates of per capita economic growth (in constant local currency) over the period 1980–2004 in a cross-section of countries.[4] In columns 1 and 4 of table 7.1, beginning of period income per capita, gover-

---

2. Although credit rationing is clearly significant in India, Mengistae, Xu, and Yeung (2006) found that Chinese firms are actually more responsive to credit access than Indian firms. Using World Bank investment climate data, they found in both countries that firms in cities exhibiting better average firm access to a bank credit line (overdraft protection) are more productive and exhibit faster growth in employment and manufacturing value added. The effect, however, is much stronger for Chinese firms.
3. Based on simple regressions of governance indicators on income per capita and country dummies.
4. The log of initial income yields similar results, as does the use of exchange rate–weighted initial income rather than purchasing power parity–adjusted initial income. These differences are 1.5 standard deviations in excess of the average lower-income country.

Table 7.1 Correlates of Growth, 1980–2004

Dependent variable[a]	India			China		
	(1)	(2)	(3)	(4)	(5)	(6)
China (1 = yes, 0 = no)				0.050 (8.10)	0.049 (7.44)	0.007 (0.37)
India (1 = yes, 0 = no)	0.018 (4.79)	0.018 (4.59)				
Income per capita (beginning of period; 1,000s of constant, PPP-adjusted dollars)	-0.0023 (6.40)	-0.002 (4.80)	-0.029 (2.61)	-0.0002 (6.33)	-0.0002 (4.62)	
Population (beginning of period, 100 millions)			0.008 (5.22)			0.006 (3.05)
Total income (beginning of period trillions of constant, PPP-adjusted dollars)			-0.005 (2.82)			-0.004 (2.29)
Governance index (beginning of period)	0.0016 (3.31)		0.001 (1.89)	0.0016 (3.34)		0.001 (1.81)
Percent of population 14 years and under (beginning of period)	-0.0016 (3.57)	-0.002 (4.62)	-0.0005 (1.22)	-0.0015 (3.46)	-0.0019 (4.51)	-0.0005 (1.29)
Percent of population rural (beginning of period)	0.00005 (0.56)	0.00005 (0.50)	0.0002 (1.68)	0.00005 (0.53)	0.00004 (0.47)	0.0002 (1.68)
Gross secondary school enrollment (beginning of period)	0.00015 (0.23)	0.00015 (1.18)	0.0002 (1.27)	0.0002 (1.33)	0.0002 (1.31)	0.0002 (1.22)
1980s (1 = yes, 0 = 1990–2004)	-0.006 (1.82)	-0.006 (1.70)	-0.008 (2.24)	-0.006 (1.74)	-0.005 (1.62)	-0.008 (2.28)
Number of countries	193 (112)	193 (112)	193 (112)	193 (112)	193 (112)	193 (112)
R^2	0.35	0.32	0.27	0.36	0.33	0.26

Sources: World Bank 2005b, World Development Indicators; International Country Risk Guide.

Note: PPP = purchasing power parity. The t-statistics appear in parentheses. Ordinary least-squares with robust standard errors (clustered). The governance index is the sum of Political Risk Service's International Country Risk Guide corruption, bureaucratic quality, and rule of law indicators. Constant not reported. A positive coefficient on the India or China variables indicates that growth is faster than predicted by the other control variables; a negative sign indicates that it is slower than predicted.

a. Per capita income growth, constant local currency, periods 1980–89 and 1990–2004.

nance, and population 14 years of age and under exhibit a large and significant association with growth.

These regressions explain about half of India's growth—the "India" coefficient indicates that 1.8 percent of India's yearly per capita growth is unexplained; and they explain less than half of China's actual annual growth (8.7 percent)—the "China" coefficient indicates that China's actual yearly per capita income growth was 5 percent faster than can be explained by its income per capita, demographic, governance, and other characteristics. We do not expect the Giants' extraordinary growth to be explained by country characteristics, such as governance, in which the two countries are merely average. Consistent with this, whether we take governance into account (in regressions 1 and 3) or not (in regressions 2 and 5), the fraction of Chinese and Indian growth that is unexplained remains the same.[5] Making comparisons with other poor countries rather than with all countries, however, we can infer from table 7.1 that Chinese governance outcomes relative to those of other poor countries enabled it to grow approximately 0.75 percent a year faster than those other countries over the period 1980–2004.

Third, China and India enjoy extraordinary potential market size that other poor countries cannot replicate and that offsets the entrepreneurial risks in weak governance environments. Holding the policy environment constant, we would expect foreign investment to gravitate to countries where the prospects of future growth are highest. Fan et al. (2006) compared foreign direct investment (FDI) received by China with that received by the rest of the world. They conclude that the burst of FDI into China in the 1990s was driven essentially by high expected growth (as represented by high past growth)—that is, by the enormous opportunities in the Chinese market that largely were opened to foreign investors by policy measures undertaken in the late 1980s and early 1990s. FDI into China is perhaps 80 percent greater than into comparator countries because of the expected rates of return. This effect dominates the (also large) influence of the institutional environment, which suppresses FDI in China by approximately 30 percent.[6]

Columns 3 and 6 in table 7.1 also shed light on this question. These regressions disaggregate two measures of market size, total income and total popula-

5. The governance variable is missing for China for the 1980s.
6. Huang (forthcoming) will argue that Chinese policy has been much friendlier to FDI than to domestic investment. This finding reinforces the essential point: foreign investors have flocked to China because high expected rates of return offset a governance regime in which property and contractual rights were moderately insecure.

tion. Country income captures two offsetting effects: the market is smaller in countries with low total incomes, thereby deterring investment, but poorer countries have lower wages and greater potential for catching up, thereby raising growth rates. Total population is an indicator of both the size of the market for a key input—labor—and the potential size of the market if per capita incomes grow—that is, the size of the option value of a current investment in the country. From columns 3 and 6 in table 7.1, we see that every increase of 100 million people in the total population is associated with a 0.6–0.8 percent increase in the annual growth of per capita income, consistent with the advantages of larger potential markets for products and larger labor markets. Every trillion-dollar *decline* in total income is associated with a 0.4–0.5 percent increase in annual growth.

These regressions offer indirect evidence that market size offsets weak governance. First, the governance coefficient drops by a third after controlling for market size. Second, Chinese growth is explained almost entirely in column 6: when policy reforms allowed the market to be exploited, potential rates of return dwarfed governance risks. In India, on the other hand, where policy reforms were less dramatic, more directly accounting for market size *reverses* the sign of the India coefficient. Rather than growing 1.8 percent faster than expected in columns 1 and 2, Indian growth was 2.9 percent *slower* than its market size would have predicted.[7]

One might argue that the market advantages of China and India are overstated here. Markets in both countries are splintered by uneven transportation networks and protective trade barriers set up by regions within these countries. But such barriers exist as well in small countries and often are worse.[8]

In addition, investors in China and India may have sought out these countries primarily for their export-based production facilities. Exports as a share of gross domestic product (GDP) rose from approximately 10 percent in 1980

---

7. Earlier "miracle" countries with weak governance environments, such as the Republic of Korea in the 1960s or Indonesia, relied much less on large markets to offset governance disadvantages, in contrast to the general experience summarized in table 7.1 These countries also were more likely to solve the governance–investment problem by relying for investment on a small number of families with close ties to the regime and/or military. Ultimately, in most cases, these institutional arrangements were unstable; in some cases, institutional changes eventually extended a secure governance environment to a larger fraction of citizens.

8. Although much smaller than its two giant neighbors, Nepal confronts worse transportation constraints because of its geography, and, like Chinese and Indian locales, Nepali towns have been known to apply such internal trade barriers as octroi taxes on goods passing through them.

to approximately 20 percent in 2000 of GDP in China, and from 6 percent to 12 percent in India. Over that period, however, per capita incomes nearly quintupled in China and more than doubled in India. Thus, although household consumption remained at approximately 50 percent of GDP in China and dropped from 74 percent to 65 percent in India, much economic growth went to satisfy the growth in domestic consumption. At the same time, even exporters have several reasons to care about domestic market size. These reasons range from any agglomeration economies that are more likely to exist in larger markets to more liquid labor markets (any single new entrant is unlikely to increase wages). Kochhar et al. (2006) have attributed Indian success to the virtues of experimentation and learning by doing; the number of experiments that an economy can conduct also rises with the size of the economy.

The evidence here strongly supports the conclusion that poor countries cannot afford to use Chinese and Indian growth experiences as reasons to downplay governance: on average, governance outcomes matter for growth; Chinese and Indian governance outcomes in any case were better than those of other poor countries; and merely matching the average governance outcomes in China and India likely will not be enough because most poor countries cannot offer the potential returns of large markets.

The next section of this chapter uses historical evidence from China and India to reach this same conclusion in another way: China and India began to grow rapidly after they had improved the governance environment significantly, even if only to average levels. It also uses the Giants to help identify the conditions that countries with and without competitive elections must meet to produce good governance outcomes.

Beneath the Cross-country Data: Political Economy and Governance Outcomes

Because growth erupted in China and India in the 1980s, we would like to know what happened to governance throughout the 1970s. There are unfortunately few data to track governance outcomes from the 1970s onward, but we can trace the evolution of Giants' political characteristics that, like voice and accountability in the World Bank governance indicators, shape the incentives of governments to pursue good governance outcomes.

The starting point is the puzzle that the voice and accountability indicators for China and India are dramatically different, but their governance outcomes are not. This finding is surprising. One might expect competition for the electoral support of a fully enfranchised citizenry to generate greater interest among political leaders in broad social welfare, including the pursuit of good governance outcomes. An influential literature argues precisely this: elections prevent elites from expropriating non-elites, thereby encouraging non-elite investment and growth (as in Acemoglu and Robinson 2006). In fact, governance scores in countries with competitive elections differ little, on average, from those in countries without.

In 1995, for example, the governance score of countries in the 50th governance percentile of all countries with competitive elections was nearly the same as the score in the 50th percentile of countries without competitive elections (11.0 versus 10.7 out of 18).[9] On the one hand, having competitive elections is not enough to ensure improved governance outcomes; on the other hand, in countries lacking competitive elections, leaders may have incentives to create institutions that strengthen the governance environment. Most measures of voice and democracy do not take these nuances into account. The cases of India and China highlight the obstacles and opportunities in both types of countries to improve governance outcomes.

The challenge in generating good governance outcomes can be framed as a question: what fraction of the population feels secure from the threat of opportunistic behavior by government? The discussion in this chapter points to a number of political characteristics of countries that influence the answer to this question. Political checks and balances are one key characteristic. Non-elected leaders can enlarge this fraction to the extent that they can build large parties with internal institutions, including internal political checks and balances on leader discretion, which make party members more secure from threats of arbitrary treatment by the leader. This was the Chinese solution to its governance problems. Political checks and balances in democracies also can expand the coverage of the good governance umbrella by expanding the range of social interests with the authority to veto arbitrary government initiatives. Although India increasingly has benefited from political checks and balances since 1977, and particularly since 1989, events of the early 1970s dismantled both external and internal checks and balances on the governing leadership of the Congress Party. In both countries, political checks and bal-

---

9. Countries are categorized as having competitive elections when they score the maximum (7) on both the executive and legislative indexes of electoral competitiveness from the Database of Political Institutions (Beck et al. 2001).

ances were weak in the 1970s, a decade of slow growth, and strengthened during the 1980s and 1990s, periods of faster growth.

Even in countries with competitive elections and checks and balances, political market imperfections can weaken political incentives to pursue good governance outcomes (see Keefer and Khemani 2005). For example, when citizens are not well informed about the connection between political decisions on particular issues and their own welfare, as is often the case with governance reforms, politicians are unlikely to compete on those policy dimensions. Lack of education and of access to information, time lags, and a noisy economic environment full of shocks all can contribute to information problems. Another political market imperfection exists when parties cannot make political promises that are broadly credible to all citizens. Parties resort to appeals to those groups of citizens to whom they *can* make credible promises—but when those groups are narrow, incentives to improve governance for all citizens dwindle (Keefer and Vlaicu 2005). Again, isolated and poor populations are less likely to know of the relationship between political actions and the governance environment, or to appreciate the importance of the country's governance environment for their own personal well-being. Similarly, in countries riven by social tension, the costs of making credible political promises to all citizens dwarf those of making promises targeted to individual groups. Each political competitor belongs to one of the groups and therefore is mistrusted by all the others.

Political market imperfections explain why political decision making in India is more likely to focus on subsidies and macroeconomic policy than on better-quality social services, better governance outcomes, and the regulatory environment for business: the political contribution to citizen welfare is harder for citizens to discern in these latter cases, allowing elected officials to be more sensitive to the pleadings of special interests opposed to reform.

Political Change and Governance in India

Most explanations of Indian growth focus on the major policy reforms of 1991. Average annual per capita growth in India, however, was about the same in the 1980s as in the 1990s (approximately 3.5 percent), compared with less than 1 percent in the 1970s.[10] Rodrik and Subramanian (2005) found no

---

10. Income is measured in constant local currency. Volatility also dropped significantly; the standard deviation of annual growth in the 1970s was more than twice the standard deviation in the 1980s and 1990s. Volatility in the 1970s is another sign of weak democratic in-

evidence of significant policy changes in the early 1980s to explain growth in that decade. Kohli (2006) has argued that there were modest policy reforms, but their importance was to signal a shift away from a redistributive development model to one friendlier to incumbent private business interests. This section points to a complementary explanation of faster growth in the 1980s. In the 1970s, both the policy and governance environments steadily deteriorated. This deterioration began to reverse just prior to the onset of growth in the 1980s.

The policy deterioration of the 1970s is well known. It was sparked by the election of 1967, in which the Congress Party's share of seats in the Parliament dropped by 19 percent, to a majority of 54 percent. As electoral weakness reduced the costs of defecting, the party began to splinter. Indira Gandhi chose to consolidate support within the interventionist wing of the party by dramatically increasing the state's role in economic activity. The government nationalized the major banks and steadily increased the profile of state-owned enterprises. Shanker and Nayak (1983) estimated that state-owned companies' gross value added in 1968–69 rose from 15 percent of the combined value added of government companies and of nongovernment, nonfinancial medium- and large-size public and private limited companies to 26 percent in 1977–78. The "License Raj" also expanded dramatically. In 1970, all large enterprises were required to register with the new Ministry of Company Affairs and could not expand without approvals from a range of ministries and, in problematic cases, from the prime minister herself. In 1976—marking at least eight successive years of growing restrictions on entrepreneurial activity—amendments to the Industrial Disputes Act obliged firms with 300 or more workers to seek government approval before laying off workers (Frankel 2005).

Weakened governance during the 1970s is less often discussed, although some of the policy changes themselves were clear evidence of it. The License Raj was not applied transparently and bank owners were not fully compensated for the losses they suffered from nationalization. Furthermore, the political drivers of good governance outcomes in India weakened in the 1970s. Events of that decade reduced both external political checks and balances and internal party checks and balances on Congress Party leaders.

Prior to 1967, competing interests had significant influence over internal Congress Party decision making; these interests limited the discretion any

---

stitutions, as Quinn and Woolley (2001) showed that democracies exhibit less volatile growth more generally.

one of them could exercise. Leaders of the Congress Party ranged from the anti-industrial Mahatma Gandhi wing of the party, to the pro-industrial but socialist wing represented by Jawaharlal Nehru, to militants prepared to take up arms in pursuit of redistributionist aims. Less ideological leaders—those who managed the Congress' well-developed clientelist network that was key to voter mobilization—also were prominent. Frankel (2005) described this network in the following terms:

> In general, national political parties did not recruit from among the poor peasantry. Instead, they accommodated themselves to the existing power structures as the easiest way to win votes. . . . [T]he major beneficiaries of [adult suffrage] were the most prosperous sections of the dominant landowning castes, individuals who could exploit a wide network of traditional caste, kinship, and economic ties (of dependent sharecroppers and laborers) to organize a large personal following (p. 20).

The interests of these landowning castes therefore were amply represented in Congress and could veto policy change. In 1946, the most powerful man in the Congress Party was Sardar Vallabhai Patel, Mahatma Gandhi's chief lieutenant, who was responsible for building up the local party. He frequently prevailed in conflicts with Nehru (for example, by blocking socialist candidates for Congress Party leadership [Frankel 2005]), and only when Patel died was Nehru able to push forward in promoting state-led industrialization (Nayar 1990).

In November 1969, the Congress Party attracted fewer than half of the votes cast (43.7 percent), dropping below 50 percent for the first time ever. Gandhi's opponents left the party, weakening internal party checks and balances.[11] Shortly thereafter, Gandhi took key functions of government out of the control of cabinet ministers and put them under her direct control. In 1970, she transferred 60 of the 100 sections of the home ministry (and 7 of 14 joint secretaries) to the cabinet secretariat, bringing under her personal oversight the major administrative, policy, and intelligence services of the national government (Frankel 2005).

The split in the party need not have led to a reduction in political checks on the exercise of executive discretion if it had forced the Congress (I) Party to govern in coalition, replacing intraparty with external checks; if it had strengthened the electoral challenge to Gandhi's party; or if she had allowed intraparty

---

11. She formed the Congress (R) Party (later I, for Indira); senior Congress officials formed the Congress (O) (Organization) Party.

checks in Congress (I) to gain strength. None of these possibilities happened. External constraints dissipated in the 1971 elections, when the refashioned Congress (I) Party increased its parliamentary majority to 68 percent.

Internally, crisis made it difficult to construct intraparty agreements that were essential to developing internal political checks and balances. In addition to foreign policy crises of the 1970s, India was struck by monsoon failure and food shortages, an economic crisis starting in 1973 triggered by the quadrupling of oil prices, and inflation exceeding 23 percent over the period 1973–74 (Frankel 2005, p. 647; Brass 1990, p. 40). Large and sometimes violent public demonstrations accompanied these shocks. Massive student-led demonstrations in Gujarat and Bihar led the government to send 40,000 troops to Bihar. Activists and demonstrators eventually earned the support of Jayaprakash Narayan, widely respected for his proximity to Mahatma Gandhi and his advocacy of the poor; and after evolving into the "J.P. Movement," the activism became an India-wide movement to challenge Indira Gandhi's government within and outside the parliament (Frankel 2005). In 1974, 700,000 railway workers went on strike—half of the sector's workforce; the strike ended 20 days later, after the government had arrested most of the union leaders and 20,000 of the workers (Frankel 2005, p. 530). In 1975, the first post-Independence assassination of a cabinet minister occurred in the bomb explosion that killed railway minister L. N. Mishra (Frankel 2005).

Faced with a foreshortened political horizon and the high costs of retaining support even inside the Congress Party, in 1975 Indira Gandhi declared an emergency, definitively relaxing both external and internal party constraints on her authority. Thousands of local-level party workers were detained, and her principal opponents were arrested (Brass 1990). She postponed parliamentary elections scheduled for 1976, thereby weakening legislative checks on executive authority (Brass 1990, p. 42). She also arranged for the late-1976 passage of the 42nd Amendment to the Constitution, which made the cabinet's advice binding on the president and removed the president as a constraint on prime ministerial discretion.

The 42nd Amendment also undercut judicial oversight of the executive. This oversight had been vigorous. For example, the Supreme Court rejected almost immediately the 1969 bank nationalization and government efforts to abolish the privy purses and privileges of ex-princely rulers. Precipitating the declaration of emergency, in June 1975 the High Court of Allahabad found Prime Minister Gandhi guilty of illegal electoral manipulation and ordered her to vacate her seat. The 42nd Amendment gave primacy to Directive Principles over Fundamental Rights. Directive Principles were constitutional goals related to the pursuit of social justice, and whose pursuit was subject to substantial executive discretion. This undercut much of the constitutional basis of judicial review. For example, the Court had used Fundamental Rights to justify the defense of property rights in the case of bank nationalization and princely privileges (Frankel 2005).

In sum, the 1970s witnessed not only significant policy deterioration with respect to private sector activity, but also deterioration in the governance environment—bank nationalization and a reduction in the checks and balances operating on the executive. It is not surprising that growth was slow in the 1970s, nor that even a gradual flattening and reversal of the hostile investment trend of policy and governance was associated with the resumption of growth in the 1980s.

Governance and Policy Reforms at the End of the 1970s

These negative trends came to a halt and began to reverse direction in 1977, when Prime Minister Gandhi called for new elections. These elections brought the Janata coalition into government in a major defeat for the Congress Party. This government implemented modest policy reforms that signaled the end of policy deterioration: coverage under the open general licensing list was expanded; access to credit and foreign exchange was liberalized; delicensing, and measures that expanded the range of products that could be produced under any given license were undertaken; and price controls were relaxed somewhat (see Kohli 2006; Kochhar et al. 2006). Also, the Communist Party decided to abandon the alliance with Congress that it had maintained since 1969, further evidence for entrepreneurs of the shift away from ever-deeper government intervention in the economy (Frankel 2005).

The governance environment improved as well. Formal, institutional checks and balances were restored. The Janata government repealed the 42nd Amendment and passed the 44th Amendment, largely restoring the pre-emergency constitution and the predominance of Fundamental Rights. The Supreme Court reestablished its right to review the consistency of laws with the Fundamental Rights of the constitution in the Minerva Mills case in May 1980 (Frankel 2005).

None of this is to say that India in the 1980s was a model of coalition government and institutionalized decision making. The Janata government, which lasted only until 1981, used all the formal and informal instruments at its disposal in attempting to remove state governors who had come to office under the Congress era. In the 1984 elections, following religious riots and the assassination of Indira Gandhi, the Congress Party won more than 70 percent of the seats in the national legislature. In his role as the new prime minister, Rajiv Gandhi was able to govern unchecked by the presence of coalition partners.

Nevertheless, the 1980s differed from the period following the 1971 elections for one significant reason: the 1977 elections proved that the Congress Party could be removed from office, thus establishing for the first time that electoral accountability was firmly entrenched in India. These elections were the first to demonstrate that no government in India was safe from poor performance and that multiparty competition was resilient in the face of such extra-institutional intrusions as mass demonstrations and declarations of emergency.[12] Even enjoying large parliamentary majorities, therefore, the governments of the 1980s confronted an electoral check on their actions that had not existed previously.

One final piece of evidence supports this conclusion. Business Environment Risk Intelligence (BERI) is an analysis and forecasting service that reported information on 45 countries in the late 1970s, among them India but not China. One of the dimensions of governance that BERI tracked was the quality of contract enforcement. This variable rose (that is, improved) from 1.15 to 1.93 (on a 4.0-point scale) from 1979 to 1980. This rise was not the product of a change in methodology or a secular improvement, for the median of the whole sample of countries (45) dropped slightly (2.43 to 2.30).

Governance and Policy Reforms in the 1990s

In 1991, the minority Congress government, led by Narashimha Rao, moved strongly to free economic activity from restraints established in the 1970s. The initial impetus behind the reforms was crisis: foreign lending on which India had relied in the 1980s dried up, debt service rose to 21 percent of current account receipts, and interest payments grew to 20 percent of government expenditures. The Rao government, however, issued executive orders that went well beyond the narrow fiscal sources of crisis, cutting back the number of industries reserved for the public sector; removing private sector compulsory licensing for starting or expanding enterprises; devaluing the ru-

---

12. The 1967 election sometimes is taken as a watershed that ended Congress hegemony. However, although the Congress Party received only 41 percent of the popular vote, its closest challenger, the Bharatiya Jana Sang, received merely 9 percent.

pee; allowing for current account convertibility; removing quantitative import quotas and reducing tariffs; lifting restrictions on foreign investment; and allowing foreign financial institutions to make portfolio investments in India's two stock markets.

These reforms were sufficient to sustain the growth rates of the 1980s without incurring the fiscal and trade disequilibria of policies of the 1980s—but not more. One reason is that substantial policy distortions remained. Subsidies remained large; state-owned enterprises were burdensome; bad loans in the banking sector were significant; and regulatory rigidity in the labor market was extreme. Reforms in these areas all required the agreement of the Lok Sabha, the lower house of India's Parliament, and they were not undertaken (Kohli 2006). The World Bank's Doing Business indicators monitor aspects of countries' legal and regulatory environments that directly affect the costs of entrepreneurial activity. By 2004, India's employment rigidity and cost of enforcing contracts were still significantly worse than those of other countries, even controlling for income per capita. India's percentile rank among all countries with respect to regulatory quality, as assessed by the World Bank governance indicators, fell from 44th to 27th from 1996 to 2004.

Governance outcomes appear to have improved during the 1990s, although the data are somewhat ambiguous. The *International Country Risk Guide* reports that India's increase in rule of law, one of the three measures used earlier to compile the 18-point governance indicator, was 3.0 or less until 1992 and 4.0 (out of 6.0) from 1994 onward. Bureaucratic quality subsequently increased from 4.0 in 1996 to 5.0 (out of 6.0). Corruption, however, changed little in the 1980s and 1990s, and it worsened in 2001 and subsequently. In addition, according to the World Bank governance indicators, India's percentile rank with respect to government effectiveness, the rule of law, or control of corruption changed little from 1996 through 2004.

Political checks and balances, however, have become more ingrained in Indian political life. Political fragmentation, which raises the likelihood of coalition governments, increased significantly from the 1980s to the 1990s. The probability that two randomly selected legislators would be from different parties rose from approximately 50 percent in the 1980s to 70 percent in the 1990s (Beck et al. 2001). Coalition governments became imperative in the 1990s: the probability that two legislators in the government coalition were from different parties was less than 2 percent in the 1980s and more than 30 percent in the 1990s. The risk of expropriatory government action therefore declined in the 1990s, consistent with the ICRG reports of improved rule of law.

Other political underpinnings of good governance outcomes, particularly political market imperfections, have changed less rapidly. Parties continued to have difficulty basing their electoral appeal on growth-related policies, including governance reforms. These policies are hard for poor, poorly educated, or isolated voters to observe. In addition, the benefits of growth reforms cut across social lines. The policy preferences that emerge from this political environment are clientelist promises or easily targeted government policies, such as subsidies (see Wilkinson 2006a). For example, not only are market-opening reforms difficult; so also are efforts to improve the quality of the bureaucracy, reduce corruption, or eliminate continuing significant regulatory impediments to growth. These efforts are more difficult because they conflict with, or are irrelevant to, the electoral basis for political success.

Political market imperfections are key to understanding slow reform generally. Most observers attribute slow reform to political fragmentation, but fragmentation is low by world standards, and, moreover, this explanation does not take into account the incentives of individual political actors.[13] Broadly beneficial economic reforms are not politically salient. It is not surprising that Kohli (2006) attributed the reluctance to open markets to a political alliance between politicians and special interests (incumbent firms), leading to policy reforms that encourage incumbents to invest, but that do not allow broad entry.

Infrastructure policy offers another glimpse into the influence of political market imperfections. The availability of infrastructure is widely agreed to be a highly constrictive bottleneck to Indian policy. Nevertheless, infrastructure spending collapsed in the 1990s, falling back to its 1970s levels (approximately 1.5 percent of GDP) from amounts exceeding 2 percent of GDP in the 1980s. This collapse certainly is related to macroeconomic and fiscal problems.[14] Macroeconomic problems, however, do not explain the allocative distortions in infrastructure toward projects with the greatest political payoff, nor do they explain the persistent difficulties in attacking bottlenecks that impose the greatest obstacles to economic growth. Here, the distortionary presence of political market imperfections offers a better explanation (Wilkinson 2006b).

---

13. India's political fragmentation in the 1990s was actually low compared with all parliamentary democracies. In the latter case, the probability that two legislators in the parliament were from different parties was approximately 67 percent.

14. This explanation is easy to overstate, however. The reallocation of spending away from politically attractive but nonproductive and scarcely equitable subsidies and improved tax administration likely would be sufficient to fund productive infrastructure.

Since 2004, annual growth has accelerated to approximately 6 percent. It is too early to analyze the roots of this dramatic increase, but it is noteworthy that the Congress Party returned to power in 2004 and, as in the 1970s, again allied with the Communist Party to form a majority. The results have been much different. In the 1970s, the alliance precipitated redistributive policies rooted in expropriation and direct government management of the economy. Growth dropped to nearly zero. A similar coalition, far from reversing the reforms of 1991, has focused instead on pursuing equity and redistribution through more efficient jobs programs. This change reflects not only learning, but also greater awareness of the electoral importance of delivering observable welfare improvements to broad segments of the population. The fact that the policy focus is persistently on redistribution rather than reforms that would promote growth, however, suggests that information and other political market imperfections continue to make it difficult for parties to benefit electorally from such policies.

Chinese Governance in the Post-Mao Era

The policy environment in China prior to 1980 is well known to have been particularly hostile to private enterprise and market incentives, perhaps among the most hostile in the world at that time. The governance environment was equally weak. Individualized rule and highly arbitrary decision making produced a strong sense of insecurity in both party and nonparty members. Shirk (1993) noted that, prior to 1978, "Mao Zedong attempted to sustain his revolutionary charisma and stem the trend of institutionalization . . . by launching mass campaigns such as the Great Leap Forward and the Cultural Revolution" (p. 8). The Cultural Revolution itself represented an effort by Mao to bypass the Communist Party and his opponents within it, and was implemented instead by the Red Guards, whom Mao directly controlled. Thousands of party officials were transferred to lower-level jobs, sent to the countryside for reeducation, or imprisoned during the Cultural Revolution (Shirk 1993). Elite politics under Mao were particularly unpredictable, again signaling the lack of constraints on opportunistic behavior. Two of Mao's "chosen successors" died politics-related deaths (Whiting 2001, p. 11).

Economic growth exploded not only after reforms relaxed the prohibition on private sector activity, but also after governance reforms relieved this insecurity. From 1952 to 1980, average annual individual incomes increased by less than 2.5 percent (Shirk 1993). From 1980 onward, growth tripled. Agricultural production rose at a yearly rate of 7 percent from 1978 to 1988, more than three times faster than in the previous 26 years (Shirk 1993). Manufacturing boomed. Between 1978 and 1987, nonstate rural enterprises rose from 8.7 percent of all industrial output to 23.1 percent (Byrd and Gelb 1990).[15] The share of total industrial output produced by nonstate firms—those not controlled by the central government—almost doubled from 1978 to 1988, rising from 22 percent to 43 percent (Shirk 1993).

The policy reforms underlying these changes were dramatic. By 1983, the Household Responsibility System, which made households residual claimants of production on their collectively owned plots, had spread throughout China. Key policy changes also stimulated private sector industrial development. Farm households were allowed to invest profits in farm machinery, trucks, and industrial equipment and to engage in private marketing and manufacturing. Collectively owned township and village enterprises (TVEs) could be leased to individuals and groups (Shirk 1993). Rural investment loomed large: private firms in the rural sector accounted for 19 percent of total fixed-asset investment in the 1980s and TVEs accounted for another 13 percent (Huang forthcoming). Decisions in 1979 expanded foreign trade and allowed foreign companies to invest in Chinese enterprises. The central government also decentralized the administration of foreign trade and investment, allowing localities to deal directly with foreign interests.

Local government officials were at the center of these reforms. Indeed, one rationale for focusing on TVEs was to channel rents to local cadres to offset their losses from decollectivization (Oi 1999).[16] The TVE focus allowed cadres who controlled an earlier variety of TVE—one established under Mao beginning in 1970 (Byrd and Gelb 1990)—to continue to use that variety to distribute jobs and other resources (Oi 1989). These cadres implemented decollectivization because land was still collectively owned at the local level. They hired the TVE managers. As Oi (1999) observed, although TVEs were usually contracted out by town and village governments to private managers, local governments—and the party officials who ran them—retained control

---

15. About two-thirds of these enterprises were owned formally by townships and villages in 1987, and about one-third were owned privately by individuals or groups.

16. The TVE focus also softened ideological opposition to the private sector. Oi (1999, p. 74), for example, quoted rural officials in one county who, in the 1980s, referred to private entrepreneurs as "underground snakes" (ditou she).

of personnel, investments, and product lines and, ultimately, they were residual claimants of profits. Whiting (2001) has written, "Indeed, township officials themselves approved the number of employees and the total wage bill of
each enterprise" (p. 204).

It is likely that local officials also were closely involved with the non-TVE
private enterprises. On the one hand, much rural private investment was driv-
en by agricultural liberalization, where the key asset—land—was controlled
by local officials. On the other hand, some evidence points to substantial pri-
vate-investor insecurity during the 1980s that would have been resolved by
taking on local officials as partners. In resource-poor Wenzhou City, although
local officials were particularly friendly to private investment because of the
lack of capital to finance TVEs, concerns about expropriatory behavior led
private entrepreneurs to make small investments; shut down their ventures
and restart them later; or, having reached a certain scale, shift their profits
from reinvestment to the purchase of "extravagant homes or even ancestral
tombs" (Whiting 2001, p. 148).

The Credibility Puzzle in Chinese Growth

Local officials would not have responded to reform with investment on a massive scale without guarantees that they would be rewarded. In fact, Oi (1999)
reported that township and village governments required collective enterprises to re-invest, on average, 50 percent of retained profits.[17] Either in their capacity as overseers of TVEs or as private individuals with close personal ties to
private investors, why did township officials believe that the central leadership would not expropriate the profits from investments *they* controlled? The
Communist Party leadership needed to make credible its promises to cadres
(its success in doing so, however, would not be captured in standard indicators
of voice and accountability because reforms would extend only to cadres and
not to citizens generally).

Che and Qian (1998a, 1998b) argued that, to induce investment, the central government allowed local governments to operate TVEs and implemented
fiscal reforms in 1980 to allow local governments to keep all revenues above a

---

17. Some fraction of this investment was not productive. For example, some of it likely
went to construct new housing for workers (Nee 1992). In addition, there is uncertainty
about whether TVEs reinvested or simply had easy access to state bank loans. In either case,
rapid output growth is indicative of significant productive investment rather than diversion
to immediate consumption.

preset amount. This gave local officials a full claim on all TVE profits above that amount, but also required them to provide local public goods, a reform described as "eating in separate kitchens" (*fenzao chifan*) (Whiting 2001, p. 76). According to Che and Qian (1998b) decentralization worked because local and central governments had similar incentives for providing local public goods, such as local roads, but particularly for maintaining order. This same strategy could not be replicated by private enterprises, which were unable to solve the collective action problems needed to provide those same local public goods.

There are two reasons to consider additional explanations. These fiscal reforms were reversed after the central government saw its revenues dry up (see Wong 1992). Investment continued, however. In addition, local and central governments turned out to have *conflicting* preferences regarding local public goods provision, and the central government exerted considerable effort to ensure the provision of the local public goods it valued. Even in the early 1980s, leaders at the center had to monitor closely the provision of education and the maintenance of social order, highlighting these public goods in performance agreements with local officials.[18] In the 1990s, local and central government interests more clearly came into conflict. For example, local officials increased social disorder by selling off collectively owned land without fully compensating farmers for their usufruct rights or by allowing local firms to ignore environmental restrictions.

Intraparty Institutions and Credible Commitments to Investors in the 1980s

An alternative explanation of the willingness of cadres to invest is the institutionalization of the CPC—checks and balances at the top and the introduction of expensive and more transparent promotion and evaluation systems. Institutionalization began when Deng Xiaoping came to power in 1977. His challenge was to increase the broad popularity of the CPC, through broadbased economic development that benefited all Chinese people, while ensuring that party cadres would have privileged access to these benefits to maintain their loyalty and commitment to the party. The key to each of these goals

18. Similar issues arose in macroeconomic policy, where the conflict of interest between local and central government officials was clearer. Huang (1996) argued that the central government used the career concerns of local officials to prevent them from adopting expansionary strategies (that is, with regard to bank credits), imposing inflationary externalities on the rest of the country.

was to increase the confidence of cadres that they would be rewarded by the party if their current decisions led to future economic growth.

The 1980 reforms assigned local officials many of the rents from reform. But to ensure that the reforms would be effective—that they would elicit investment beneficial to all citizens—the rewards promised to cadres needed to be credible. As Huang (2003) noted, because township enterprises were run by government officials with formal civil service status, Deng focused on making the rules for promotion and cadre evaluation more credible. Deng "governed by rules, clear lines of authority, and collective decision-making institutions to replace the over-concentration of power and patriarchal rule that had characterized China under Mao" (Shirk 1993 p. 9; see also Whiting 2006). By 1983, the Organization Department of the CPC had implemented concrete and tangible criteria in cadre evaluations, ranging from gross output and investment in the early years to finer measures of economic growth and social stability in the 1990s. The party also created more room at the top to reward cadres by instituting mandatory retirement for party cadres (Manion 1992).

A number of conditions raised the central government's cost of abandoning these rules. First, the rules were expensive to implement, involving retraining of thousands of cadres and constructing a costly bureaucratic process for evaluation. This investment was lost to the leadership if it disregarded the newly established rules.

Second, Deng Xiaoping was personally credible. He had incurred significant personal costs in advocating the same cadre management system under Mao: Mao used the Cultural Revolution not only to dismantle the system, but also to purge Deng himself (Manion 1985). By having paid a high price for his advocacy of systematic cadre management under Mao, Deng was credible in advocating support for the system when he came to power in 1978.

Third, the plan passed through a series of intraparty checks and balances, the most important of which was the core group of senior leaders. With the death of Mao, authority was spread to a greater extent among the top leadership of the party. Deng, for example, deferred to party elders. Leadership succession at least loosely followed formal rules, but clearly was also a shared decision of 30 or more leaders (Shirk 1993).[19] Shirk further pointed out that policy movement in the 1980s was slowed by lack of consensus among leaders

19. Here is a prominent example of this looseness: although the collective consent of numerous top leaders was essential to oust Hu Yaobang as general secretary of the CPC in 1987, the leadership chose to ignore the formally required procedure of seeking the ratification of the Central Committee (Shirk 1993).

at the top. Although this made reform more difficult, it also made reform more difficult to overturn. In the context of personnel reform, the difficult decision to eliminate lifetime tenure for almost 20 million cadres was agreed by the top leadership only after meaningful compromise to satisfy the interests of multiple leaders (Manion 1992). These same checks and balances impeded unilateral changes to the rules for cadre promotion or the disregard of promotion criteria for cadres. In practice, as well, the promises were kept. Between 1978 and 1995, Li and Zhou (2005) have found that the likelihood of promotion for provincial leaders increased with a province's economic performance, and the likelihood of termination decreased.

Sources of Investment and Good Governance after 1990

In the 1990s, the development model shifted, and investments from non-cadres, especially from foreign investors, substantially increased. Combined TVE and rural private fixed-asset investment dropped steadily as a fraction of total fixed-asset investment, whereas the share of urban and foreign-invested firms rose to approximately 14 percent of total investment in 2001–03, compared with less than three percent in the period 1986–1990 (Huang forthcoming). This shift in strategy raises two questions: how did governance arrangements of the 1980s change to encourage foreign and noncadre domestic investment? and how did this change enable the leadership to continue to balance cadre interests with those of citizens more broadly?

The 1980s model of growth that relied heavily on local cadres confronted three difficulties. First, local cadres had strong political and private incentives to maximize revenues and employment, but weaker incentives to maximize profits, thus encouraging them to take on debt and build up tax liabilities that were sustainable only as long as growth continued. In 1989, approximately 18 percent of TVEs had severe difficulties: the government allowed 800,000 TVEs to close and another 2.2 million to merge with other enterprises or be restructured (Nee 1992). The process culminated in 1997, when the central government shifted influence over lending decisions away from local governments, closing hundreds of local banks and financial institutions and transferring lending authority within the four major state banks away from local and provincial offices to Beijing (see Shih 2004).

Second, the 1980s model starved the central government of revenues, which fell as a fraction of GDP from 30 percent in 1970, to 23 percent in 1985, to 12.6 percent in 1993, to 10 percent in 1995. This loss left central leaders with little choice but to modify the fiscal arrangements developed in the 1980s that had left local governments with the lions' share of revenues (Yang 2004).

Third, local officials proved to be less reliable agents of the party than leaders had hoped. Concerns about the erosion of the central government's authority were voiced widely in the late 1980s and early 1990s (see Nee 1992). On the economic front, the most obvious manifestation of this erosion was the establishment of interlocality trade barriers to protect local firms from outside competition.

At the same time, the party's always high need for committed cadres was lower in 1990 than in 1980. Early in the reform process, party leaders could not be confident that market reforms would deliver the large payoffs to average citizens that they eventually did. Given the risks of failure, it was particularly important to sustain the loyalty of the cadres. This necessity had diminished by 1990, when market-oriented reforms had demonstrated their success. The cost of maintaining cadre loyalty also had risen because party members had better outside opportunities in the 1990s than in the 1980s. Nee and Opper (2006) noted, "The lure of lucrative career opportunities in the thriving market economy has led many government bureaucrats to seek jobs in local businesses after leaving the government" (p. 11).

Instead of TVE and cadre-driven investment, therefore, the center turned also to FDI and, later, to domestic, private investment. In 1991, private firms of all kinds accounted for only 5.7 percent of industrial output value, compared with almost 52.7 percent for all nonstate firms, largely TVEs (Huang 2003). FDI increased from 0.9 percent of fixed-asset investment in all firms in 1983 to 15.0 percent in 1997. Relative to all nonstate firms (TVEs, essentially), FDI was 2.6 percent of fixed investment in 1983 and 31.7 percent in 1997. By mid-2003, TVEs (collectives) accounted for a small fraction of sales and profits—a share that continued to fall rapidly, dropping by almost half in mid-2005. Private firms financed by foreign or domestic investment produced the lion's share of manufacturing sales, holding nearly 60 percent by mid-2005 (World Bank Office 2005).

Huang (2003) attributed the upswing in FDI to government financial and legal policies that favored foreign investors over domestic ones. These policies also can be seen, however, as efforts to maintain rewards for local cadres. For example, until the mid-1990s domestic private firms were obligated to register as collective firms, which formally placed them under local government control (Huang 2003).

In any case, in 1992 the environment for domestic private enterprises also began to change when Deng called for more private firms. In 1998 the central bank relaxed lending quotas that had severely disfavored private firms, and the government finally allowed these firms to export. By 1999 the private sector was recognized in the Chinese Constitution as an integral part of the Chinese economy and placed on equal footing with other firms.[20] In July 2001, Jiang Zemin announced that private entrepreneurs should be allowed to join the ranks of the Communist Party (Huang 2003). The ratio of foreign-financed to private fixed investment fell from 48 percent in 1996 to 29 percent in 2000 (Huang 2003). One sign of policy friendliness to private investment is that China seems to have vaulted ahead of other poor countries in lowering costs to investors. According to the World Bank Doing Business indicators, by 2004 China's employment rigidity and contract enforcement costs were almost one standard deviation better than those of other countries, controlling for income per capita.

As before, the key question is, why did investors, particularly foreign investors, respond to these policy changes? The credibility of the cadre evaluation system that protected local officials from arbitrary treatment by the party in the 1980s would not seem to offer similar protection to foreign investors in the 1990s. Recalling the evidence in Fan et al. (2006), the size of the Chinese market alone might have attracted huge amounts of private capital when investment prohibitions were eased. At the central government level, intra-elite competition continued to exhibit increasing regularization through the 1980s and 1990s. Under Mao, intra-elite struggles sometimes ended violently. This was less the case under Deng and even less so after him, when the penalties associated with losing a leadership contest have fallen farther and are no longer as dramatic as arrest or worse. The growing institutionalization of intra-CPC political checks and balances increased the difficulties confronting any single party leader seeking to act opportunistically.

Increasing political checks and balances provided a credible underpinning for continuing administrative and judicial reforms throughout the 1990s. Under the auspices of the Administrative Litigation Law of 1989, nearly 10,000 cases were filed against government agencies in 1989; this rose to 98,000 in 1998. Of the 460,000 total cases filed over the period, plaintiffs won 35 percent of the time (Yang 2004). Clarke, Murrell, and Whiting (2006) have

---

20. Foreign-invested enterprises had enjoyed constitutional recognition since the 1982 Constitution (Huang 2003).

pointed to the growing institutionalization of legal dispute resolution, replac-ing the administrative, cadre-centered resolution of disputes that would have favored TVEs. Administrative reforms culminated in 2005 with the passage of a comprehensive legal code governing civil service, consolidating the regula-tory effort to modernize China's state bureaucracy (Nee and Opper 2006).

At least in part, these efforts all were aimed at creating a safe climate for in-vestment. As Yang (2004) wrote, "For Deng Xiaoping, political stability, par-ticularly the continuity of Communist Party leadership, was a necessary con-dition for further economic reforms. Deng clearly recognized that the promotion of economic development through further economic reforms would be essential if the ruling elite were to regain the sort of performance le-gitimacy it had acquired in the 1980s" (p. 6).

Finally, the Chinese government has used its enhanced fiscal position to increase investor rates of return directly, using massive infrastructure invest-ment—investments that precisely expanded the size of markets, magnifying one of China's principal advantages. From 1990 to 1995, for example, China increased its total road network by 23 percent, and by 50 percent in 2002 (World Bank 2005b, *World Development Indicators*). This attracted private in-vestment for two reasons. First, although most observers agree that much pub-lic investment in China has low returns, partly because it is targeted ahead of demand to poor areas of the country, high-return productive infrastructure has increased dramatically. Chinese ports, for example, are world class, thus raising rates of return to private investment in the production of tradables. Second, productive public investments constitute a bond that the govern-ment has put up: they have a high political payoff only if private investors take advantage of the new infrastructure. If the government acts opportunisti-cally, investors depart and the investment in infrastructure is lost, just as the earlier investments in cadre evaluation systems would have been lost if the government returned to opaque criteria for cadre advancement.

Governance Stress in the 1990s

Why have other one-party states not adopted the strategies of the CPC and enjoyed similar economic success? In fact, as the Chinese example makes clear, it is costly for leaders to establish large parties that are organized to pro-tect members from arbitrary decisions by the party leadership; hence their rar-ity (Gehlbach and Keefer 2006). For example, to engender party member loy-alty, members must receive larger rents than they could receive outside the party. As their numbers rise, so too does the share of rents owed to party members as a whole.[21] Investments in elaborate intraparty evaluation and promotion processes, such as those China introduced in the 1970s and 1980s, are also expensive and they limit executive discretion.

Power sharing also is less likely when a single leader of the unelected government commands disproportionately more influence (military, popular, or otherwise) than do the others. When this is not the case, political checks and balances emerge naturally as the consequence of a balance of power among key leaders. When the distribution of power within the leadership group is unbalanced, as in China under Mao, it is difficult to establish political checks and balances.

Therefore, although the significant adjustments of the 1990s demonstrate the adaptability of the Chinese leadership to shifting political and economic challenges, it should not be surprising that the new bargain between party leaders and cadres has not been an easy one to sustain. The 1990 adjustments—the decline of TVEs, falling access to capital, and reduced tax shares—moved substantial rents and authority away from local officials. To soften the loss of rents to cadres, the central government privatized 250,000 small- and medium-size enterprises in 1997, selling many at low prices to party members. Nevertheless, the net effect of these reforms appears to have increased the relative benefits to cadres of pursuing privately beneficial actions that impose costs on society, and specifically on the party. Corruption, land grabs, and a lack of vigilance with regard to provision of local public goods (education, environmental safety, and so forth) are activities that disgruntled cadres might pursue. Strengthened institutional checks and balances at the top may not have offset weaker incentives to pursue good governance at the local level.

To the extent that the shifting cadre–leadership bargain has weakened cadre discipline and governance at the local level, we would expect to see some citizen reaction. According to Huang (forthcoming), the total number of demonstrations that occurred annually between 1993 and 1997 rose from 8,700 to 32,000. Officially reported incidents of social unrest rose from 58,000 in 2003 to 74,000 in 2004. These increases seem directly tied to efforts by local officials to raise their rents, including the transfer of land away from farmers to industrial and other uses and weak oversight of the environmental degradation caused by local enterprises. For example, results of a survey, conducted by Anthony

---

21. The exception here is ideological motivation. To the extent that party leaders can use ideology to mobilize followers, they can provide fewer financial rents to supporters.

Saich of Harvard, showed that support for the central government has remained "extremely high" over the period 2002–05; this is not the case for local governments ("Good Things" 2006, p. 15). In his report to the 16th National Congress in November 2002, Jiang Zemin insisted, "If we do not crack down on corruption, the flesh-and-blood ties between the party and the people will suffer a lot and the party will be in danger of losing its ruling position, or possibly heading for self-destruction" (Yang 2004, p. 257).

In principle, the leadership should be able to clamp down on corruption and nonperformance by local cadres. In fact, the government increased its prosecution of local corruption, targeting especially senior cadres in province, prefecture, and county governments and demonstrating its intent to stifle local officials who shirk their duties or collect illicit rents at the expense of the party's ability to deliver growth. The share of party members disciplined who were senior cadres was three times higher in 2000 as in 1993. Every year between 1995 and 2000, from 4,000 to 6,000 senior cadres at the province, prefecture, or county levels were punished by the disciplinary inspection committee (DIC) system. Economic offenses, including corruption, were 22 percent of the cases that province-level DICs filed in 1987, but 48 percent of the cases filed in 1997; major cases—those involving more than 10,000 yuan—increased from 6 percent to more than 30 percent in 2000. Of those offenders subject to disciplinary action, 25 percent were expelled from the party, 69 percent were subjected to milder party sanctions, and 6 percent were referred to the judiciary (Wedeman 2004).

The government does not have a free hand here, however. Cadre loyalty rests on the transparency with which cadres are evaluated. Transparency is easier to sustain when the goals are few and easily documented. When they are many and hard to measure, as is the case in battling corruption, the aggressive prosecution of corruption creates a risk of leadership being perceived as arbitrary by cadres. For example, the leadership still places significant weight on economic growth and job creation. Whereas social peace and environmental improvement enter into cadre evaluation schemes, economic growth is the most important factor. Without undermining the clarity of its promotion criteria processes to all cadres, the government cannot easily punish cadres who succeed with respect to growth but are less successful on other margins. As a consequence, anticorruption crackdowns have been sporadic, incomplete, and sometimes politically motivated (Yang 2004).

The costs of an ill-fought campaign against corruption—that is, the costs of alienating cadres—are significant. Connections to local cadres still provide security for private investors, which would be lost if the credibility of leadership promises to cadres were to fall. Local cadres collect taxes, are responsible for law and order, and conduct other indispensable and hard-to-monitor tasks for the center. In addition, some of the troublesome rents earned by cadres bind them more closely to the party: cadres can earn these only if the party remains in power and only if they remain in the party.

To offset increased governance problems at the local level, the party has strengthened institutions to oversee local officials and offered expanded avenues of redress. These institutions all work from the top down and maintain control over cadre careers firmly in leadership hands. They also are more accessible to individuals with more resources and a bigger stake in the outcome: it is costly to pursue legal appeals, to travel to Beijing, and to gain access to the right officials. Bottom-up institutions for the evaluation of local cadres, particularly local elections, have been adopted more tentatively. These institutions have the advantage of vesting the responsibility for sanctioning cadre malfeasance in the hands of better-informed citizens. They do, however, have the severe disadvantage of detaching cadre career advancement from the decisions of the top party leadership.

Regardless of its specific evolution of governance in the 1990s, China is noteworthy for having strengthened institutions to improve governance and support broad-based growth. This distinguishes China from other countries without competitive elections, where reliance on cronyism has been more marked. For example, Mexico under Porfirio Díaz managed to use crony relationships (personal relationships between entrepreneurs and political leaders) to generate investment and growth. But the concentration of economic activity and the concentration of rewards among Díaz's cronies became a target for revolt, ultimately culminating in the Mexican Revolution in the early 1900s (Haber, Razo, and Maurer 2003).

What the Future Holds

The experiences of China and India in the 1980s and 1990s underline, first, the importance of governance for growth and, second, the importance for good governance outcomes of institutional and political arrangements that enable government leaders to make credible promises to a large fraction of their citizenry. Both of these countries only started to grow after they improved their governance environments from low levels. Although governance outcomes in both countries generally have been average, the two countries make clear the challenges of achieving even average outcomes, whether in countries with competitive elections or in countries without them. China has reached a delicate balance between satisfying party members and the population as a whole, while institutionalizing competition between leaders at the top of the party, that has eluded leaders in other countries. Governance in India has advanced despite the shadow of clientelist politics that diminish political incentives to maintain it. Both countries highlight the role of political checks and balances, whether between parties or branches of government, as in India, or between factions of a party, as in China.

The Chinese government's continued success in balancing popular and cadre demands has been key to achieving average governance outcomes. As wages rise and extraordinary profits from large markets fall, still better governance will be key to continued fast growth. This will require that the leadership succeed in advancing farther its agenda of institutionalizing intraparty constraints on opportunism by government officials. For example, local and national people's congresses have exercised increased influence over lawmaking, appointment ratification, budget and policy reviews, and the monitoring and supervision of agency's and officials' behavior (Whiting 2006). Evidence of their growing importance is the number of provincial party secretaries who chair provincial people's congresses—a number that has risen from 13 out of the 31 held in 1998 to 23 out of 31 in 2003 (Yang 2004). Future governance outcomes will depend on the extent to which these institutions can provide greater security to investors and citizens without jeopardizing the rewards to CPC cadres.

As the CPC shifts rents and control away from local cadres, it will need to provide them with exceptional rewards, above and beyond what they can achieve outside of the party. For example, to the extent that greater institutionalization requires more aggressive crackdowns on corruption or the subordination of local cadres to local courts of peoples' congresses, increased compensation may be needed to maintain cadre loyalty. Singapore has been very successful in using this model.

The stability of the cadre–leadership bargain rests as well on the entrenchment of the party. If the government experiences severe popularity shocks, or if social unrest increases more rapidly than the government can move in renegotiating the cadre–leadership contract to improve local governance, the price of cadre loyalty will rise, making governance more difficult to improve. China's cautious approach to major macroeconomic policy changes, such as financial sector reform or exchange rate flotation, underlines its sensitivity to popularity shocks, such as those precipitated by adverse economic events or unexpected citizen dismay at particular aspects of government policy. The experience of 1989 demonstrates, as well, that reactions to popularity shocks have been directed at the domestic private sector: following the Tiananmen Square events that year, the official attitude toward private entrepreneurs deteriorated dramatically (Huang 2003). To the extent that growth depends more on private investment, as it does to a much greater extent in China now than it did in 1989, such a strategic shift would have more noticeable effects on growth and investment.

India is well endowed with external institutions of credibility—political checks and balances, for example, that do not depend on any particular party. These have been sufficient to yield average governance even in the face of economic shocks and significant political instability. Economic and political shocks are unlikely to pose a particular threat to governance and growth in India. In the face of political market imperfections, however, political checks and balances that are the key to moderately secure property rights in India are also a barrier to reform. The key issue for the future is improving governance and policy generally: greater opening of the economy to allow more entry, more innovation, and wider participation across all markets. Political market imperfections have reduced the electoral payoffs to pursuing this agenda. Cleavage-riven social settings, lack of education, isolation, and poverty itself conspire to make voters responsive primarily to clientelist promises and easily observed subsidies.

India, however, also has embarked on a vast program of decentralization, instituting local elections and putting greater revenue and public service responsibilities in the hands of local governments. It has experimented aggressively with institutions to bring the disadvantaged into politics, including reserved seats on local government councils for women and for lower castes. These new local governments hold the promise of overcoming some of the obstacles to improved governance—for example, by removing some of the information barriers that make electoral accountability difficult to generate at higher levels of government.

Finally, India and China provide hopeful signs of a virtuous circle, signs that growth can help propel governance reforms in countries able to achieve even a moderate level of governance to begin with. Wilkinson (2006b) has argued that growth in India seems to be creating a constituency less tolerant of clientelist political appeals. In China, growth in the 1990s gave the Communist Party leadership sufficient confidence in the party's public approval that it risked opening up the economy to private investment and cracking down on excessive rent-seeking by party members in the 1990s. It has enabled the leadership to demand more of cadres than mere growth, where the benefits have been easy to share between party members and citizens more broadly; to embrace higher quality public services, reduced pollution, and more transparent local land management, where the sharing is more difficult.

References

Acemoglu, Daron, and James A. Robinson. 2006. *Economic Origins of Dictatorship and Democracy*. New York: Cambridge University Press.

Aghion, Philippe, Eva Caroli, and Cecilia Garcia-Peñalosa. 1999. "Inequality and Economic Growth: The Perspectives of the New Growth Theories." *Journal of Economic Literature* 37 (4): 1615–60.

Ahluwalia, M. S. 2000. "Economic Performance of States in Post-Reforms Period." *Economic and Political Weekly*, May 6, 1637–48.

"Air-conditioners Wilt under Cold Blast of Competition in China." 2005. *Financial Times*, September 24.

Aizenman, Joshua, and Jaewoo Lee. 2005. "International Reserves: Precautionary Versus Mercantilist Views, Theory and Evidence." Working Paper 11366, National Bureau of Economic Research, Cambridge, MA.

Allen, Franklin, Jun Qian, and Meijun Qian. 2005. "China's Financial System: Past, Present, and Future." Photocopy. Wharton School, Philadelphia.

Amiel, Yoram, and Frank Cowell. 1999. *Thinking about Inequality: Personal Judgment and Income Distributions*. Cambridge, UK: Cambridge University Press.

"An Alpha Delta." 2006. *Financial Times*, May 8.

"An Urgent Political and Moral Imperative." 2006. *Financial Times*, April 24.

Ananthakrishnan, Prasad, and Sonali Jain-Chandra. 2005. "The Impact on India of Trade Liberalization in the Textiles and Clothing Sector." Working Paper 05/214, International Monetary Fund, Washington, DC.

Ando, M., and F. Kimura. 2003. "The Formation of International Production and Distribution Networks in East Asia." Working Paper 10167, National Bureau of Economic Research, Cambridge, MA.

Arora, Ashish, and Suma Athreye. 2001. "The Software Industry and India's Economic Development." Discussion Paper 2001/20, United Nations University/World Institute for Development Economics Research, Helsinki.

Arora, Ashish, and Alfonso Gambardella. 2004. "The Globalization of the Software Industry: Perspectives and Opportunities for Developed and Developing Countries." Working Paper 10538, National Bureau of Economic Research, Cambridge, MA.

"Attempting a Steel Revolution." 2005. *Business China*, May 23.

Au, Chun-Chung, and J. Vernon Henderson. 2006. "How Migration Restrictions Limit Agglomeration and Productivity in China." *Journal of Development Economics* 80: 350–88.

"Automotive." 2006. *Business China*, June 5.

Bai, Chong-En. 2006. "The Domestic Financial System and Capital Flows: China." Background paper for *Dancing with Giants: China, India, and the Global Economy*. Institute for Policy Studies and the World Bank, Washington, DC.

Balakrishnan, Karthik, Ananth Iyer, Sridhar Seshadri, and Anshul Sehopuri. 2006. "Indian Auto Supply Chain at the Cross-Roads." Photocopy. Purdue University, West Lafayette, IN.

Banerjee, Abhijit, Shawn Cole, and Esther Duflo. 2003. "Bank Financing in India." Photocopy. Department of Economics, Massachusetts Institute of Technology, Cambridge.

Banerjee, Abhijit, and Thomas Piketty. 2003. "Top Indian Income: 1956–2000." Photocopy. Department of Economics, Massachusetts Institute of Technology, Cambridge.

Bardhan, P. 2005. "The Nature of Opposition to Economic Reforms in India." *Economic and Political Weekly*, November 26. http://www.epw.org.in/showArticles.php?root=2005&leaf=11&filename=9388&filetype=html.

Beck, Thorsten, George R. Clarke, Alberto Groff, Philip E. Keefer, and Patrick P. Walsh. 2001. "New Tools in Comparative Political Economy: The Database of Political Institutions." *World Bank Economic Review* 15 (1): 165–76.

Beck, Thorsten, Asli Demirgüç-Kunt, and Ross Levine. 2006. "A New Database on Financial Development and Structure (1960–2004)." Policy Research Working Paper 2146, World Bank, Washington, DC.

Bergsten, C. Fred, Bates Gill, Nicholas Lardy, and Derek J. Mitchell. 2006. *China: The Balance Sheet: What the World Needs to Know Now about the Emerging Superpower*. New York: Public Affairs/Institute for International Economics/Center for Strategic and International Studies.

Bhalla, Surjit. 2002. *Imagine There's No Country: Poverty, Inequality and Growth in the Era of Globalization*. Washington, DC: Institute for International Economics.

"Big Players in Chip Design Buy Into India." 2006. *IEEE Spectrum* March.

Blanchard, Olivier, and Francesco Giavazzi. 2005. "Rebalancing Growth in China: A Three-handed Approach." Working Paper 05-32, Massachusetts Institute of Technology, Cambridge.

BP. 2006. "Quantifying Energy: Statistical Review of World Energy 2006." http://www.bp.com/statisticalreview.

Bradley, R. 2006. "Transforming the Way We Use Energy." Presentation at World Bank Energy Week, Washington, DC, March 6–8.

Brandon, Carter J., and Kirsten Hommann. 1995. "The Cost of Inaction." Internal document, South Asia Environment Unit, World Bank, Washington, DC.

Branstetter, Lee, and Nicholas Lardy. 2006. "China's Embrace of Globalization." Working Paper 12373, National Bureau of Economic Research, Cambridge, MA.

Brass, Paul R. 1990. *The Politics of India since Independence*. The New Cambridge History of India, vol. IV.1. Cambridge, UK: Cambridge University Press.

Briscoe, John. 2005. *Bracing for a Turbulent Water Future*. Washington, DC: World Bank.

Broadman, Harry. 2007. *Africa's Silk Road: China and India's New Economic Frontier*. Washington, DC: World Bank.

Bruno, Michael, Martin Ravallion, and Lyn Squire. 1998. "Equity and Growth in Developing Countries: Old and New Perspectives on the Policy Issues." In *Income Distribution and High-Quality Growth*, ed. Vito Tanzi and Ke-young Chu. Cambridge, MA: MIT Press.

Byrd, William, and Alan Gelb. 1990. "Township, Village and Private Industry in China's Economic Reform." Policy Research and External Affairs Working Papers 406 (April), World Bank, Washington, DC.

Caballero, Ricardo, Emmanuel Farhi, and Pierre-Olivier Gourinchas. 2006. "An Equilibrium Model of Global Imbalances and Low Interest Rates." Working Paper 11996, National Bureau of Economic Research, Cambridge, MA.

Cai, Hongin, Hanming Fang, and Lixin Colin Xu. 2005. "Eat, Drink, Firm, Government: An Investigation of Corruption from Entertainment and Travel Costs of Chinese Firms." Working Paper 11592, National Bureau of Economic Research, Cambridge, MA.

Chameides, William L., H. Yu, S. C. Liu, M. Bergin, X. Zhou, L. Mearns, G. Wang, C. S. Kiang, R. D. Saylor, C. Luo, Y. Huang, A. Steiner, and F. Giorgi. 1999. "Case Study of the Effects of Atmospheric Aerosols and Regional Haze on Agriculture: An Opportunity to Enhance Crop Yields in China through Emission Controls?" *Proceedings of the National Academy of Sciences* 96 (2): 13626–33.

Chamon, Marcos, and Eswar Prasad. 2005. "Determinants of Household Saving in China." Photocopy. International Monetary Fund, Washington, DC.

Chan, Sarah, and Qingyang Gu. 2006. "Investment in China Migrates Inland." *Far Eastern Economic Review* May.

Chaudhuri, Sudip. 2004. "The Pharmaceutical Industry." In *The Structure of Indian Industry*, ed. Subir Gokarn, Anindya Sen, and Rajendra R. Vaidya. New York: Oxford University Press.

Che, Jiahua, and Yingyi Qian. 1998a. "Insecure Property Rights and Government Ownership of Firms." *Quarterly Journal of Economics* 113 (2): 467–96.

———. 1998b. "Institutional Environment, Community Government, and Corporate Governance: Understanding China's Township-Village Enterprises." *Journal of Law, Economics and Organization* 14 (1): 1–23.

Chen, Jian, and Belton M. Fleisher. 1996. "Regional Income Inequality and Economic Growth in China." *Journal of Comparative Economics* 22: 141–64.

Chen, Kun, and Martin Kenney. Forthcoming. "Universities/Research Institutes and Regional Innovation Systems: The Cases of Beijing and Shenzhen." *World Development*.

Chen, Shaohua, and Martin Ravallion. 2004. "How Have the World's Poorest Fared Since the Early 1980s?" *World Bank Research Observer* 19 (2): 141–70.

———. 2006. "Inequality and Poverty Comparisons between Consumption and Income." Photocopy. Development Research Group, World Bank, Washington, DC.

Chen, Shaohua, Martin Ravallion, and Youjuan Wang. 2006. "*Dibao*: A Guaranteed Minimum Income in China's Cities?" Policy Research Working Paper 3805, World Bank, Washington, DC.

"China Looms Large on India's Pharma Frontier." 2006. http://www.bain.com/bain web/publications/in_the_news_detail.asp?id=24912&menu_url=for_the_media.asp.

"China: Pharmaceuticals Sector Has Unrealized Potential." 2005. *Oxford Analytica*, September 8.

"China's Hi-Tech Success Is Not Patently Obvious." 2005. *Financial Times*, October 25.

"China: Water Shortage Poses Significant Risks." 2006. *Oxford Analytica*, February 13.

"Chinese Fridge Magnate Becomes Hot Property." 2005. *Financial Times*, November 18.

Chinese Statistical Abstract. 2005. Beijing: China Statistics Press.

Clarke, Donald, Peter Murrell, and Susan Whiting. 2006. "The Role of Law in China's Economic Development." Public Law and Legal Theory Working Paper 187, George Washington University, Washington, DC.

Clarke, George R., and Scott J. Wallsten. 2006. "Has the Internet Increased Trade? Developed and Developing Country Evidence." *Economic Inquiry* 44 (3): 465–84.

Cohen, Aaron J., H. Ross Anderson, Bart Ostro, Kiran Dev Pandey, Michal Krzyzanowski, Nino Künzli, Kersten Gutschmidt, Arden Pope, Isabelle Romieu, Jonathan M. Samet, and Kirk Smith. 2004. "Mortality Impacts of Urban Air Pollution." In *Comparative Quantification of Health Risks: The Global and Regional Burden of Disease Attributable to Selected Major Risk Factors*, vol. 2, ed. M. Ezzati Majid, A. D. Lopez, A. Rodgers, and C.J.L. Murray, 1353–433. Geneva: World Health Organization.

Commander, Simon, Rupa Chanda, Mari Kangasniemi, and L. Alan Winters. 2004. "Must Skilled Migration Be a Brain Drain? Evidence from the Indian Software Industry." Discussion Paper 1422, Institute for the Study of Labor, Bonn, Germany.

Cooper, Richard N. 2006. "How Integrated Are Chinese and Indian Labor into the World Economy?" Background paper for *Dancing with Giants: China, India, and the Global Economy*. Institute for Policy Studies and the World Bank, Washington, DC.

Corbett, Jenny, and Tim Jenkinson. 1996. "The Financing of Industry, 1970–1989: An International Comparison." *Journal of the Japanese and International Economies* 10: 71–96.

Crassous, Renaud, Jean-Charles Hourcade, Olivier Sassi, Vincent Gitz, Sandrine

Mathy, and Meriem Hamdi-Cherif. 2006. "IMACLIM-R: A Modeling Framework for Sustainable Development Issues." Background paper for *Dancing with Giants: China, India, and the Global Economy*. Institute for Policy Studies and the World Bank, Washington, DC.

Dasgupta, Susmita, Hua Wang, and David Wheeler. 1997. "Surviving Success: Policy Reform and the Future of Industrial Pollution in China." Policy Research Working Paper 1856, World Bank, Washington, DC.

Datt, Gaurav, and Martin Ravallion. 2002. "Has India's Post-Reform Economic Growth Left the Poor Behind?" *Journal of Economic Perspectives* 16 (3): 89–108.

D'Costa, Anthony. 2006. "Exports, University-Industry Linkages, and Innovation Challenges in Bangalore, India." Policy Research Working Paper 3887, World Bank, Washington, DC.

Deaton, Angus. 2001. "Adjusted Indian Poverty Estimates for 1999–00." Photocopy. Research Program in Development Studies, Princeton University, Princeton, NJ.

———. 2005. "Measuring Poverty in a Growing World (or Measuring Growth in a Poor World)." *Review of Economics and Statistics* 87 (1): 1–19.

Deaton, Angus, and Jean Drèze. 2002. "Poverty and Inequality in India: A Re-Examination." *Economic and Political Weekly*, September 7, 3729–48.

Deaton, Angus, and Valerie Kozel. 2005. *The Great Indian Poverty Debate*. Delhi, India: Macmillan.

Devlin, Robert, Antoni Estevadeordal, and Andres Rodríguez-Clare. 2006. *The Emergence of China: Opportunities and Challenges for Latin America and the Caribbean*. Cambridge, MA: David Rockefeller Center, Harvard University.

DfID (Department for International Development). 2005. "The Effect of China and India's Growth and Trade Liberalisation on Poverty in Africa." DCP 70, Final Report, London.

Dimaranan, Betina V., ed. Forthcoming. *Global Trade, Assistance, and Production: The GTAP 6 Data Base*. West Lafayette, IN: Center for Global Trade Analysis, Purdue University.

Dollar, David, and Aart Kraay. 2006. "Neither a Borrower Nor a Lender: Does China's Zero Net Foreign Asset Position Make Economic Sense?" *Journal of Monetary Economics* 53 (5): 943–71.

Dooley, Michael, David Folkerts-Landau, and Peter Garber. 2003. "An Essay on the Revived Bretton Woods System." Working Paper 9971, National Bureau of Economic Research, Cambridge, MA.

Drèze, Jean, and Amartya . 1995. *India: Economic Development and Social Opportunity*. Delhi, India: Oxford University Press.

Dutta, P. 2005. "Accounting for Wage Inequality in India." Poverty Research Unit Working Paper 29, Department of Economics, University of Sussex, UK.

Edmonds, James A., M. Wise, and D. Barns. 1995. "Carbon Coalitions: The Cost and Effectiveness of Energy Agreements to Alter Trajectories of Atmospheric Carbon Dioxide Emissions." *Energy Policy* 23: 309–36.

Edmonds, James A., M. A. Wise, and C. MacCracken. 1994. "Advanced Energy Technologies and Climate Change: An Analysis Using the Global Change Assessment Model (GCAM)." Pacific Northeast Laboratory, Richland, Washington.

Eichengreen, Barry. 2004. "Global Imbalances and the Lessons of Bretton Woods." Working Paper 10497, National Bureau of Economic Research, Cambridge, MA.

Eichengreen, Barry, and Pipat Luengnaruemitchai. 2004. "Why Doesn't Asia Have Bigger Bond Markets?" Presentation at the Korea University/BIS Conference, "Asian Bond Market Research," Seoul, March.

Eichengreen, Barry, and Yung Chul Park. 2003. "Why Has There Been Less Financial Integration in Asia Than in Europe?" Working Paper PEIF-4, Institute of European Studies, University of California, Berkeley.

European Central Bank. 2006. "The Accumulation of Foreign Reserves." Occasional Paper 43, International Relations Committee Task Force, Frankfurt, Germany.

Evenett, Simon J., and Anthony J. Venables. 2002. "Export Growth in Developing Countries: Market Entry and Bilateral Trade Flows." http://www.alexandria.un isg.ch/Publikationen/22177.

Fan, Joseph P. H., Randall Morck, Lixin Colin Xu, and Bernard Yeung. 2006. "Does 'Good Government' Draw Foreign Capital? Explaining China's Exceptional FDI Inflow." Background paper for *Dancing with Giants: China, India, and the Global Economy*. Institute for Policy Studies and the World Bank, Washington, DC.

Fan, Shenggen. 1991. "Effects of Technological Change and Institutional Reform on Growth in Chinese Agriculture." *American Journal of Agricultural Economics* 73: 266–75.

FAO (Food and Agriculture Organization of the United Nations). 2006. "Rapid Growth of Selected Asian Economies: Lessons and Implications for Agriculture and Food Security: China and India." Regional Office for Asia and the Pacific. Bangkok: FAO.

Farrell, Diana, and Aneta Marcheva Key. 2005. "India's Lagging Financial System." *McKinsey Quarterly* 2.

Fehr, Hans, Sabine Jokisch, and Laurence Kotlikoff. Forthcoming. "Will China Eat Our Lunch or Take Us Out to Dinner? Simulating the Demographic, Fiscal, and Economic Transition Paths of the U.S., EU, Japan, and China." In *Fiscal Policy and Management in East Asia*, ed. Takatoshi Ito and Andrew Rose. Chicago: University of Chicago Press.

Fernandez, Juan Antonio, and Laurie Underwood. 2006. *China CEO*. Singapore: John Wiley & Sons.

"Figures Show China as Net Vehicle Exporter." 2006. *Financial Times*, February 11.

Fleisher, Belton, and Xiaojun Wang. 2004. "Skill Differentials, Return to Schooling and Market Segmentation in a Transition Economy: The Case of Mainland China." *Journal of Development Economics* 73: 315–28.

Frankel, Francine R. 2005. *India's Political Economy 1947–2004: The Gradual Revolution*. New Delhi: Oxford University Press.

Freund, Caroline, and Caglar Ozden. 2006. "The Effect of China's Exports on Latin American Trade with the World." Photocopy. World Bank, Washington, DC.

Friedman, Edward, and Bruce Gilley, eds. 2005. *Asia's Giants: Comparing China and India*. New York: Palgrave Macmillan.

Fujita, Masahisa, and Nobuaki Hamaguchi. 2006. "The Coming Age of China-Plus-One: The Japanese Perspective on East Asian Production Networks." Background paper for *Dancing with Giants: China, India, and the Global Economy*. Institute for Policy Studies and the World Bank, Washington, DC.

Gallagher, Kelly Sims. 2006. "Limits to Leapfrogging in Energy Technologies? Evidence from the Chinese Automobile Industry." *Energy Policy* 34 (4): 383–94.

Gehlbach, Scott, and Philip Keefer. 2006. "Credible Commitments in Autocracies." Photocopy. University of Wisconsin-Madison.

Genberg, Hans, Robert McCauley, Yung Chul Park, and Avinash Persaud. 2005. *Official Reserves and Currency Management in Asia: Myth, Reality and the Future*. London: Centre for Economic Policy Research.

Ghosh, Madhusudan. 2006. "Economic Reforms, Growth and Regional Divergence in India." Photocopy. Visva-Bharati University, West Bengal, India.

Gill, B. 2006. "China's Domestic Transformation: Democratization or Disorder?" In *China: The Balance Sheet: What the World Needs to Know Now about the Emerging Superpower*, ed. C. Fred Bergsten, Bates Gill, Nicholas Lardy, and Derek J. Mitchell, ch. 3. New York: Public Affairs/Institute for International Economics/Center for Strategic and International Studies.

"Global Transformation." 2006. *Business China*, June 19.

Gokarn, Subir, Anindya Sen, and Rajendra R. Vaidya, eds. 2004. *The Structure of Indian Industry*. New York: Oxford University Press.

Gokarn, Subir, and Rajendra R. Vaidya. 2004. "The Automobile Components Industry." In *The Structure of Indian Industry*, ed. Subir Gokarn, Anindya Sen, and Rajendra R. Vaidya. New York: Oxford University Press.

Goldstein, Andrea, Nicolas Pinaud, Helmut Reisen, and Xiaobao Chen. 2006. "The Rise of China and India: What's in It for Africa?" Development Centre, OECD, Paris.

Goldstein, Morris, and Nicholas Lardy. 2005. "China's Role in the Revived Bretton Woods System: A Case of Mistaken Identity." Working Paper 05-2, Institute for International Economics, Washington, DC.

Goodfriend, Marvin, and Eswar Prasad. 2006. "A Framework for Independent Monetary Policy in China." Working Paper 06/111, International Monetary Fund, Washington, DC.

"Good Things in Tiny Packages." 2006. *The Economist*, March 25, 14–16.

Gordon, James, and Poonam Gupta. 2005. "Understanding India's Services Revolution." In *India's and China's Recent Experience with Reform and Growth*, ed. Wanda Tseng and David Cowen. New York: Palgrave Macmillan.

Government of India, Ministry of Power. 2003. "Statistics 2003." http://powermin.nic.in/JSP_SERVLETS/internal.jsp.

Government of India, Planning Commission. 2002. *India Vision 2020*. New Delhi.

Grace, Cheri. 2005. "A Briefing Paper for DfID: Update on China and India and Access to Medicines." London: Department for International Development.

Haber, Stephen, Armando Razo, and Noel Maurer. 2003. *The Politics of Property Rights: Political Instability, Credible Commitments, and Economic Growth in Mexico, 1876–1929*. Cambridge, UK: Cambridge University Press.

"Haier to Create 1,000 Jobs in Kershaw County." 2006. *The State*, April 11. http://www.thestate.com/mld/thestate/.

Hamilton, James D. 2003. "What Is an Oil Shock?" *Journal of Econometrics* 113: 363–98.

Han, Chunping, and Martin King Whyte. 2006. "The Social Contours of Distributive Injustice Feelings in Contemporary China." Photocopy. Harvard University, Cambridge, MA.

Hanson, Gordon, and Raymond Robertson. 2006. "China and the Recent Evolution of Latin America's Manufacturing Exports." Photocopy. World Bank, Washington, DC.

Hao, Jiming, and Litao Wang. 2005. "Improving Air Quality in China: Beijing Case Study." *Journal of the Air and Waste Management Association* 55: 1298–305.

Hausmann, Ricardo, and Dani Rodrik. 2003. "Economic Development as Self-discovery." *Journal of Development Economics* 72: 603–33.

Heckman, James, and Xuesong Li. 2004. "Selection Bias, Comparative Advantage and Heterogeneous Returns to Education: Evidence from China in 2000." *Pacific Economic Review* 9 (3): 155–71.

Hellman, Joel. 1998. "Winners Take All: The Politics of Partial Reform in Postcommunist Transitions." *World Politics* 50 (2): 203–34.

"Here Come the Wal-Mart Wannabes." 2005. *BusinessWeek*, April 4.

Hertel, Thomas W., ed. 1997. *Global Trade Analysis, Modeling and Applications*. Cambridge, UK: Cambridge University Press.

Holz, Carsten A. 2006. "China's Reform Period Economic Growth: How Reliable Are Angus Maddison's Estimates?" *Review of Income and Wealth* 52 (1): 85–119.

"Honda to Invest $652m in Drive on Indian Market." 2006. *Financial Times*, July 5.

Huang, Yasheng. 1996. *Inflation and Investment Controls in China*. Cambridge, UK: Cambridge University Press.

————. 2003. *Selling China: Foreign Direct Investment during the Reform Era*. New York: Cambridge University Press.

————. Forthcoming. "Just How Capitalist Is China?" In *International Handbook of Development Economics*, ed. Amitava Krishna Dutt and Jamie Ros. Aldershot, UK: Edward Elgar.

Huang, Yasheng, and Tarun Khanna. 2005. "Indigenous Versus Foreign Business Models." In *Asia's Giants: Comparing China and India*, ed. Edward Friedman and Bruce Gilley. New York: Palgrave Macmillan.

Hummels, David, and Peter Klenow. 2005. "The Variety and Quality of a Nation's Exports." *American Economic Review* 95 (3): 704–23.

Ianchovichina, Elena. 2004. "Trade Policy Analysis in the Presence of Duty Drawbacks." *Journal of Policy Modeling* 26: 353–71.

Ianchovichina, Elena, and Pooja Kacker. 2005. "Growth Trends in the Developing World: Country Forecasts and Determinants." Policy Research Working Paper 3775, World Bank, Washington, DC.

Ianchovichina, Elena, and Will Martin. 2004. "Economic Impacts of China's Accession to the World Trade Organization." *World Bank Economic Review* 18 (1): 3–28.

"IBM to Build Its Presence in India with $6bn Investment." 2006. *Financial Times*, June 7.

IEA (International Energy Agency). 2002. *World Energy Outlook 2002*. Paris: OECD.

————. 2004. *World Energy Outlook 2004*. Paris: OECD.

————. 2005a. "Energy Balances of Non-OECD Member Countries—Extended Balances," vol. 2005, release 01. OECD, Paris.

————. 2005b. "CO_2 Emissions from Fuel Combustion," vol. 2005, release 01. OECD, Paris.

————. 2006. "Energy Prices and Taxes—Crude Oil Spot Prices (US$/bbl)," vol. 2006, release 01. OECD, Paris.

————. Various years. "Oil Market Report." http://www.oilmarketreport.org.

IMF (International Monetary Fund). 2005a. "Will the Oil Market Continue to Be Tight?" *World Economic Outlook*, ch. IV. Washington, DC.

————. 2005b. *World Economic Outlook: Building Institutions*. Washington, DC.

————. 2006a. *Global Financial Stability Report*. April. Washington, DC.

————. 2006b. *World Economic Outlook* database, accessed in September 2006. http://www.imf.org/external/pubs/ft/weo/2006/02/data/index.htm.

"India: China Eats Into Textile Exports." 2005. *Oxford Analytica*, May 20.

"India: Poor Infrastructure Hampers Urban Growth." 2006. *Oxford Analytica*, July 11.

Jalan, Jyotsna, and Martin Ravallion. 2002. "Geographic Poverty Traps? A Micro Model of Consumption Growth in Rural China?" *Journal of Applied Econometrics* 17: 329–46.

"Japanese White Goods Get High Recognition in India." 2006. *Jiji Press*, April 17.

Jean, Sébastien, David Laborde, and Will Martin. 2005. "Consequences of Alternative Formulas for Agricultural Tariff Cuts." In *Agricultural Trade Reform and the Doha Development Agenda*, ed. Kym Anderson and Will Martin, ch. 4. Washington, DC: World Bank.

Jenkins, Rhys, and Chris Edwards. 2006. "The Asian Drivers and Sub-Saharan Africa." *IDS Bulletin* 37 (1): 23–32.

Jian, Tianlun, Jeffrey Sachs, and Andrew Warner. 1996. "Trends in Regional Inequality in China." *China Economic Review* 7 (1): 1–21.

Joseph, K. J. 2004. "The Electronics Industry." In *The Structure of Indian Industry*, ed. Subir Gokarn, Anindya Sen, and Rajendra R. Vaidya. New York: Oxford University Press.

Ju, Jiandong, and Shang-Jin Wei. 2006. "A Solution to Two Paradoxes of International Capital Flows." Photocopy. International Monetary Fund, Washington, DC.

Kaminsky, Graciela, and Sergio Schmukler. 2003. "Short-run Pain, Long-run Gain: The Effects of Financial Liberalization." Working Paper 9787, National Bureau of Economic Research, Cambridge, MA.

Kanbur, Ravi. 2001. "Economic Policy, Distribution and Poverty: The Nature of Disagreements." *World Development* 29 (6): 1083–94.

Kanbur, Ravi, and Xiaobo Zhang. 1999. "Which Regional Inequality: The Evolution of Rural-Urban and Coast-Inland Inequality in China." *Journal of Comparative Economics* 27: 686–701.

Kaplinsky, Raphael, Dorothy McCormick, and Mike Morris. 2006. "The Impact of China on Sub-Saharan Africa." China Office, U.K. Department for International Development, Beijing.

Kaufmann, Daniel, Aart Kraay, and Massimo Mastruzzi. 2005. "Governance Matters IV: Governance Indicators for 1996–2004." Policy Research Working Paper 3630 (June), World Bank, Washington, DC.

Keefer, Philip, and Stuti Khemani. 2005. "Democracy, Public Expenditures, and the Poor: Understanding Political Incentives for Providing Public Services." *World Bank Research Observer* 20 (1): 1–28.

Keefer, Philip, and Razvan Vlaicu. 2005. "Democracy, Credibility and Clientelism." Policy Research Working Paper 3472, World Bank, Washington, DC.

Keidel, Albert. 2005. "The Economic Basis of Social Unrest in China." Paper presented at the Third European-American Dialogue on China, Washington, DC, May 26–27.

Khanna, Tarun, and Krishna Palepu. 2004. "The Evolution of Concentrated Ownership in India: Broad Patterns and a History of the Indian Software Industry." Working Paper 10613, National Bureau of Economic Research, Cambridge, MA.

Kletzer, Kenneth M. 2005. "Liberalizing Capital Flows in India: Financial Repression,

Macroeconomic Policy, and Gradual Reforms." In *India Policy Forum 2004*, ed. Suman Bery, Barry Bosworth, and Arvind Panagariya, 1–40. Washington, DC: Brookings Institution Press.

Knack, Stephen, and Philip Keefer. 1995. "Institutions and Economic Performance: Cross-country Tests Using Alternative Institutional Measures." *Economics and Politics* 7 (3): 207–27.

Kochhar, Kalpana, U. Kumar, R. Rajan, A. Subramanian, and I. Tokatlidis. 2005. "India's Pattern of Development: What Happened, What Follows?" Paper presented at the Carnegie-Rochester Conference Series on Public Policy, Tepper School of Business, Carnegie-Mellon University, Pittsburgh, PA, November 18–19.

———. 2006. "India's Pattern of Development: What Happened, What Follows." Working Paper 06/22, International Monetary Fund, Washington, DC.

Kohli, Atul. 2006. "Politics of Economic Growth in India, 1980–2005, Parts I and II." *Economic and Political Weekly*, April 1, 1251–60, and April 8, 1361–70.

Korinek, Anton, Johan Mistiaen, and Martin Ravallion. 2006. "Survey Nonresponse and the Distribution of Income." *Journal of Economic Inequality* 4 (2): 33–55.

KPMG International. 2006. *Manufacturing in India: Opportunities, Challenges, and Myths*. Report No. 211-786.

Kuijs, Louis. 2005. "Investment and Savings in China." Policy Research Working Paper 3633, World Bank, Washington, DC.

———. 2006. "China in the Future: A Large Net Saver or Net Borrower?" Background paper for *Dancing with Giants: China, India, and the Global Economy*. Institute for Policy Studies and the World Bank, Washington, DC.

Kypreos, K. 2000. "The MERGE Model with Endogenous Technological Change." Presentation at the Workshop on Economic Modeling of Environmental Policy and Endogenous Technological Change, Amsterdam, November 16–17.

Lall, Sanjaya, and Manuel Albaladejo. 2004. "China's Competitive Performance: A Threat to East Asian Manufactured Exports?" *World Development* 32 (9): 1441–66.

Lall, Sanjaya, and John Weiss. 2004. "China's Competitive Threat to Latin America: An Analysis for 1990–2002." Queen Elizabeth House Working Paper 120, University of Oxford, UK.

Lall, Somik, and Sanjoy Chakravorty. 2005. "Industrial Location and Spatial Inequality: Theory and Evidence from India." *Review of Development Economics* 9 (1): 47–68.

Lane, Philip. 2006. "The International Balance Sheets of China and India." Background paper for *Dancing with Giants: China, India, and the Global Economy*. Institute for Policy Studies and the World Bank, Washington, DC.

Lane, Philip, and Gian Maria Milesi-Ferretti. 2002. "Long-term Capital Movements." In *NBER Macroeconomics Annual 2001*, ed. Ben S. Bernanke and Kenneth S. Rogoff, 73–116. Cambridge, MA: MIT Press.

————. 2006. "The External Wealth of Nations Mark II: Revised and Extended Estimates of Foreign Assets and Liabilities, 1970–2004." Working Paper 06/69, International Monetary Fund, Washington, DC.

Lane, Philip, and Sergio Schmukler. 2006. "The International Financial Integration of China and India." Discussion Paper 5852, Center for Economic Policy Research, London.

Lardy, Nicholas R. 2004. "China: The Great New Economic Challenge?" In *The United States and the World Economy: Foreign Economic Policy for the New Decade*, ed. C. Fred Bergsten. Washington, DC: Institute for International Economics.

Lewis, W. Arthur. 1954. "Economic Development with Unlimited Supplies of Labour." *The Manchester School of Economic and Social Studies* 22: 139–91.

Li, David D. 2006. "Large Domestic Non-intermediated Investments and Government Liabilities: Challenges Facing China's Financial Sector Reform." Background paper for *Dancing with Giants: China, India, and the Global Economy*. Institute for Policy Studies and the World Bank, Washington, DC.

Li, Hongbin, and Li-An Zhou. 2005. "Political Turnover and Economic Performance: The Incentive Role of Personnel Control in China." *Journal of Public Economics* 89 (9/10): 1743–62.

Lim, Edwin, Michael Spence, and Ricardo Hausmann. 2006. "China and the Global Economy: Medium-term Issues and Opinions." Working Paper 1265, Center for International Development, Harvard University, Cambridge, MA.

Lin, Justin. 1992. "Rural Reforms and Agricultural Growth in China." *American Economic Review* 82: 34–51.

Lin, Xiannuan. 1996. *China's Energy Strategy: Economic Structure, Technological Choices, and Energy Consumption*. Westport, CT: Praeger.

Lindert, P. H. 2000. "Three Centuries of Inequality in Britain and America." In *Handbook of Income Distribution*, vol. I, ed. A. B. Atkinson and F. Bourguignon, 167–216. Amsterdam: North Holland.

Liu, Gang. 2004. "Estimating Energy Demand Elasticities for OECD Countries: A Dynamic Panel Data Approach." Discussion Paper 373, Research Department, Statistics Norway, Oslo.

Liu, Shijin. 2003. "Challenges and Development Goals of China's Energy Industry in 2020." Presentation at the China Development Forum 2003, China's National Energy Strategy and Reform, November 15–17.

Loayza, Norman, P. Fajnzylber, and C. Calderon. 2005. *Economic Growth in Latin America and the Caribbean: Stylized Facts, Explanations, and Forecasts*. Washington, DC: World Bank.

Ma, Jun, Nam Ngyuen, and Jin Xu. 2006. *China's Innovation Drive*. Hong Kong (China): Deutsche Bank, May 18.

Maddison, Angus. 2003. *The World Economy: Historical Statistics*. Paris: OECD.

Manion, Melanie. 1985. "The Cadre Management System, Post-Mao: The Appointment, Promotion, Transfer and Removal of Party and State Leaders." *China Quarterly* 102 (June): 203–33.

———. 1992. "Politics and Policy in Post-Mao Cadre Retirement." *China Quarterly* 129 (March): 1–25.

Manne, Allen. 1978. "Energy-Economy Interactions: The Fable of the Elephant and the Rabbit?" In *Advances in the Economics of Energy and Resources*, vol. 1, ed. R. Pindyck. Greenwich, CT: JAI Press.

Markusen, J., T. Rutherford, and D. Tarr. 2005. "Trade and Direct Investment in Producer Services and the Domestic Market for Expertise." *Canadian Journal of Economics* 38 (3): 758–77.

Martin, Will. 1993. "The Fallacy of Composition and Developing Country Exports of Manufactures." *World Economy* 16 (2): 159–72.

Mattoo, Aaditya, Deepak Mishra, and Anirudh Shingal. 2004. *Sustaining India's Services Revolution: Access to Foreign Markets, Domestic Reform and International Negotiations*. Washington, DC: World Bank.

McKinsey Global Institute. 2005. *The Emerging Global Labor Market*. New York: McKinsey & Company.

Mehta, Pratap Bhanu. 2003. "A Problem Not Named—India's Economy Is Not Well Poised to Generate Employment." *The Telegraph*, December 17.

Mengistae, Taye, Lixin Colin Xu, and Bernard Yeung. 2006. "China vs. India: A Microeconomic Look at Comparative Macroeconomic Performance." Background paper for *Dancing with Giants: China, India, and the Global Economy*. Institute for Policy Studies and the World Bank, Washington, DC.

Min, Weifang. 2006. "Recent Trends of Higher Education Development in China." May 8.

Mishra, Deepak. 2006. "Financing India's Rapid Growth and Its Implications for the Global Economy." Background paper for *Dancing with Giants: China, India, and the Global Economy*. Institute for Policy Studies and the World Bank, Washington, DC.

Mitra, A. P., and C. Sharma. 2002. "India Aerosol: Present Status." *Chemosphere* 49: 1175–90.

Mitra, Devashish, and Beyza P. Ural. 2006. "Indian Manufacturing: A Slow Sector in a Rapidly Growing Economy." Background paper for *Dancing with Giants: China, India, and the Global Economy*. Institute for Policy Studies and the World Bank, Washington, DC.

Modigliani, Franco, and Shi Larry Cao. 2004. "The Chinese Saving Puzzle and the Life-cycle Hypothesis." *Journal of Economic Literature* 42 (1): 145–70.

Morita, Tsuneyuki, Mikiko Kainuma, Hideo Harasawa, and Keiko Kai. 1994. "Asian-Pacific Integrated Model for Evaluating Policy Options to Reduce Greenhouse Gas

Emissions and Global Warming Impacts." National Institute for Environmental Studies, Ibaraki, Japan.

Mukherji, Joydeep. 2005. "The Causes of Differential Development: Beyond Regime Dichotomies." In *Asia's Giants: Comparing China and India*, ed. Edward Friedman and Bruce Gilley. New York: Palgrave Macmillan.

Murgai, Rinku, and Martin Ravallion. 2005. "Employment Guarantee in Rural India: What Would It Cost and How Much Would It Reduce Poverty?" *Economic and Political Weekly*, July 30, 3450–55.

National Bureau of Statistics of China. 2005. *China Statistical Yearbook 2005*. Beijing.

Naughton, Barry. 1995. *Growing Out of the Plan: Chinese Economic Reform, 1978–1993*. New York: Cambridge University Press.

———. 2006. "Top-down Control: SASAC and the Persistence of State Ownership in China." Photocopy. University of California, San Diego.

Nayar, Baldev Raj. 1990. *The Political Economy of India's Public Sector*. London: Sangam Books.

Nee, Victor. 1992. "Organizational Dynamics of Market Transition: Hybrid Forms, Property Rights, and Mixed Economy in China." *Administrative Science Quarterly* 37 (1): 1–27.

Nee, Victor, and Sonja Opper. 2006. "China's Politicized Capitalism." PBackground paper for *Dancing with Giants: China, India, and the Global Economy*. Institute for Policy Studies and the World Bank, Washington, DC.

Nichols, Theo, and Surhan Cam. 2005. "The World of White Goods: Markets, Industry Structure and Dynamics." In *Labour in a Global World: Case Studies from the White Goods Industry in Africa, South America, East Asia and Europe*, ed. Theo Nichols and Surhan Cam, 1–22. New York: Palgrave Macmillan.

Nikomborirak, Deunden. 2006. "A Comparative Study of the Role of the Service Sector in the Economic Development of China and India." Background paper for *Dancing with Giants: China, India, and the Global Economy*. Institute for Policy Studies and the World Bank, Washington, DC.

Noble, Gregory W. 2006. "The Emergence of the Chinese and Indian Automobile Industries and Implications for Other Developing Countries." Background paper for *Dancing with Giants: China, India, and the Global Economy*. Institute for Policy Studies and the World Bank, Washington, DC.

North, Douglass C. 1990. *Institutions, Institutional Change and Economic Performance*. Cambridge, UK: Cambridge University Press.

"Now for the Hard Part." 2006. *The Economist*, June 3.

Obstfeld, Maurice. 2005. "The Renminbi's Dollar Peg at the Crossroads." Photocopy. University of California, Berkeley.

Obstfeld, Maurice, and Kenneth Rogoff. 2005. "Global Current Account Imbalances and Exchange Rate Adjustments." *Brookings Papers on Economic Activity* 1: 67–146.

Office of the Registrar General, India. 2003. "Household Assets in India from Census 2001." http://www.censusindia.net/2001housing/S00-020.html.

Oi, Jean Chun. 1989. *State and Peasant in Contemporary China: The Political Economy of Village Government*. Berkeley: University of California Press.

———. 1999. *Rural China Takes Off: Institutional Foundations of Economic Reform*. Berkeley: University of California Press.

Padhi, Asutosh, Geert Pauwels, and Charlie Taylor. 2004. "Freeing India's Textile Industry." *McKinsey Quarterly* October.

Panagariya, Arvind. 2004. "India in the 1980s and 1990s: A Triumph of Reforms." Working Paper 04/43, International Monetary Fund, Washington, DC.

———. 2006. "India and China: Trade and Foreign Investment." Photocopy. Columbia University, New York.

Park, Albaret, Xiaoqing Song, Junsen Zhang, and Yaohui Zhao. 2004. "The Growth of Wage Inequality in Urban China, 1988 to 1999." Photocopy. Department of Economics, University of Michigan, Ann Arbor.

Patnaik, Ila, and Ajay Shah. 2006. "The Interplay between Capital Flows and the Domestic Indian Financial System." Background paper for *Dancing with Giants: China, India, and the Global Economy*. Institute for Policy Studies and the World Bank, Washington, DC.

———. Forthcoming. "India's Experience with Capital Flows: The Elusive Quest for a Sustainable Current Account Deficit." In *Capital Controls and Capital Flows in Emerging Economies: Policies, Practices, and Consequences*, ed. Sebastian Edwards. Chicago: University of Chicago Press.

Paul, Shyamal, and Rabindra N. Bhattacharya. 2004. "CO_2 Emission from Energy Use in India: A Decomposition Analysis." *Energy Policy* 32: 585–93.

Pecht, Michael, and Y. C. Chan. 2004. *China's Electronics Industry*. College Park, MD: CALCE EPSC Press.

Pei, Minxin. 2006. *China's Trapped Transition: The Limits of Developmental Autocracy*. Cambridge, MA: Harvard University Press.

Petri, Peter A. 2006. "Is East Asia Becoming More Interdependent?" *Journal of Asian Economics* 17 (3): 381–94.

Prasad, Eswar, and Raghuram Rajan. 2005. "Controlled Capital Account Liberalization: A Proposal." Policy Discussion Paper 05/7, International Monetary Fund, Washington, DC.

———. 2006. "A Framework for Independent Monetary Policy in China." Working Paper 06/111, International Monetary Fund, Washington, DC.

Prasad, Eswar, Kenneth Rogoff, Shang-Jin Wei, and Ayhan Kose. 2003. *Effects of Financial Globalization on Developing Countries: Some Empirical Evidence*. Occasional Paper 220. Washington, DC: International Monetary Fund.

Prasad, Eswar, and Shang-Jin Wei. 2005. "China's Approach to Capital Inflows: Patterns and Possible Explanations." Working Paper 05/79, International Monetary Fund, Washington, DC.

PROBE Team. 1999. *Public Report on Basic Education*. New Delhi, India: Oxford University Press.

Puga, Diego, and Anthony Venables. 1999. "Agglomeration and Economic Development: Import Substitution vs. Trade Liberalization." *Economic Journal* 109: 292–311.

Quinn, Dennis P., and John Woolley. 2001. "Democracy and National Economic Performance: The Preference for Stability." *American Journal of Political Science* 45 (3): 634–57.

Radhakrishnan, K. G. 2006. "India's Adolescent Software Industry." *Far Eastern Economic Review*.

Raiser, Martin. 1998. "Subsidizing Inequality: Economic Reforms, Fiscal Transfers and Convergence across Chinese Provinces." *Journal of Development Studies* 34: 1–26.

Ranciere, Romain, Aaron Tornell, and Frank Westermann. 2005. "Systemic Crises and Growth." Working Paper 11076, National Bureau of Economic Research, Cambridge, MA.

Ravallion, Martin. 2000. "Should Poverty Measures Be Anchored to the National Accounts?" *Economic and Political Weekly*, August 26, 3245–52.

———. 2003. "Measuring Aggregate Economic Welfare in Developing Countries: How Well Do National Accounts and Surveys Agree?" *Review of Economics and Statistics* 85: 645–52.

———. 2004a. "Competing Concepts of Inequality in the Globalization Debate." In *Brookings Trade Forum 2004*, ed. Susan Collins and Carol Graham, 1–38. Washington, DC: Brookings Institution Press.

———. 2004b. "Pro-Poor Growth: A Primer." Policy Research Working Paper 3242, World Bank, Washington, DC.

———. 2005. "Externalities in Rural Development: Evidence for China." In *Spatial Inequality and Development*, ed. Ravi Kanbur and Anthony Venables, 137–62. New York: Oxford University Press.

Ravallion, Martin, and Shaohua Chen. 1999. "When Economic Reform Is Faster Than Statistical Reform: Measuring and Explaining Inequality in Rural China." *Oxford Bulletin of Economics and Statistics* 61: 33–56.

———. 2003. "Measuring Pro-Poor Growth." *Economics Letters* 78 (1): 93–99.

———. 2005. "Hidden Impact: Household Saving in Response to a Poor-Area Development Project." *Journal of Public Economics* 89: 2183–204.

———. Forthcoming. "China's (Uneven) Progress against Poverty." *Journal of Development Economics*.

Ravallion, Martin, and Gaurav Datt. 1996. "How Important to India's Poor Is the Sectoral Composition of Economic Growth?" *World Bank Economic Review* 10: 1–26.

———. 2002. "Why Has Economic Growth Been More Pro-Poor in Some States of India Than Others?" *Journal of Development Economics* 68: 381–400.

Ravallion, Martin, and Dominique van de Walle. 2006. "Does Rising Landlessness Signal Success or Failure for Vietnam's Agrarian Transition?" Policy Research Working Paper 3871, World Bank, Washington, DC.

Rawski, Thomas. 2006. "International Dimensions of China's Long Boom: Trends, Prospects, and Implications." Presentation at the Yale East Asia Forum on Political Economy, New Haven, CT, May 31.

Reisen, Helmut, Andrea Goldstein, and Nicolas Pinaud. 2006. "China and India: What's in It for Africa?" Paper presented at the Seventh Annual Global Development Conference, St. Petersburg, Russia, January 18.

"Risks Mount Alongside Growth." 2006. *Oxford Analytica*, February 20.

Rodrik, Dani. 2006a. "The Social Cost of Foreign Exchange Reserves." *International Economic Journal* 20 (3): 253–66.

———. 2006b. "What's So Special about China's Exports?" Photocopy. Kennedy School, Harvard University, Cambridge, MA.

Rodrik, Dani, and Arvind Subramanian. 2005. "From Hindu Growth to Productivity Surge: The Mystery of the Indian Growth Transition." *IMF Staff Papers* 52 (2): 193–236.

Roland-Holst, David, and John Weiss. 2005. "People's Republic of China and Its Neighbors: Evidence on Regional Trade and Investment Effects." *Asia-Pacific Economic Literature* 19 (2): 18–35.

Roy, Tirthankar. 2004. "The Textile Industry." In *The Structure of Indian Industry*, ed. Subir Gokarn, Anindya Sen, and Rajendra R. Vaidya. New York: Oxford University Press.

Sala-i-Martin, Xavier. 2002. "The World Distribution of Income (Estimated from Individual Country Distributions)." Working Paper 8933, National Bureau of Economic Research, Cambridge, MA.

"Sanyo Seeks India Boost." 2006. *Nihon Keizai Shimbun*, April 3.

Sarma, E.A.S, J. N. Margo, and A. S. Sachdeva. 1998. "India's Energy Scenario in 2020." Paper presented at the 17th World Energy Congress, Houston, TX, September 13–18.

Saxenian, AnnaLee. 2006. *The New Argonauts*. Cambridge, MA: Harvard University Press.

Schiff, Jerald, Enric Fernandez, Renu Kohli, Sudip Mohapatra, Catriona Purfield, Mark Flanagan, and Dimitri Rozhkov. 2006. "India: Selected Issues." Country Report No. 06/56, International Monetary Fund, Washington, DC.

"Selling Generics Used to Be So Easy." 2006. *Business Week*, February 27.

Sen, Abhijit, and Himanshu. 2004a. "Poverty and Inequality in India 1." *Economic and Political Weekly*, September 18, 4247–63.

————. 2004b. "Poverty and Inequality in India 2: Widening Disparities during the 1990s." *Economic and Political Weekly*, September 25, 4361–75.

Setser, Brad. 2005. "The Chinese Conundrum: External Financial Strength, Domestic Financial Weakness." Presentation at the CESifo Conference, "Understanding the Chinese Economy," Munich, June.

Shalizi, Zmarak. 2005. "Sustainable Development and the Wise Use of Natural Resources in China." Presentation at the 21st Century Forum, Beijing, September 5–7.

————. 2006. "Addressing China's Growing Water Shortages and Associated Social and Environmental Consequences." Policy Research Working Paper 3895, World Bank, Washington, DC.

————. Forthcoming. "Energy and Emissions: Local and Global Effects of the Rise of China and India." Policy Research Working Paper, World Bank, Washington, DC.

Shanker, Kripa, and T. G. Nayak. 1983. "Shifts in the Factor Income Shares—A Comparative Study of the Public and Private Indian Corporate Sector, 1960–61 to 1977–78." *Occasional Papers, Reserve Bank of India* 4 (June): 82–109.

"Sharp India Chalking Out Come Back Plan." 2006. *Economic Times*, April 25.

Shi, Xinzheng, Terry Sicular, and Yaohui Zhao. 2004. "Urban–Rural Income Inequality in China in the 1990s." Photocopy. China Center for Economic Research, Beijing University.

Shih, Victor. 2004. "Dealing with Non-performing Loans: Political Constraints and Financial Policies in China." *China Quarterly* 922–44.

Shirk, Susan L. 1993. *The Political Logic of Economic Reform in China*. Berkeley: University of California Press.

Sigurdson, Jon. 2005. *Technological Superpower China*. Northampton, MA: Edward Elgar.

Sinton, Jonathan. 2001. "Accuracy and Reliability of China's Energy Statistics." *China Economic Review* 12 (4): 373–83.

Sinton, Jonathan E., and David G. Fridley. 2000. "What Goes Up: Recent Trends in China's Energy Consumption." *Energy Policy* 28: 671–87.

————. 2003. "Comments on Recent Energy Statistics from China." *Sino Sphere Journal* 6 (2): 6–14.

Sinton, Jonathan E., Mark D. Levine, and Qingyi Wang. 1998. "Energy Efficiency in China: Accomplishments and Challenges." *Energy Policy* 26 (11): 813–29.

"Smooth Drive." 2006. *Economic and Political Weekly*, February 25.

Srinivasan, T. N. 2003a. "China and India: Economic Performance, Competition, and Cooperation, An Update." Working Paper 199, Stanford University Center for International Development, Palo Alto, CA.

————. 2003b. "Indian Economic Reforms: A Stock-taking." Paper 190, Stanford Center for International Development, Stanford University, Stanford, CA.

————. 2006. "China, India, and the World Economy." Background paper for *Dancing with Giants: China, India, and the Global Economy*. Institute for Policy Studies and the World Bank, Washington, DC.

Stevens, Christopher, and Jane Kennan. 2006. "How to Identify the Trade Impact of China on Small Countries." *Institute of Development Studies Bulletin* 37 (1): 33–42.

Streifel, Shane. 2006. "Impact of China and India on Global Commodity Markets: Focus on Metals and Minerals and Petroleum." Background paper for *Dancing with Giants: China, India, and the Global Economy*. Institute for Policy Studies and the World Bank, Washington, DC.

Sull, Donald N., and Yong Wang. 2005. *Made in China: What Western Managers Can Learn from Trailblazing Chinese Entrepreneurs*. Boston: Harvard Business School Press.

Summers, Lawrence. 2006. "Reflections on Global Account Imbalances and Emerging Markets Reserve Accumulation." L. K. Jha Memorial Lecture, Reserve Bank of India, Mumbai, March.

Sun, Haishun, and Dilip Dutta. 1997. "China's Economic Growth during 1984–93: A Case of Regional Dualism." *Third World Quarterly* 18 (5): 843–64.

Sundaram, Krishnamurty, and Suresh D. Tendulkar. 2003. "Poverty in India in the 1990s: Revised Results for All-India and 15 Major States for 1993–94." *Economic and Political Weekly*, November 15, 4865–73.

Suri, K. C. 2004. "Democracy, Economic Reforms and Election Results in India." *Economic and Political Weekly*, 39 (51), 5404–11.

Sutton, John. 2004. "The Auto-Component Supply Chain in China and India: A Benchmarking Study." Photocopy. Suntory and Toyota International Centres for Economics and Related Disciplines, London School of Economics.

Swamy, Subramanian. 2005. "Chasing China: Can India Bridge the Gap?" In *Asia's Giants: Comparing China and India*, ed. Edward Friedman and Bruce Gilley. New York: Palgrave Macmillan.

Tan, Kong-Yam. 2004. "Market Fragmentation and Impact on Economics Growth." Paper prepared for the 11th Five-Year Plan of China. World Bank, Washington, DC.

"Tata Steel Girds Itself to Meet Indian Demand with Good Technology and Access to Cheap Ore." 2006. *Financial Times*, March 24.

"Telecoms and Technology." 2006. *Business China*, June 5.

TERI (The Energy and Resources Institute). 2004. *TERI Energy Data Directory and Yearbook 2004*. New Delhi, India: TERI Press.

"Today India, Tomorrow the World." 2005. *The Economist*, April 2.

"Toshiba Forays into Indian Home Appliances Market." 2006. *Business Line*, May 5.

Tseng, Wanda, and Markus Rodlauer, eds. 2003. *China: Competing in the Global Economy*. Washington, DC: IMF.

UNCTAD (United Nations Conference on Trade and Development). 2005. *Trade and Development Report, 2005.* New York: United Nations.

UNDP (United Nations Development Programme). 2002. *Human Development Report 2002: Deepening Democracy in a Fragmented World.* New York: Oxford University Press.

United Kingdom, Department of Trade and Industry. 2005. *The 2005 R&D Scoreboard.* London.

"Up to the Job? How India and China Risk Being Stifled by a Skills Squeeze." 2006. *Financial Times*, July 20.

USEIA (U.S. Energy Information Administration). 2003. "An Energy Overview of the People's Republic of China." http://www.fe.doe.gov/international/EastAs ia_and_Oceania/chinover.html.

———. 2005. *International Energy Annual 2003.* http://tonto.eia.doe.gov/bookshel f/SearchResults.asp?title=International+Energy+Annual&submit=Search&product.

———. 2006. *International Energy Annual 2004.* http://www.eia.doe.gov/iea/.

Van Vuuren, Detlef, Zhou Fengqi, Bert de Vries, Jiang Kejun, Cor Graveland, and Li Yun. 2003. "Energy and Emission Scenarios for China in the 21st Century—Exploration of Baseline Development and Mitigation Options." *Energy Policy* 31: 369–87.

Virmani, Arvind. 2005. "Policy Regimes, Growth and Poverty in India: Lessons of Government Failure and Entrepreneurial Success." Working Paper 170, Indian Council for Research on International Economic Relations, New Delhi.

Walmsley, Terrie, Betina Dimaranan, and Robert McDougall. 2002. "A Base Case Scenario for the Dynamic GTAP Model." Paper prepared for the GTAP Advisory Board Meeting, Taipei, Taiwan (China), June 2–3.

Warnock, Francis, and Veronica Warnock. 2006. "International Capital Flows and U.S. Interest Rates." Photocopy. Darden School of Business, University of Virginia, Charlottesville.

"Watch Out, India." 2006. *The Economist*, May 6.

Wedeman, Andrew. 2004. "The Intensification of Corruption in China." *China Quarterly* 895–921.

Whalley, John. 2006. "The Post MFA Performance of Developing Asia." Working Paper 12178, National Bureau of Economic Research, Cambridge, MA.

Whiting, Susan H. 2001. *Power and Wealth in Rural China: The Political Economy of Institutional Change.* New York: Cambridge University Press.

———. 2006. "Growth, Governance and Institutions: The Internal Institutions of the Party-State in China." Background paper for *Dancing with Giants: China, India, and the Global Economy.* Institute for Policy Studies and the World Bank, Washington, DC.

Wilkinson, Steven I. 2006a. "Explaining Changing Patterns of Party-Voter Linkages in India." In *Patrons, Clients and Policies: Patterns of Democratic Accountability and*

Political Competition, ed. Herbert Kitschelt and Steven I. Wilkinson. Cambridge, UK: Cambridge University Press.

———. 2006b. "The Politics of Infrastructural Spending in India." Background paper for *Dancing with Giants: China, India, and the Global Economy*. Institute for Policy Studies and the World Bank, Washington, DC.

Wong, Christine P. W. 1992. "Fiscal Reform and Local Industrialization: The Problematic Sequencing of Reform in Post-Mao China." *Modern China* 18 (2): 197–227.

World Bank. 1994. *China: Foreign Trade Reform*. Washington, DC.

———. 2002. "Box 2.3: Round-tripping of capital flows between China and Hong Kong (China)." In *Global Development Finance 2002: Financing the Poorest Countries*, 41. Washington, DC.

———. 2003a. *Global Economic Prospects and the Developing Countries 2004*. Washington, DC.

———. 2003b. *World Development Report 2003: Sustainable Development in a Dynamic World*. New York: Oxford University Press.

———. 2004a. *India Investment Climate Assessment 2004: Improving Manufacturing Competitiveness*. Washington, DC.

———. 2004b. "Trade Policies in South Asia: An Overview." Report 29949, Washington, DC.

———. 2005a. "For a Breath of Fresh Air: Ten Years of Progress and Challenges in Urban Air Quality Management 1993–2002." Washington, DC.

———. 2005b. *World Development Indicators*. http://web.worldbank.org/WBSITE/EXTERNAL/DATASTATISTICS/0,,contentMDK:20899413~menuPK:232599~pagePK:64133150~piPK:64133175~theSitePK:239419,00.html.

———. 2005c. *World Development Report: Equity and Development*. New York: Oxford University Press.

———. 2006a. "The China Environmental Cost Model." Photocopy. Washington, DC.

———. 2006b. *Global Economic Indicators*. Washington, DC.

———. 2006c. *India: Inclusive Growth and Service Delivery: Building on India's Success*. New Delhi, India.

———. Forthcoming. *Latin America and the Caribbean Respond to the Growth of China and India*. Regional Study of the Office of the Chief Economist for Latin America and the Caribbean, Washington, DC.

World Bank Office, Beijing. 2005. *China Quarterly Update—November 2005*, table 2, p. 16.

———. 2006. "GDP Revisions—What Has Changed and What Has Remained the Same?" *Quarterly Update: February 2006*. http://siteresources.worldbank.org/INTCHINA/Resources/318862-1121421293578/cqu_feb06.pdf, downloaded April 3, 2006.

World Energy Council. 1999. *Energy Efficiency Policies and Indicators*. London.

WHO (World Health Organization). 2002. *The World Health Report*. Geneva.

Wu, Jinglian. 2005. *Understanding and Interpreting Chinese Economic Reform*. Cincinnati, OH: Thomson/South-Western.

Wu, Yanrui, and Zhangyue Zhou. 2006. "Changing Bilateral Trade between China and India." *Journal of Asian Economics* 17 (3): 509–18.

Xiao, Geng. 2004. "People's Republic of China's Round-tripping FDI: Scale, Causes and Implications." Discussion Paper 7, Asian Development Bank Institute, Tokyo.

Yang, Dali L. 2004. *Remaking the Chinese Leviathan: Market Transition and the Politics of Governance in China*. Stanford, CA: Stanford University Press.

Yang, Yongzheng. 2006. "China's Integration into the World Economy: Implications for Developing Countries." *Asia-Pacific Economic Literature* 20 (1): 40–56.

Yusuf, Shahid, and Kaoru Nabeshima. 2006a. *China's Development Priorities*. Washington, DC: World Bank.

———. 2006b. *Post Industrial East Asian Cities*. Stanford, CA: Stanford University Press.

Yusuf, Shahid, Shuilin Wang, and Kaoru Nabeshima. 2005. "Fiscal Policies for Innovation." Photocopy. World Bank, Washington, DC.

Zhang, Xiaobo, and Ravi Kanbur. 2005. "Spatial Inequality in Education and Health Care in China." *China Economic Review* 16: 189–204.

Zhang, Zhongxiang. 2000. "Can China Afford to Commit Itself to an Emissions Cap? An Economic and Political Analysis." *Energy Economics* 22: 587–614.

Zhao, Min. 2006. "External Liberalization and the Evolution of China's Exchange System: An Empirical Approach." Background paper for *Dancing with Giants: China, India, and the Global Economy*. Institute for Policy Studies and the World Bank, Washington, DC.

Zhao, Wei, Theo Nichols, and Surhan Cam. 2005. "China: White Goods and the Capitalist Transformation." In *Labour in a Global World: Case Studies from the White Goods Industry in Africa, South America, East Asia and Europe*, ed. Theo Nichols and Surhan Cam, 92–119. New York: Palgrave Macmillan.

Zhou, Ping, and Loet Leydesdorff. 2006. "The Emergence of China as a Leading Nation in Science." *Research Policy* 35 (1): 83–104.

Index

‮

manufacturing sector, 35, 37
research and development investment share, 43
services sector share, 45
trade shares and, 14
Gross domestic product, world, 1, 10, 107, 145–46
Growth incidence curve, 188
Growth of Giants
auto and auto parts production and consumption, 58–60
benefits for developing countries, 68
carbon emissions, 140–41
constraints to. *See* Constraints to growth
distribution of foreign direct investment and, 22–24
economic policy of other countries in response to, 31–34, 64
energy production and consumption, 16, 26, 135–40, 144, 145. *See also* Energy and emissions trajectories
environmental concerns, 24–27
global effects of Giants' capital accumulation, 97
global effects of Giants' human capital accumulation, 97
global significance, 1–2, 4–5, 10–11, 31, 35, 67
global trade outcomes, 19–22, 82–94, 99–100
governance factors, 3–4, 28–31, 211, 212, 214–18, 239, 241–42
historical comparisons, 7–11
implications of international integration, 128–31
international comparison, 6–7
market size as factor in, 216–18
modeling methodologies, 2–3, 4, 13, 74–82
moderators of effects of, 67–69
per capita incomes, 188–89, 213
pharmaceutical industry, 56–57
poverty reduction and, 175
projected growth rate, 2–3
quality and variety of exports, 80–81, 84–94
recent history, 175
services exports, 70–72
societal distribution. *See* Distribution of growth and wealth in India and China
socioeconomic factors, 3–4
sources. *See* Sources of growth
steel industry, 60–61
total factor productivity, 13
trade between India and China and, 93
transportation system, 138–39

H
High-income countries. *See* Middle- and high-income countries
High-technology capability
Giants' exports, 14
implications of Giants' growth for other countries, 33–34, 99–100
trends in China, 43

Historical comparisons of economic growth, 7–11
Households
consumption, 218
savings, 116, 118, 126–27
See also Per capita incomes
Human resources
China's, 41–43
future prospects, 65–66
global effects of Giants' growth in, 97
global output modeling, 82–84
India's, 44
information technology-enabled services, 17
labor regulations, 198, 206
manufacturing sector, 18–19, 50, 51, 65
See also Educational attainment; Population patterns and trends
Hydroelectric power, 137, 140, 155

I
IMACLIM-R model, 151–53
Imports
China's, 14, 35, 39–41, 73
Giants' share, 13–14
India's, 35, 43–44, 60, 73
India
agricultural sector, 12, 28
domestic financial policy and performance, 117–19
educational attainments, 12–13, 15–16, 17–18
energy efficiency, 26
finance sector, 48–49
financial crisis of 1990s, 117, 118
future governance challenges, 30, 241
GDP, 1, 6
governance reform experiences, 29–30, 220–28
human resources, 44
manufacturing sector, 19, 37, 43–45, 49–50, 51–53, 65
political environment, 241
population patterns and trends, 11–12, 28
production sharing participation, 69, 74
services sector, 45–49, 65, 68
share of world economic growth, 6
trade liberalization effects, 77–78
trade patterns, 17, 35, 43–44, 45, 50, 51, 60, 62, 65–66, 68, 69, 73–74
trade protection, 53, 69, 77
water resources, 25
white goods industry, 56
white goods market, 54–55, 56
See also Economies of China and India; Growth of Giants
Industrial production
auto and auto parts, 58–60
China's policy, 229
differences between India and China, 99